Praise for *Soil and Sacrament*

"This is a spiritual memoir with real dirt under its fingernails, as deep and gritty and rich as well-tended soil—or Holy Scripture. Fred Bahnson's vision matters, and the work he writes so beautifully and unsentimentally about has the power to change communities. An important and moving book."

—Sara Miles, author of *Take This Bread* and *City of God*

"This is a very moving as well as a wonderfully intelligent meditation on what is involved in care for our earth. Fred Bahnson succeeds in showing how our practices of cultivating the environment and producing our food can become an integral part of a 'gospel for all creation.' In a culture obsessed with both growth and control, his spiritual insight is a gentle but clear challenge."

—Rowan Williams, former Archbishop of Canterbury

"There's been an explosion of activity at the intersection of food and faith in the last ten years. Fred Bahnson's book is superb—it's incredibly readable, it's exciting, and most of all, it's inspirational."

—Nigel Savage, founder and president of Hazon

"About once in a generation, an American writer delivers a memoir that unites the spiritual longing of every soul with the particular challenges of their day. I think of Merton's *Seven Storey Mountain* or Dillard's *Pilgrim at Tinker Creek*. These books resonate because they are a distillation of one person's hope, which echoes in the heart of every reader. I realized this book may be one of them when I not only couldn't put it down but also couldn't stop thinking of all the people I wanted to give it to when I was finished."

—Jonathan Wilson-Hartgrove, author of *Strangers at My Door*

"Fred Bahnson's *Soil and Sacrament* reminds us that among the most necessary recoveries that may serve to heal a splintered personhood and a splintered community is the essentially *agnostic*—the *not* Gnostic—return to a love for and the care of the stuff of creation. As we are wooed away from false and debilitating dichotomies— of body and spirit, of substance and essence—we find before us a people and a land laden with spirit. We know now that our hunger is not for transcendence, but for immanence."

—Scott Cairns, author of *The End of Suffering*

ALSO BY FRED BAHNSON

Making Peace with the Land

SOIL AND SACRAMENT

A Spiritual Memoir of
Food and Faith

FRED BAHNSON

Simon & Schuster
New York   London   Toronto   Sydney   New Delhi

Simon & Schuster
1230 Avenue of the Americas
New York, NY 10020

First Simon & Schuster hardcover edition August 2013

SIMON & SCHUSTER and colophon are registered trademarks
of Simon & Schuster, Inc.

For information about special discounts for bulk purchases,
please contact Simon & Schuster Special Sales at
1-866-506-1949 or business@simonandschuster.com.

The Simon & Schuster Speakers Bureau can bring authors
to your live event. For more information or to book an event,
contact the Simon & Schuster Speakers Bureau at
1-866-248-3049 or visit our website at www.simonspeakers.com.

Designed by Akasha Archer

Manufactured in the United States of America

10 9 8 7 6 5 4 3 2 1
Library of Congress Cataloging-in-Publication Data
  Bahnson, Fred, date.
    Soil & sacrament : a spiritual memoir of food and faith / Fred Bahnson.
—First Simon & Schuster hardcover edition.
      pages   cm
1. Gardeners—Religious life. 2. Gardening—Religious aspects—Christianity.
3. Gardens—Religious aspects—Christianity I. Title. II. Title: Soil and sacrament.
BV4596.G36B34 2013
261.8'8—dc23   2013007992
ISBN 978-1-4516-6330-3
ISBN 978-1-4516-6333-4 (ebook)

For Elizabeth, Carsten, Elijah, David:

ALL MY LOVE

Contents

Prologue   1

1. The Underground Life of Prayer   15
   Advent, Mepkin Abbey, South Carolina

2. Dwellers in the Dust   56

3. At Play in the Fields of the Lord   82
   Eastertide, the Lord's Acre, North Carolina

4. Out of Africa, Into Babylon   107

5. A New Heaven, A New Earth   132
   Pentecost, Tierra Nueva, Washington

6. Significant Soil   174

7. Surpassing Civilization   196
   Sukkot, Adamah Farm, Connecticut

Epilogue   243

Acknowledgments   257

Recommended Reading   259

Index   263

SOIL AND SACRAMENT

"The glory of God is a human being fully alive."
—Saint Irenaeus

Prologue

Winter is my favorite growing season. Anyone can toss down a few seeds in June and get a crop, but it takes a disciplined hope to garden in the dark of December. And what rewards. After several frosts, plant starches become sugars. Carrots attain the sweet crunch of apples, and kale loses all hint of bitterness. Turnips become so sugary you can eat them raw.

Mid-morning on the first Sunday in Advent, I stood beside the red-roofed barn and looked out at Anathoth Community Garden. Down the hill the greenhouse was shedding its frost in the first light. Along the creek sat the children's playhouse, and beyond that the site of our future orchard. But the sight that always drew my eye was the wide expanse of the field itself, a wave-and-trough succession of raised vegetable beds lying dark and still in the low winter light, pregnant with life waiting to be born. Soon I would need to drive a mile down the road to the little Methodist church where my wife and sons would be arriving for the morning service, but first I needed to come here, to this five-acre piece of land that had come to feel like an extension of my own body. Over the past three years of working here I had grown attached to this garden and its people. They had fed me in so many ways. Perhaps too many ways.

I walked downhill to the greenhouse, a Gothic arch structure where we grew most of our winter crops and started all our seed. Heated entirely by the sun and ventilated by wax pistons, it was off the grid. This was my favorite of winter places, my sanctuary; I could lose myself in here for hours. What a thrill I received each morning as I entered this congregation of plants, lit as if from within by the low winter sun. The world outside the greenhouse was nineteen degrees cold; dry and lifeless. Once I stepped across the wooden threshold, the temperature rose to a balmy forty, lush and humid and alive with the earthy aroma of plants seeking light.

The soil here was deeper than in the rest of the garden, the color and consistency of chocolate sponge cake. Even on the coldest of winter days, black organic matter in the soil absorbed the sun's heat and slowly released it at night, keeping the plants alive. The beds, each four feet wide and thirty feet long, were double-dug. While the topsoil of a rototilled garden descends a mere eight inches, our greenhouse beds reached a depth of at least two feet, mimicking the fertile, loamy soils of the American prairie or the Russian steppe. With such deep beds, roots have better access to water and minerals deep in the ground. Plants can be spaced closer together, quadrupling yield. Thousands of years ago the Greeks realized that plants grew better in mountain landslides. The deep soil there was loose and friable, allowing the roots easy access to nutrients. A double-dug bed is like an underground landslide. Roots flourish in such deep tilth, creating a vast subterranean network that feeds aboveground life.

I spent much of my time at Anathoth preparing and working and thinking about the soil. There is an entire ecosystem in a handful of soil: bacteria, fungi, protozoa, nematodes, earthworms. Through their breeding and dying such creatures vivify the world.

This pattern of relationships I find a captivating mystery; I love plants, but I am most attracted to the fervent and secret work that goes on beneath the surface.

Soil is not dirt. It is a living organism, or rather a collection of organisms, and it must be fed. Soil both craves life and wants to produce more life, even a hundredfold.

The true profundity of our soil was difficult to gauge. One day I slid my hand into one of the greenhouse beds. I gently pushed down and kept pushing until my arm vanished and my shoulder touched the soil's surface. It had seemed then as if I could keep burrowing downward, until my entire body was swallowed by the warm, dark earth.

Soil is a portal to another world.

That Sunday morning I was alone in the garden.

Anathoth was a food garden for the community—our sixty members worked the land in common and shared its bounty—yet more and more I had found myself going there at such times to escape people. I was by nature reclusive, yet my role as Anathoth's director required me to act as a public figure, putting on a smile and chatting up the members, who worked a minimum of two hours a week in exchange for produce. The truth was that I had less and less energy for people—even my own family. Increasingly I felt accosted by so many people needing something from me, and no matter how deeply I wanted to give them what they needed, all I wanted to do was withdraw.

The Sunday morning service down the road at Cedar Grove United Methodist Church would begin soon, but I remembered that there were beds that needed cover cropping; I had a sudden desire to plant. Leaving the greenhouse I walked back up to the barn and reached for the blue hand-cranked seed spreader, opened a bag of rye, and poured in the seed. I mixed rhizobium inoculant into a bucket full of hairy vetch and crimson clover seed, added a few drops of water, and stirred them together with the rye. Vetch and clover are legumes, plants that form a beneficial relationship with rhizobium bacteria. Their roots would supply nitrogen not only to the rye but also to the crops that would follow in the rotation. It's a beautiful symbiosis: legume roots provide the bacteria with sugars and in exchange the bacteria fix nitrogen into tiny pink nodules that cling like barnacles to the legume roots. The bacteria and legumes serve one another. The rye stalk provides a structure for the legumes to climb, and rye's fibrous roots mine minerals from the subsoil, reaching ten feet down into the earth. It's a trinity of abundance—rye, vetch, and clover—each freely giving up its body for the other's nourishment, each dying so that the other may live.

I knew something of that sacrifice. For years I had labored for Anathoth, but only recently did I realize the toll it had taken on me and my family. There were too many days when I would come back to our farm and instead of being with the family who needed me, I would retreat to my little shack in the woods. My wife, Elizabeth, sacrificed her own needs for the needs of Anathoth, and mostly suffered my absences in silence. But our young sons were confused. "Why does Daddy need so much time alone?" they asked. I had started to ask that question, too.

By early May the cover crops would be five feet tall. When the rye reached milk stage and the vetch and clover flowered purple and crimson, I would walk up and down the beds swinging a scythe, the stalks falling before me, the air growing redolent with grassy perfume, and then I would rake up the cuttings to make compost. First the green layer: fresh rye, vetch, and clover stalks. Then a brown layer: old hay or leaves. The third layer would be a dusting of garden soil, containing the spark of bacteria that would set this biological pyre aflame. In a week the tiny hordes inside the compost pile would expend their oxygen, slowing their combustion, and I would turn the pile with a pitchfork to give them air. All kinds of organic matter could go into a compost pile. Once I even composted a dead field rat; a few months later there was nothing but bones.

I loved making compost. The bright green of freshly mown rye, vetch, and clover; steam arising from the pile on a cold morning; the smell of the forest floor in your hands. There is a secret joy, a kind of charity to be found in this act, transforming a pile of grass and dirt and old leaves into an offering of humic mystery. On those days I became a priest dispensing the elements to a microbial congregation. Lord, take these humble gifts: grass, leaves, soil. Make them be for us the body and blood of the world, holy vessels of self-emptying glory. *All things come of thee, O Lord; and of thine own have we given thee.* After several months of heating and cooling and turning, the pile of well-cooked humus would be ready to spread onto the soil. Into that I would plant Speckled Trout lettuce, Kuri squash, or Sugarsnap peas, which would feed the hungry people of Cedar Grove. The people's hunger could be slackened, but it would never end, and all the while the secret life of soil would continue, the gift waiting to be found. Like a ceaseless hymn of praise, this cycle went on with or without you, winter and summer, rain and drought, seedtime and harvest, a process of creation beyond your control that had been in motion since the foundation of the world. It is a song of life that sings even when things around and within you no longer seem certain.

I was beginning my fourth year as the director of Anathoth, and the experience had been deeply fulfilling and profoundly frustrating. The garden was a ministry of Cedar Grove UMC, but only a minority of the congregants worked there. Visitors came from around the country to learn how to build communities through working the land, but some church members stubbornly refused to have anything to do with the garden. Some were afraid of liability. Others feared the garden's racially inclusive vision for our town.

I was weary of defending the project before our own church, but that wasn't the only thing. I was questioning what I had for years been certain was my life's calling.

After sowing the rye, vetch, and clover, I walked back again to the greenhouse and stood in the quiet air, letting the winter sun warm my bones. I would be a few minutes late for church, but I could still slip in. After all: when our Lord sought refuge, when his heart was troubled, it was not to the temple that he went to pray. It was to the garden.

The night's frost evaporated from the broccoli heads like gauzy veils lifting from upturned faces. Dinosaur kale, Napoli carrots, Arcadia broccoli, Bronze Arrow lettuce—these were our winter savings account, available to the garden members for free withdrawal. Carrots grew happily inter-planted with lettuce. Kale, broccoli, and cabbage—all benevolent brassicas—rubbed shoulders good-naturedly. Each crop cluster formed a dark green microclimate of contentment. The congregants of this tiny cathedral thrived in each other's company. I could not always say the same for our little Methodist church down the road.

The points of overlap between the church and garden were not always harmonious. Many did support the garden. Pastor Grace Hackney was one of Anathoth's cofounders and often praised the garden in her sermons. The church's accountant kept our books, others served on the advisory board, and some were regular volunteers on our Saturday workdays. As the garden's director, I was employed by the church as a minister of the land. But there was also a small group of naysayers on the church's administrative council, those whose families had owned land here since the king's grants of the 1700s. They were threatened by new ideas like community gardens, and were adamant that the garden would receive none of the church's money. I wrote grants and sought individual donations to fund Anathoth's yearly budget, but when funds would arrive, inevitably someone would ask, with feigned piety, why didn't we just use that money to buy food and give it to the poor.

But Anathoth was not just a hunger relief ministry. It was a whole new way to be a church. And therein lay the struggle.

We took Anathoth's mission from the book of Jeremiah: "plant gardens and seek the peace of the city," and here at the beginning of my fourth year I think we had that mission half right. We had planted a lush and abundant acre of biointensive beds that provided our members with everything from arugula to Zapotec tomatoes; we had planted blueberry bushes, a native plants garden, and a greenhouseful of winter produce. We had planted the events calendar with biweekly potlucks and concerts, children's programs and community service days for troubled teens. We planted so many things that churches from all over the South came to ask how they, too, could plant such gardens and seek the peace of their city. Anathoth had sprouted from an empty field, and on its best days it afforded a glimpse of the messianic feast, Jesus's abundant smorgasbord where all were fed. But I'd begun to question if feeding people was truly my calling. I couldn't bear to see the crestfallen faces of Elizabeth and the boys when yet another Saturday afternoon would come and I would head off to hide exhausted in my hermitage.

Inside the greenhouse I watered the spinach bed, then snapped off a piece and raised it to my mouth. Chewing slowly, I savored the wafer-thin leaf, remembering the summer Eucharist services we held in the garden. How beautiful it was to bring the gifts of the altar out into the fields.

The cold truth that morning was inescapable: I had given my-self so completely to this vocation that there was little left over for my family. Work was all I thought about: when Elizabeth tried to talk to me at dinner or one of my boys wanted me to wrestle, my thoughts went to the garden: the Brussels sprouts needed transplant-ing; I needed to order strawberry plants for the fall; and I couldn't forget that email to the garden members about our upcoming sweet potato harvest. Anathoth was all I thought about and yet, that work was also draining me of life and energy.

That Sunday morning at the beginning of another Christian year, standing in the greenhouse, I realized I could not stay.

The garden is our oldest metaphor. In Genesis God creates the first *Adam* from the *adamah,* and tells him to "till and keep" it, the fertile soil on which all life depends. Human from humus. That's our first etymological clue as to the inextricable bond we share with the soil. Our ecological problems are a result of having forgotten who we are—soil people, inspired by the breath of God. "Earth's hallowed mould," as Milton referred to Adam in *Paradise Lost*. Or in Saint Augustine's phrase, *terra animata*—animated earth.

The command to care for soil is our first divinely appointed vocation, yet in our zeal to produce cheap, abundant food we have shunned it; we have tilled the *adamah* but we have not kept it.

Tilling is, in fact, often harmful to soil structure and creates ero-sion. Since World War II, as a result of excessive tillage and use of petrochemicals, we've managed to squander a third of our country's topsoil. With the combined challenges of climate change, peak oil, and the global food crisis, the balance of life on earth is rapidly ap-proaching a tipping point. In the ways we grow our food and in the food we choose to eat, we have largely lost our connection with the *adamah;* we have failed to live in the garden.

Anathoth taught me that to live and work in a garden is to relearn the most basic realities of life. Rather than an escape from the world's problems, a garden—especially a communal food garden—confronts us with those very problems. Referring to Voltaire's famous dictum *We must cultivate our garden,* cultural critic Robert Pogue Harrison says in *Gardens:* "*Notre jardin* is never a garden of merely private concerns into which one escapes from the real; it is that plot of soil on the earth, within the self, or amid the social collective, where the cultural, ethical, and civic virtues that save reality from its own worst impulses are cultivated. Those virtues are always *ours.*"

We left the following August, four years to the day after I'd become director of Anathoth, and our leaving happened, from my perspective at least, on good terms. Elizabeth and I had been talking about how we wanted to live closer to our extended families while our children were young. I had received a generous two-year writing grant, and this was our chance. We moved back to the mountains of western North Carolina, planted our own gardens and orchards, and I set about relearning how to be a husband to her and a father to our children.

By 2011 nearly two years had passed, two lovely years of building a new life on the land with my family, yet since leaving Anathoth something within me remained unsettled. A decade ago in Chiapas, Mexico, I had discovered the connection between the cultivation of crops and the cultivation of the spirit. I had sensed a calling to feed people, and my subsequent years at Anathoth had been a crucible in which I'd leaned into that calling. But now, despite a contented family life on our own piece of land, I felt an acute spiritual hunger that could not be filled. I would need to revisit those years from my past, only this time from a different vantage point.

While I knew something about soil—feed the soil, the soil will feed the plants, and plants will feed the people—I was only just beginning to embrace a sacramental life, a life of drawing nearer to God. I grew up in a Christian home, was a missionary kid in Nigeria for three years, attended divinity school, taught the New Testament to undergrads, and started a communal garden ministry for a Methodist church, which is to say that all my life I've been immersed in various Christian subcultures. Yet I realized at age thirty-eight that I was only just beginning my spiritual journey. When I went to church I mostly felt bored. But I believed that the Living Christ was real—I had met Him at Anathoth in the faces of strangers, even enemies—and I wanted to find Him again.

I somehow needed to start from scratch, to approach the faith with the eyes of a new convert. I wanted answers to some fairly simple questions: What does it mean to follow God? How should I live my life? And what does all this have to do with the soil, the literal ground of my existence? These most basic questions had become incessant preoccupations. What I was really after, I realized, was that age-old quest for a life of holiness. A life of wholeness.

In Luke's story of the disciples meeting Jesus on the road to Emmaus, they knew him not. Only when they broke bread at the same table did they recognize him. For two thousand years, through the sacramental elements of the Eucharist and in table fellowship, people have sought Jesus in the breaking of the bread. Perhaps, I thought, one could also seek him in the growing of the wheat.

During my Anathoth years I had experienced God's presence in the act of growing food with others. In order to understand those experiences, I embarked on a new journey to seek out others, both living and dead, whose calling was similar to my own. I plumbed the riches of living Christian and Jewish tradition. I decided to dig deep into the soil of the burgeoning twenty-first-century food and faith movement about which I'd been hearing many good things, to learn about the cultivation of soul and soil from the examples of those I encountered.

The search for an authentic life is an old one. When the early Christians went to the desert, this is what they prayed: *We beg you, God, make us truly alive.* That fourth-century prayer was not the prayer of people patiently awaiting their ticket to heaven, just biding their time on earth; it was the urgent and anguished and utterly rooted prayer of people who wanted God to make them more fully here now. Those fourth-century monastics fled to the desert because they were being drawn toward life. They knew that their society, a bloated culture of excess and spiritual emptiness, prevented them from becoming the humans God wanted them to be. Like these early monastics, I had a desire to live a life of integrity and wholeness, to become more fully alive. And I decided to look for the fulfillment of those desires not in the desert, but in the garden.

Over the course of a year I would visit a different garden for each of the four seasons, each visit coinciding with a liturgical holiday. I traveled as an immersion journalist, but also as a pilgrim. This journey was a quest to find those modern prophets who might teach all of us better ways to be at home in the world. I visited a Trappist monastery in the South Carolina low country where I prayed the Divine Office with the monks and learned to grow mushrooms. At a model community garden started by several Protestant churches in the mountains of North Carolina I asked a blessing over a potluck meal and renewed my faith in community. I ran a prayer gauntlet with Pentecostal organic farmers and meth-cooks-turned-coffee-roasters in Washington's Skagit Valley. And finally, in what struck me as the completion of a sacred circle, I traveled to a Jewish organic farm in the Berkshires where I davened in a red yurt in the predawn hours, celebrating the bounty of the fall harvest according to ancient tradition. Each of these garden communities arose out of their particular place and context. They were small, even obscure, which meant they were in little danger of being commodified or otherwise co-opted. Over the course of that year I would discover many things: That times of intentional solitude deepened, rather than distanced, my relationship with others. That manual labor disciplined not only the body but also the spirit. That trying to save an imperiled world is for naught unless that work is undergirded by a rigorous prayer life. And everywhere I went, I witnessed how our yearning for real food is inextricably bound up in our spiritual desire to be fed.

During my four years at Anathoth there were times when I caught a glimpse of what the biblical writers called *shalom,* a right relation not only with God and people but with the *adamah;* I had experienced profound moments when people and the land coexisted in blessèd armistice, times free of struggle, and in those moments it seemed as if God's glory had come to dwell in the land, as the Psalmist promised, a time when justice and peace would kiss. And so I went looking for these glimpses of *shalom* among others who were trying to live again in the garden, in the most expansive sense of the word.

I began my journey in Advent, the beginning of the Christian year, and as the time drew near to embark, I began to think of my quest as really a journey to four spiritual strongholds, fortresses of power both sacred and profane. It was this balance of the holy and the mundane that attracted me. In each place I felt a palpable and immediate sense of the Divine Presence, yet that mystery arose from the daily tasks of growing mushrooms, milking goats, planting carrots. Each of these communities produced some of their own food, making them less dependent than most of us on a centralized, oil-addicted food system that is already showing signs of collapse. That simple act of growing food gave them something most of us don't possess: agency. As such, they had regained a measure of freedom from anxiety. But there was also something more mysterious at work in these places. A merciful Presence brooding over the bent world. The answer to our hunger for more than just bread.

To grow and share food with others in a garden is to enter a holy country. American spirituality is discovering itself anew as people of faith reconnect with the land. But while the *buy local, eat organic* movement is increasingly in the public eye, the faith-based food movement remains virtually unknown by the wider public. At times it intersects with its larger cousin, but mostly it charts a parallel course, comprised of many people who've neither heard of Michael Pollan nor set foot in a Whole Foods. Many of those I've come to meet in this loosely woven movement view soil as a sacrament: a physical manifestation of God's presence, a channel of Divine grace. They know soil is a portal that joins us to the world to come even while rooting us more deeply in this one.

Through the practices of caring for the soil, those I encountered had discovered a way to become more fully alive.

What follows are the stories of people who have aligned their lives with *the real*. They have sought from God, and been given to find, the patterns of life that made them more holy. More whole. More human.

This was the way I was seeking, and this was the way I was given to find.

We beg you, make us truly alive.

CHAPTER ONE

The Underground Life of Prayer

Advent

Mepkin Abbey, South Carolina

I see you are fired by a very great longing.
—Abba Moses, fourth-century Egyptian monk, to a pilgrim

Vigils, 3:20 A.M.

Prayer began in darkness.

At 3 A.M. a buzzer rang in my cell. I dressed quickly and stepped out into the twenty-degree December night. The moon was full and by its light a host of dark, silent forms glided across the cloistered lawn and into the abbey church. Inside a faint aroma of incense lingered from Vespers the night before. The walls were unadorned. Next to the bare, granite altar a leafless poplar tree stood in an earthen pot, a symbol of the barrenness of winter. Some of the monks walked to a stone font in the center of the nave and dipped their fingers before crossing themselves. As I walked past the font and dipped my right forefinger, I glanced at the opposite wall. A thin, vertical slit in the wall, no wider than my hand, opened into an adjoining room. Through the opening I saw a long chain hanging from the ceiling, and attached to this chain was a candle, illuminating the space beyond. The room was a tiny chapel for solitary prayer. A lone, hooded monk knelt on the cement floor.

I took my seat next to Brother Gregory and watched the other monks arrive. At 3:20 A.M. a bell began to ring. After a few moments the ringing slowed, and everyone stood and turned to face the altar. From somewhere behind me a set of knuckles knocked once on the wooden choir seats, and all bowed toward the altar. We then recited two lines from Psalm 51, the first words to pass our lips since the end of last night's Compline, sanctifying the night as those words have sanctified every night for the past 1,500 years: *O Lord, open my lips*, a lone monk said, and in unison we joined him: *And my mouth shall declare your praise*.

According to the Monastic Guest Handbook I found on the desk in my narrow cell, "It is in living out the *horarium* and doing the ordinary tasks of the day that you will discover the wisdom of this way of life." The *horarium,* or Divine Office, consisted of the services beginning with Vigils, spiritual reading, and manual labor: the threefold path of Benedictine life. In my search to find life, where the cultivation of the spirit went hand in hand with cultivation of the land, it seemed apt to begin with people who, for one and a half millennia, have been living just that.

The brothers knew which Psalm to sing next, but I had trouble finding my way through the prayer book. Brother Gregory reached a clawed hand over and turned the page in my psalter. We sang the first verse of Psalm 57—*Have mercy on me, God, have mercy, for in you my soul has taken refuge*—and sat down. The prior's side of the choir picked up the next verse, and then we traded verses, bowing at the end and singing *Glory be to the Father and to the Son and to the Holy Spirit,* our words lifting slightly on "Spirit," and our bodies lifting, too.

At ninety-two, Gregory was the last of the original founders of

Mepkin Abbey. He would be my stalwart companion all week, guiding me through each day's seven services. Despite his age, Gregory's voice rose to meet the others—*O God, arise above the heavens; may your glory shine on earth!*—and I found my own voice growing in confidence.

I looked around at the brothers, some wearing the signature black and white Trappist garb, others clad in long white robes. Brother Dismas was the guitar-playing choir leader. When monks join an order they take a new name, and he had taken the name Christian tradition gave to the good thief on the cross beside Jesus. Though it was only 3:30 in the morning, Brother Dismas had already been up for two hours drinking strong coffee and writing confessional poetry. To his right sat Brother Theophilus, whose name meant "friend of God." He was a loquacious, cigar-smoking monk who would teach me about Mepkin's mushroom operation. Behind him was Father Kevin, the prior, my spiritual director for the week. When I asked Father Kevin how to go deeper in prayer, he told me a story about a younger monk who had approached an older monk with that very question. "Limit the input," was the answer. "God pursues *us*. The challenge is to slow down enough to recognize it."

My heart is ready, O God, my heart is ready, we sang from the psalter. This life of prayer was like the tiny chapel next door, a hidden room of which I could see only a glimpse. I desired more and I knew that slowing down enough to recognize God's voice would require keeping my body close to the ground, like the kneeling monk. I was not seeking the airy heights of transcendence. I wanted a rooted spirituality; wanted to meet Jesus crouching there in the dirt, scribbling a few words. Whatever experience of God I might have here in this quiet place, it would need to take root in the mundane soil of my own life, in everything I did and touched and saw, or it would not flourish.

Awake my soul, we chanted, *awake lyre and harp; I will awake the dawn.*

When Vigils ended at four we would leave in silence, each returning to our cells for nearly two hours of *lectio divina*—spiritual reading—until we would gather again at daybreak to sing Lauds. When the abbot's knuckles knocked and the monks stood to depart, Brother Gregory remained seated. At first he seemed to still be praying, but then I noticed a bit of drool on his lower lip. He had only dozed off, his head slumped so low that his chin nearly grazed his lap. To me it seemed as if Brother Gregory was returning to the fetal position, as if through all those years of bowing and rising, God had been slowly curling him up again before bringing him home.

The two hours of reading were no chore; I had good books at hand. First among these was *Thoughts in Solitude,* short meditations by Thomas Merton, perhaps the most famous Trappist monk of the twentieth century and one of my inspirations for coming to Mepkin Abbey. I arrived at Mepkin during the season of Advent, the beginning of the Christian year. It was also during Advent on December 10, 1941, that Thomas Merton joined Gethsemani, a Trappist monastery in Kentucky. "Liturgically speaking," Merton wrote in *The Seven Storey Mountain,* "you could hardly find a better time to become a monk than Advent. You begin a new life, you enter a new world at the beginning of a new liturgical year. And everything that the Church gives you to sing, every prayer that you say in and with Christ in His Mystical Body is a cry of ardent desire for grace, for help, for the coming of the Messiah, the Redeemer." Merton had become one of the foremost saints in my personal pantheon. Four of the monks at Mepkin Abbey had known Merton: Gregory, Joseph, Robert, and Abbot Stan. I wanted to hear their memories of the man

I knew only through his books, hoping that some of Merton's wisdom might somehow pass to me.

Along with Merton I carried one of the staples of monastic spirituality: *The Conferences* by fifth-century monk and interpreter of early monasticism John Cassian; Rainer Maria Rilke's *Book of Hours* rode along for lyrical inspiration. A mushroom grower's guide by mycologist Paul Stamets called *Mycelium Running* came as well, and finally a short book by the late Francis Kline, former abbot of Mepkin Abbey, called *Lovers of the Place.* In the predawn hours of that first morning I began with Kline, who spoke to me right where I sat. "The word enters our dreams and images more easily at the time before the sun's light. Only in the darkness are certain, more choice intuitions of God received."

As I read, my mind traveled past the abbey church across the fields to a cluster of sheds, where millions of tiny threads of mycelium worked in the darkness. A stringlike network of fungal cells, mycelium is the organism that produces mushrooms. The brothers cultivate mycelium, whose "fruit" supports their life of prayer. This relationship with fungi was relatively new for them; they had taken up mushroom cultivation after many years in the egg business. But the relationship of fungi to life as we know it goes back nearly 450 million years. Indeed, without mycelium, there would be no life at all. Only recently have we come to understand the true magnitude of our dependence on these organisms. We now know, for instance, that at least 90 percent of all plants on earth form symbiotic relationships with a fungus called mycorrhizae. Greek for "fungus-root," mycorrhizae are ubiquitous, found in nearly every ecosystem in the world.

The relationship works like this: the fungus penetrates a plant's roots and provides the plant with nutrients and water from the surrounding soil, which the fungus accesses through its mycelial network. The fungus in turn receives starches from the plant. When mycelium grows out into the surrounding soil it is said to "run," and in so doing it not only forms symbiotic relationships with single plants; it provides links between plant species. In 1964, two North Carolina scientists chopped down a red maple tree and poured radioactive liquid into the stump. Eight days later they found that, within a radius of twenty-two feet, the leaves of nearly half of all the trees, shrubs, vines, and herbs contained radioactivity; mycelium provided the pathway through which the radioactive material spread. The experiment confirmed fungi's link to every living thing. And every dead thing. Fungi are our biological go-betweens to the world beyond animate life. And like monks at prayer, fungi do their best work in darkness.

I knew something of the benefits of early morning darkness. Back home on winter mornings I had lately been rising at 6 A.M. I would fire up the woodstove, set the kettle on top, and for the thirty minutes it took for the water to boil, I would try to pray. But my mind wandered easily. I got bored. Many mornings when the kettle boiled, I would awake from a fire-trance stupor, my thoughts far from God. Despite my lifelong faith I'd arrived at age thirty-eight only to realize that I didn't know the first thing about prayer. In *The Conferences,* John Cassian described prayer as "an uncontrollable grasping fire." The only fire I knew was the one burning in front of me in the woodstove while a clear day dawned. When I did manage to actually *pray,* I often became trapped in litanies of petitions, pleas for forgiveness, or cesspools of self-recrimination for past wrongs. My prayer repertoire was limited to the *juswanna* prayer: Lord, I *juswanna* thank you . . . God, I *juswanna* ask you . . . Jesus, I *juswanna* . . . But prayer is not simply a matter of technique. The monk's way of life is not about learning to pray for a few hours a day; it is about turning one's entire life toward God. Some viewed such a life as escapist, yet that was a misunderstanding. As Father Kevin put it, "Monasteries do not exist to say 'the world is bad—let's hide.' They exist because in order to go deeper into the heart of God we have to let go of other things that are constantly calling our attention." I questioned my decision to leave Elizabeth and the boys behind to begin this journey. Was it selfish of me to leave them now when I had often been emotionally absent during those four years at Anathoth? Far from leaving our bodies behind, prayer leads us to engage more fully with them, for God cannot be separated from the things of this world. I sought a life of prayer lived in intimacy not only with God, but also with the land and with a community of fellow pilgrims. That was why I came to the Trappists; they were known for a life of *ora et labora,* prayer and manual labor.

"To sit on the side and gaze at our navel," Abbot Stan wrote in an essay on work, "is to miss the great reality of life. We are co-creators with God of the earthly city." Creation was not a one-time event, Stan said, it is ongoing, and we are called to participate in it with the work of our hands. For the monks at Mepkin there was a constant back-and-forth between work and prayer, action and contemplation, the one feeding the other. For the first five and a half hours of the day they prayed and studied, but from 8:30 A.M. onward they worked to co-create an earthly city in miniature. "If our work is to share in the creative activity of God," Abbot Stan continued, "then it is precisely not a dominion of power or self-aggrandizement. It is one of humility before the creative presence of God; work must serve to realize our humanity, to fulfill the calling to be a person. . . . We do not dominate by lording it over nature, but by treading lightly, knowing that we are all in this together."

An austere order, the Trappists were modern-day ascetics who practiced silence and contemplation following the sixth-century monastic *Rule of Saint Benedict*. While the *Rule* would become the foundational text for Western monasticism, in the centuries following Benedict's death his followers grew lax, softening the *Rule* to suit their own slovenly habits, in some cases forsaking it altogether. In 1098 in Cîteaux, France, a small group of Benedictine monks returned to the rigorous life of manual labor and unceasing prayer that had marked the monasticism of the fourth-century Desert Fathers. The Trappists, as they came to be known, reclaimed the agrarian arts of the early Benedictines. Through their hard work they became known for taking swampland that nobody wanted and converting it into productive farmland.

Saint Bernard, the most famous of the early Trappists, often wrote admiringly of the fields and meadows around his monastery. While the later Romantic poets would find their inspiration in a world untouched by human hands, Saint Bernard wrote of the beauty of *tilled* fields and *hay* meadows. Working farmland, in other words, not pristine wilderness, was what caught his eye. Becoming co-creators with God means that our cultivation of the earth should not only feed us, but express beauty as well. How many modern farms, I wondered, could witness to that truth?

The brothers of Mepkin Abbey were heirs of the oldest Christian agrarian community in the world. Though most of them were too old to do much farm work, the Trappist agrarian ethos lives on at the abbey. In 2008 the monks gave up their long-standing egg operation for the new venture into mushrooms, looking for a business that was profitable while also being more ecologically sustainable. That change also inspired them to plant an organic vegetable garden. Father Guerric grows some of the vegetables that appear on the refectory table, as well as Muscadine grapes, blackberries, and figs. "I think it's a moral imperative to have a vegetable garden," Father Guerric told me. "It saves energy costs, we eat healthier. You may get your hands red peeling beets," he said with a smile, "so there are minor inconveniences."

In addition to the gardens and mushroom operation, the monks' ecological footprint is made smaller by their life together. "When people live in community," Father Guerric said, "they need less, spend less, use fewer resources." Guerric was quick to acknowledge that they haven't taken a vow of poverty. "We'll use a good piece of machinery. But we still live frugally, we don't have many possessions. We have what we need, not necessarily what we want."

The monks aren't entirely self-sufficient; they do hire some outside help. But self-sufficiency is, ecologically speaking, a contradiction in terms and hardly a goal worth pursuing. The abbey's economy overlaps with the local economy and, to a lesser extent, the national economy, but they maintain a certain sphere in which they don't depend on those larger, inherently unstable forces. They have what the ancient Greeks called an *oikos,* from which we get *oikonomia:* a household that includes fields, people, and home. It is an ancient pattern of living, with much to say to my own situation. I had lived in eleven different houses before I left for college and I'd newly rooted myself, moving onto a piece of land in western North Carolina. Elizabeth and I planted an orchard, grape vines, asparagus—perennials you put in only when you plan to stay. But it felt as though something was missing. As the day dawned outside the monastery window, providing the only light in my cell, out on the Cooper River a blue heron glided into the marsh for breakfast. A flock of crows squawked at the intruder, but the heron took no notice, stalking knee-deep through the still water, a creature utterly at home. "Taming the heart requires a sense of place," Kline wrote. "It roots not just the mind to a set of principles, but also the body to a piece of land." By coming to Mepkin I hoped to learn patterns of work and worship that I might take back to my own life on our small farm, learning how the monks' work helping mycelium to run also fed their life of prayer. I also came to escape the messiness of human life. Years ago I'd felt called to a life on the land, but now I knew my spiritual resources for sustaining that life were too few. I hoped to learn from the monks how to nurture those inner resources, both through deeper prayer and through discovering the balance of solitude and community.

Lauds, 6:30 A.M.

O God, come to my assistance, a lone monk sang at the opening of Lauds, and in reply we sang: Lord, make haste to help me. If only every morning began like this.

After Lauds came breakfast in the refectory, a reminder that being a monk is harder than it looks. I'd been to the abbey twice before on shorter visits and I'd learned that the monks don't eat very much: breakfast consists of a few thin slices of pumpernickel bread, a slice of cheese, maybe some PB&J. Supper is not much different. Though they occasionally eat fish, Trappists are otherwise vegetarians. The main meal at noon was always a hearty affair—butternut squash and lentil curry with rice or oyster mushroom lasagna and fresh garden salad—but the daily caloric intake still left me in a constant state of hunger. Which is the idea. By ordering our bodily desires, fasting helps us better understand ourselves. Being less occupied about the tasks of preparing and consuming food, we can use that energy to turn our thoughts inward and give in to our desire for God.

Nonetheless, on this third trip to Mepkin I decided that, while I would engage the rigors of bodily denial at some meals, I would also bring a cooler of food which could be secretly stashed in the guest fridge. Just a backup, a little something to take the edge off. Elizabeth sent along a big loaf of her peasant bread, jam, and hummus, all of it homemade. I packed organic almond butter, bananas, and oranges. For suppers I brought fresh winter produce from our garden: Napoli carrots, Hakurei turnips, Winterbor kale. To maintain healthy intestinal function during my week of spiritual rigor I brought a big jar of home-fermented kimchi, loaded with lacto-bacilli and probiotics. For snacks I packed organic BBQ potato chips, miso soup, almonds and hazelnuts, and six bars of dark chocolate (78 percent cacao). I know it sounds like I was bringing Oreos to fat camp, but aside from skipping Vigils a few times, my mealtime laxity was my one concession to an otherwise complete adoption of the rigors of Trappist life. Well, that's not the whole truth. I confess I did smuggle in several beers and a bottle of single-malt for nightcaps. Benedict's *horarium* was a good invention, I reasoned, but it needed the addition of cocktail hour to make it complete.

As I stood one morning in front of the open guest fridge perusing my secret stash, Brother Dismas walked over to refill his coffee. In the hours between Vigils and Lauds when most monks were deep into *lectio divina,* Brother Dismas was down in the laundry room rowing. It was his only time of day for exercise, so the abbot agreed. In the glare of the kitchen light, I could see scars on Dismas's shaved head, remnants of childhood surgeries for cerebral palsy. His waist was wrapped by a leather belt, to which were attached two leather cords hanging well past his knees. I pointed to them and mouthed a question. We were still in Grand Silence, the period from the end of Compline to the next day's Mass during which talk was strictly forbidden. As an answer Brother Dismas gave a grim smile. He picked up the leather cords and made a whipping motion on his shoulders.

Uncovering the hidden beers in the fridge, I tipped my right hand thumb-to-mouth, pinkie extended. Did he want to join me for a cold one that evening? He grasped my shoulder and whispered, "Bless you, my son. Bless you."

"Gaelic Ale or Fat Tire?" I whispered back.

"Oh, I'm a Fat Tire man for sure."

We agreed to meet that night after Vespers in the little dining room. Then it was time for Mass, and we hurried off through the breezeway toward the church.

Eucharist, 7:30 A.M.

Though I had attended church services all my life—evangelical, Methodist, Lutheran, Mennonite—none quite prepared me for the stark beauty of Advent Mass with the brothers of Mepkin. The songs were unadorned, like the empty branches of the poplar tree standing beside the altar, yet amidst the season's barrenness hung a palpable expectation in everything we read or sang.

I have come to think Advent is the church's loveliest liturgical season. From the Latin word for "coming," Advent is the season of waiting. In my younger years I had naively viewed that wait as a tedious march of days leading up to Jesus's birth. *Why drag it out?* I wondered. But if this time is simply about waiting for Jesus's birthday, then we miss the point, writes Benedictine sister Joan Chittister in *The Liturgical Year*. That's the soft, sentimental "baby Jesus" version of Advent, "a simple, soothing story that makes few, if any, demands on the soul." A more robust understanding of Advent is as a time when we learn, says Chittister, "to wait for what is beyond the obvious. Advent makes us look for God in all those places we have, until now, ignored."

Saint Bernard described Advent as a threefold coming of the Lord: Jesus came at Bethlehem, he will come at the end of the ages, and he comes now, in our hearts. "Advent," Father Kevin told me, "is about hope for what is yet to be. A farmer cannot tell you exactly how his crops are going to produce. But he trusts. Like the seed in the ground, there's a whole process of life that goes on in a hidden way, that's not visible to us. The monastic life is about waiting in expectation that God's hidden life in us will reveal itself. But it is an active waiting, not passive waiting."

This active waiting is enacted by living out Saint Benedict's *Rule*. Getting your tired body out of bed at 3 A.M. for Vigils. Working the mushrooms. Spiritual reading. All these things wear down the hardened heart and prepare it to receive God. Benedict likened the monastery to a workshop; it was the anvil on which the soul's blade was forged. "As our lives and faith progress," he wrote, "the heart expands." Perhaps that's what I needed most, I thought. To make my heart a big enough place in which God could be born.

We gathered for Eucharist first in the choir seats that ran down the length of the nave. Father Joe, the abbey's cook, preached on the classic text from Isaiah, *Comfort, O comfort my people, says your God.* God is a shepherd, Father Joe said, a shepherd who is always searching for us, waiting to comfort us. Advent is the time when we wait for Jesus to be born, but really Jesus is being born in us every day. Through the Eucharist, through silence, through others. God is always coming for us, Father Joe said. Pursuing us. Hunting us down with unrelenting mercy. But what will be our response to God's pursuit? Following God is not simply assenting to certain doctrines or subscribing to the right beliefs. It is rather a way to be walked. "The spiritual life is first of all a life," wrote Thomas Merton in *Thoughts in Solitude.* "It is not merely something to be known and studied, it is to be lived."

After Father Joe's sermon it was time for the Passing of the Peace. I turned to Brother Robert, an eighty-year-old brother who never wore a coat or socks, even in winter, and who in his younger days preferred roaming the woods to sitting in chapel. As the peace was passed, Robert turned to speak to another monk and they locked arms in embrace, greeting each other like brothers who had been separated by a long absence. Which, in a sense, they had. Since this time yesterday they had swum through oceans of silence, and now seemed pleasantly surprised to have landed together on this island. For a short time here among other solitary swimmers, they would share a morsel of bread, a sip of wine, and a brief embrace before returning to the water. There was an austerity of human connection among these men that I found immensely appealing. They spent much of their day with limited human contact, which made the few interactions they did have—a friendly nod passing one another in the mushroom shed, a simple embrace at Mass—all the more powerful. Men like Gregory and Robert, it was clear, had deep, meaningful friendships, yet they seemed to manage on very few words.

I walked over to shake Brother Gregory's hand. He was seated and I stooped above him. As our hands clasped, his head curled upward from its fetal position near his lap, his meek smile turning my way, and said, "Peace, Brother Fred." We had exchanged a total of maybe five words, he was fifty-four years my senior, yet he called me *brother*. It was good to be so recognized. Sometimes there's not much more than that we need do or say for one another in this life. A smile of friendship. An embrace of peace.

When the paten and chalice were lifted above the altar and Jesus's body was mystically united with the bread and wine and all the hosts of heaven sang in unison, I looked over in the corner at Father Christian. His head was bowed, his right arm raised, palm upward. Though hunched at age ninety-seven and recently in need of a walker, Father Christian was still spry. He wore a beard sans mustache, like the Amish, and spoke with a slight Irish lilt, giving thanks earlier in the service for the "clement weather." In his spare time, Father Christian liked to read books on quantum physics.

The other monks who were priests now gathered around the altar. They, too, lifted their right arms. They did this at every Mass; I found it a powerful gesture.

Father Christian hung back in the corner, his lips moving silently in unison with theirs. *This is my body, this is my blood.* Being a child of the 1980s raised on *Star Wars,* I found a certain image suddenly forcing its way into my mind. With his tightly shut eyes, silently moving lips, and shaky right arm extended outward, Father Christian looked like a Trappist Yoda, ready to wield the Force. I would not have been surprised if in that moment the stone altar had lifted slightly off the floor. I don't mean to sound glib, the image soon passed, but what I knew for certain was that something was happening here that I did not understand—real power surged from Father Christian and the other priests and traveled through the room—but it was not the kind of power that enables backflips or dislodges stuck Lightsabers with a flick of the wrist; this power was at once more subtle, more overwhelming, and also more humbling. It was something heavy laid on your shoulders, but the kind of weight your body was made to carry, reminding me of Jesus's words about his yoke being easy, his burden light. The heaviness bowed you over in gratitude, pressed you earthward with a desire to genuflect, and each morning during Mass at this moment—the Lifting of the Hands—I was so burdened with this welcomed weight that it was all I could do not to drop to my knees.

I was running low on sleep. Perhaps I was hallucinating. But after those long predawn hours of reading, prayer, and forced wakefulness, this spare, holy feast of bread and wine felt so lavish, so undeserved—*The body of Christ, broken for you,* said Father Joe, placing a wafer in my outstretched hands, *The blood of Christ, shed for you*—that all my inner defenses were overcome. I was being fed, my hunger was being subsumed.

On his first Mass at Gethsemani in 1941, Thomas Merton was similarly overwhelmed. In *The Seven Storey Mountain* he wrote that to him this liturgy proclaimed "one simple, cogent, tremendous truth: this church, the court of the Queen of heaven, is the real capital of the country in which we are living. This is the center of all the vitality that is in America. This is the cause and reason why the nation is holding together. These men . . . are doing for their land what no army, no congress, no president could ever do as such: they are winning for it the grace and the protection and the friendship of God." What Merton saw that day in 1941 was a vision extending backward and forward in time, touching down wherever people have seriously devoted themselves to God. What I saw at Mepkin is that such prayer was not disembodied or ethereal, did not exist up in the ether; it was utterly rooted in the fecund soil of this place, a constant interplay of *ora et labora,* prayer and work. Among these men prayer was itself a form of labor, and difficult labor at that. It is prayer that keeps the world from spinning off its axis.

At the culmination of the Mass we sang the Lord's Prayer to a melody that reminded me of Sibelius's *Finlandia*. The Lord's Prayer, wrote John Cassian in his visit to the fourth-century Egyptian monastics, lifts the heart of the one praying it "to that prayer of fire known to so few. It lifts them up to that ineffable prayer which rises above all human consciousness, with no voice sounding, no tongue moving, no words uttered." I wouldn't say I got that far with it, but each morning at Mepkin when I prayed the Our Father I found myself at once lifted up and pressed down. My knees wobbled, my eyes brimmed, my sense of connection to God was given a new potency. Moments like these were not entirely new; I had felt a similar connection to God at times during my years as the garden manager at Anathoth, like the times we celebrated the Eucharist out among the garden beds, or the time Sister Doris raised two heads of freshly harvested Jericho lettuce and shouted praises to God. But while in that place I often felt overwhelmed by the amount of human interaction, I was here beginning to glimpse a yearned-for balance of solitude and intimacy, of being both connected to others and standing apart in silence with the Lord; a piece of ground providing the anchor for both.

Terce, 8:15 A.M.

After Mass we sang Terce, a short service of Psalms and readings, and by then it was 8:30. We had been awake for five and a half hours, yet our workday was just beginning. As I left the sanctuary my head was abuzz with prayers and chants. *I will awake the dawn. Comfort, O Comfort my people.* When we gathered in the chapter room to receive work assignments, I was sent to work the oyster mushroom columns with Brothers Dismas and Anthony-Maria. Hopping on one of the monastery bicycles, I pedaled out to join them at the mushroom sheds.

"Get ready fellas," Dismas shouted. "I'm hauling in some Christmas gifts."

"I hope it's cheeseburgers," Anthony-Maria said.

Hardly. Dismas entered the growing shed wheeling a dolly with a hundred-pound barrel of pasteurized wheat chaff and cottonseed hulls. Into this substrate we would mix spawn and pack the mixture into long plastic tubes—the columns. A foot wide and five feet long when filled, each cylindrical plastic tube weighed sixty to seventy pounds. After they were packed came three weeks of waiting, the mycelium running along its ancient pathways, slowly turning death into life until suddenly, out of the darkness, the mushrooms would emerge.

Dismas and Anthony-Maria were in charge of making the columns. I stood beside Anthony-Maria, an African American man. He had a quiet, serious demeanor, though his smile suggested a lively humor. He reminded me of a monastic Mr. T without the Mohawk. Aside from a few terse directives—"Kneepads on that hook," "Spray some denatured alcohol on those tarps"—Anthony-Maria had uttered very few words. I was curious how he had ended up in a Trappist monastery and taken such an intriguing name. Once we knelt on the concrete and started packing tubes with mushroom substrate, I asked him.

"Well, I was driving cab up in Philly, and somebody said, 'Man, you too good-*lookin'* to be living in Philly—you need to move to North Carolina.' And somehow this is where I ended up. You may not have heard, but I was voted Best Looking Monk in *Monastic Quarterly* four years running."

"I thought you were just runner-up," Dismas said.

"Naw, I was runner-up at Internationals. Got beat there by a double cheeseburger." The two tried to hold a straight face, but Anthony-Maria erupted in belly laughter. I'd been had. In church, Anthony-Maria's visage was inscrutable, but out here in the mushroom shed, the man who had been the gregarious cab driver from Philly emerged. Slowly he shared more of his story.

Before he became Brother Anthony-Maria, his name was Rodney. After driving a cab for a few years he started a small business in computers. He tended a small garden and mostly kept to himself. People told him he was shy, but really he was just comfortable being alone. He started reading about Zen Buddhism, which led him to Christian monastic literature, and when he read *The Life of Saint*

Anthony, "that was it." He became a Catholic. "I wanted to pray like Saint Anthony," he said, lifting his hands, "and become light."

Saint Anthony (251–356), the son of well-to-do peasants, was sitting in church one day when a text from the Gospels was read, and in Jesus's words to a rich young ruler Anthony heard instead a command addressed directly to himself: "Go, sell all you have and give to the poor and come and follow me." He left everything behind and set out for the desert, where he discovered an abandoned fort and walled himself in. There was a spring inside the fort, and friends would bring him bread twice a year, but he otherwise had no human company. Later he moved into a cave, which became his permanent dwelling. For the next twenty years, Anthony fasted and prayed and fought demons, uniting himself to Christ. Word spread of Anthony's holiness, and soon others were leaving their homes to become hermits in the desert of Egypt, marking the beginnings of Christian monasticism.

When Rodney finished reading *The Life of Saint Anthony* he knew he would become a monk. At first he thought he needed to go live in a cave, but then he learned that modern monasticism was much less rigorous than it was in the fourth century. For a time he continued working in Philly, leading a monkish life of prayer mostly on his own, and attending Mass. Then he moved to Charlotte, North Carolina, thinking he would join a Benedictine abbey there, but that monastery was located in the center of a co-ed college. During his visit he took one walk across campus with all the pretty women sauntering about and said, "No way." Then he discovered Mepkin. That was two years ago. Now he had received the novice habit, an important first step toward becoming a Trappist, and assumed the name Anthony-Maria after his twin guides in the faith: Maria, the Virgin of Guadalupe, and Anthony, the first monk. "Many times you hear something and it speaks to your whole being," he said. "You want to respond to it, but nobody else is doing it so you don't. But then you do it. And it turns out it wasn't as difficult as you thought."

After packing several hundred pounds of pasteurized wheat chaff, cottonseed hulls, and mushroom spawn into a dozen plastic columns, Anthony-Maria and I carted them over to a truck, where we hung them lengthwise on movable racks. The columns were sealed on one end and tied with yellow twine on the other. Now we needed to punch holes in them so the growing mycelium would send out fruiting bodies. To do this, Anthony-Maria produced a wicked looking tool: a two-by-four with razor-sharp arrowheads screwed on. He went down the line, punching the upright columns like a seasoned street fighter, then handed the device to me. "Next row is yours." After I punched holes in the remaining columns, we drove the truck around to a long line of tractor-trailers—temperature- and humidity-controlled grow rooms—and hung the columns from metal hooks. Here they would stay for the next month, producing several crops of oyster mushrooms.

It was clear that Anthony-Maria loved this life, but I wanted to know about its challenges. "Giving up romance," he said, "that's been hard." Other monks I asked, especially the younger ones like Dismas, said the same thing. I recalled reading in the introduction to the *Rule* that Benedict, whenever he felt lust rising within him, would roll naked in a patch of stinging nettles. If there's anything that could quell thoughts of lust, I imagined, it would certainly be nettle-stung nethers.

Another big challenge for Anthony-Maria was giving up cheeseburgers. When Brother Vincent recently traveled to Scotland, Anthony-Maria asked him to bring him back his favorite food. Instead Vincent mailed Anthony-Maria a postcard with some cows on it. "This is all Homeland Security would allow me to send," Vincent wrote. But cheeseburger deprivation for Anthony-Maria was minor. Dealing with himself had been the hardest. "You're confronted by yourself here in a way that you're not out in the world."

Yes, I thought. Hope for this kind of confrontation with myself had brought me to Mepkin.

We drove back to the shed and found Dismas wrestling a second batch of columns onto a cart. "Working the columns" it was called, and Dismas reveled in it. Though slight of build, the man possessed a wiry strength. After a morning hoisting columns, I was eager to rest, but Dismas never really stopped moving. One reason he came to the Trappists was because after four years of studying academic theology at Notre Dame he realized he couldn't even fix a kitchen sink. "I needed to put the faith in *my hands*." He had learned that certain mental and spiritual problems could not be resolved intellectually; they needed to be worked out physically, with one's own body. Manual labor was the ancient monastic cure for many a spiritual ailment. "I see work as very incarnational. Jesus became flesh, muscle, sinew. He put his body where the question was. And then he walked the question."

I asked Dismas what he meant by the question.

"Human sin. Broken relationships. Loneliness. Take the most agonizing question of your life—that's the question Jesus came into and walked." Which seemed a good way to think about what drove men like Dismas and Anthony-Maria to become monks. An agonizing question for which there were no immediate answers, a yearning without apparent remedy.

That is, until a way avails itself to the seeker. A way which becomes the Way, followed by a sudden and overwhelming desire to walk in it. This is the nature of the calling. With its rigors and rituals the monastic life offered a well-worn path to follow. The monastery anchored your spiritual life through life in the body: getting up at 3 A.M., packing cottonseed hulls into columns, putting the faith in your hands.

You put your body where the question is, then you walk the question.

As the days passed, I was to learn that the monks of Mepkin felt called to this life in different ways, and from very different backgrounds. One day shortly before Sext, the noonday prayer before lunch, I was pedaling along the road under a canopy of live oaks and Spanish moss when Brother Theophilus passed me in a golf cart and waved. I waved back. Earlier in the week I had spent several mornings helping him in the shiitake grow rooms.

Incredulity. That's the reaction Theophilus had when he realized God was calling him to this life. "Most Trappists are introverts by nature," he said, "but I'm more of an extrovert. People call me an evangelical Catholic."

Our first task was to release the submerged shiitake logs, which had been soaking overnight in a giant plastic tub. They weren't actually logs, but were made from a blended substrate similar to the oyster mix, only these had been pressed into four-pound logs the size of a football. Mottled brown with white splotches, they looked like overgrown Tootsie Rolls that had been sitting out in the rain for a couple of years. The vat held forty or fifty logs, and after fishing them out and placing them on plastic trays, we wheeled them on dollies into the grow rooms, where they would sit for two weeks before fruiting.

Before landing here Theophilus had been Alan, a district supervisor for a family grocery store chain in eastern Tennessee, then a manager of several Love's truck stops in Kentucky and South Carolina. He was also a rabid sports nut. Alan loved to call in to talk radio sports shows, where his handle was "Tennessee Big Al." For many years he ran a website called Sports Parlor South, a gathering place for other sports fanatics like himself who wished to pay homage to their teams, especially the University of Tennessee Volunteers. Alan and some fans launched a big campaign to get a statue of General Neyland, the UT football coach, installed outside the stadium. After much time and effort at what became a quasi-religious pursuit, Alan began to wonder if this sports craze of his wasn't masking some deeper hunger.

He began to get more involved in his local church, and his prayer life deepened, even as his marriage faltered. As his own faith grew, he and his wife grew apart, and against his wishes she filed for divorce. With his four children mostly grown, Alan found himself living alone. Though pained at his divorce, he enjoyed his newfound hermit's life of prayer. Something was happening to him. Once, after leaving a Denny's restaurant where he had counseled a despairing friend, he was speeding down the highway and had to pull over. He felt as if waves were pouring over him. He thought, "Either I'm having a heart attack or this is the Holy Spirit." After that he decided to go on retreat at Gethsemani Abbey in Kentucky. Standing in the balcony during Compline, the final night prayers, he suddenly experienced something momentous, unexplainable, completely losing track of time. When he opened his eyes everyone was gone. "You know when you're making love to a woman and you just lose yourself? It was like that. You're just utterly at peace."

After stacking our shiitake logs in one of the grow rooms, we checked on the oyster columns made several weeks previously. Some were fruiting, the whitish blue mushroom caps rising with humble beauty toward the light. In the fluorescent glow they appeared strange, as if they had come from another world. Alan showed me around the other grow rooms, old tractor-trailers in which he had cobbled together fans, humidity controls, and lights with timers.

Because the abbey couldn't always afford new equipment, they used what was on hand. I pointed to a fifty-gallon plastic trash can suspended from the ceiling. It had been converted into a ventilation shaft, held loosely in place by bungee cords and duct tape. "Looks like a MacGyver rig," I said. Theophilus chuckled. "Almost everything we do around here is a MacGyver rig."

For much of his adult life Alan was a tailgater—not just the beers-before-ballgames kind, but the riding-your-bumper kind. He would habitually drive fifteen to twenty miles over the speed limit. If people didn't move to the right lane, he would tailgate them and hurl insults. "Pull over, speed up, or blow up, I don't care—just get out of my way." Prior to what he called his reconversion, Alan knew he was hungry for truth. "I wanted to love God, but I didn't know God to an extent that I could love him." One night after his experience in Gethsemani, he knelt down and made God three promises. Every day from then on he vowed to read his Bible, make his bed, and stop tailgating people. "Then I passed the ball back to God. I said, 'Lord, that's the best I can do, please help me to find my way.'"

"Did you stop speeding?" I asked.

"Nope. But I did stop tailgating people."

Our mushroom duties complete, we hopped into the golf cart and zoomed off to one of the sheds. Along the way Theophilus lit a cigar, stopped to unload a manure spreader full of mushroom substrate, then jumped into the Bobcat and mixed this with leftover manure from the chicken houses. He was making compost and hoped to sell this rich soil to home gardeners around Charleston as another potential income stream. The earth was sustaining the monks' life of prayer in ever increasing ways.

After his experience in the balcony at Gethsemani and the visitation on the highway, Alan knew that God was pursuing him. One morning he was praying downstairs in his condo, and decided to go up to his bedroom and lie down, desiring to go deeper in prayer. When he lay down on his bed, face toward the ceiling, he unconsciously stretched out his arms. He realized his body was forming the shape of a cross, and a thought came to him: *I wonder what it would be like to be pinned like this.* "And then—bam. All kinds of images came pouring in. I heard God pretty clearly saying, *Okay, it's time to follow me.*" He went downstairs, lit a cigarette, made a pot of coffee, and began making a list. There were many things he would need to do before joining the monastery. Though he thought he would join Gethsemani, God led him to Mepkin.

He remains incredulous and not a little amused that God would want to make him, a garrulous evangelical Catholic, into a monk, and a Trappist no less, known for their practice of silence, though during my visit most of the brothers of Mepkin were kind enough to relax that practice to chat with me. Most times Theophilus follows this practice, though he's found that in a community silence can occasionally become poisonous, hindering reconciliation between the brothers. "Sometimes you just gotta cut through the bull crap and speak the truth, you know?" he told me. Even in his new life, the old Alan sometimes returns. One day he was in the golf cart on his way to the noon prayer, when he came upon a tour group blocking the road. "My first thought was: *Crap—another bunch of old farts in my way.*" Instead of waiting for them to move, he swerved into the grass and sped past. Telling me the story he shook his head, amazed that he was still capable of such blunders. "I was trying to get to church," he said, "to learn such things as patience, peace, and lovingkindness."

In the oyster grow rooms most of the columns were black plastic, but I noticed a few smaller ones that were clear. The clear ones, Theophilus said, allowed the monks to watch for possible contaminations of mold, which could ruin an entire batch. So why not make all the columns clear?

"Because mushrooms grow better in darkness," he said. "It forces them to reach toward the light."

Sext, 12:00 noon

During my previous year's visit to the abbey, Father Leonard, one of the older monks, passed away after a long decline. It was during Sext on that visit that we gathered in the breezeway's cold wind and sprinkled holy water on his body.

Father Leonard was from Charleston and had joined the monastery in 1960. A black man, he suffered from a rare skin disease that, over the course of his lifetime, turned his skin completely white. On my first visit here, in fact, I thought he was white. Which confirmed just how little skin color has to do with anything. "He was a soul brutha," Dismas told me, equally comfortable speaking Gullah as he was in the contemplative silence of the monastery. Every so often Father Leonard would slip into that dialect with Dismas. *Make you dun come on in heah.* He was a funny man, said Dismas, and a complex man. In the late 1960s Father Leonard left Mepkin to join the civil rights movement. He ran for a seat in the South Carolina House of Representatives and nearly won, quite a feat in the South of the late 1960s. At a time when the rest of the nation was trying to keep black people out of sight and certainly out of public office, the brothers of Mepkin had welcomed him as one of their own, and supported his run for the legislature. And when his political energy was expended, they welcomed Father Leonard back to the monastery, where he lived out the rest of his years. A few days before he died, he asked for his last meal. Defying the order's vegetarian standards, he requested—and received—a fried baloney sandwich.

The morning Father Leonard's death was announced, I had been wandering aimlessly around the cloister when Brother Vincent approached. Vincent was an old Catholic radical from the 1960s, tall and lanky with a gray beard. He once had a farm near Kent State, and was active in the protests after the National Guard shot four students there.

"Young man," Vincent said, "what are you doing for the next ten minutes?"

"Going to read the Desert Fathers," I said.

"Want to join me on a fool's errand?"

"Sure, why not."

We went into the music room and Vincent pointed to a longish wood box. We needed to wrap a sheet around the foam pad inside the box, and he showed me how. We worked and talked for the next fifteen minutes or so, until it occurred to me that this box had a strangely familiar shape. We were preparing Father Leonard's bier.

Trappists don't use coffins. They put the monk's body on a bier and carry it to the graveside where, clad in his habit, he is removed and lowered into the hole. The brothers each put a shovel full of soil on the body, connecting themselves to their brother in death as they had been connected in life. I had to leave the day before Leonard's funeral and was sorry to miss it. I had come to appreciate the way the monks dealt with death. The monastic funeral made death a part of life. When I go, I'd like my friends to just put me in a hole and shovel some dirt on me in the same way. No fancy casket, no chemicals pumped through my veins. I'd like them to sing a few Psalms and lay me in the soft ground where I'll await the Resurrection, slowly becoming compost.

In the breezeway that day, Leonard was laid out on what I now thought of as "my" bier. Whether I wanted to or not, I felt strangely connected to this man. I knew him very little, yet the choreography of life here at the abbey brought me into intimate contact with him even in death. I'd never been so close to a corpse before. Even at my own grandparents' funerals, I'd kept my distance. I prayed and sang and shed a tear during the service, and the funeral home took care of the rest. But here the brothers were each other's funeral home. On the one hand you might go years and only exchange a handful of words with your brother, but meanwhile you shared an intimacy of daily contact through the dishes you washed and the mushrooms you grew and the Psalms you chanted in unison, until the day one of you would cover the other with soil.

The choreography of life for the monks was a constant movement between retreat and connection, a dance whose moves had been rehearsed for 1,500 years. Abbot Stan had asked me if I would be a pallbearer, which seemed a perfectly reasonable request, considering that the septua- and octo- and nonagenarian monks couldn't do much heavy lifting. I was happy to agree. When I grabbed a corner of the bier and hoisted Leonard onto the stretcher, I thought about how Father Leonard was ending his journey just as I was beginning mine, and I remembered these lines from Rilke:

> *The stir of departure—*
> *Someone being carried to his grave,*
> *and another, taking up the pilgrim's staff,*
> *to ask in unknown places for the path*
> *where he knows you are waiting.*

We walked to the church singing hymns. I held the foot of the bier, Leonard's black Velcro Reeboks swinging back and forth in front of my hands. Once inside the church we sang a brief antiphon, then each person in turn walked forward with a sprig of juniper, dipped it in the font of holy water, and sprinkled the water onto Leonard's head. One of the monks remained behind with Leonard's body, reading him Psalms through the afternoon. The rest of us filed out of the church and walked in silence to the refectory and there, with the ravenous hunger of the living, we ate our fill.

One day toward the end of lunch, as Sinatra crooned about doing it "my way," Brother Robert shuffled past me on his way to the kitchen carrying his brothers' dirty dishes. Trappists eat most of their meals in silence. During the noon meal, however, one of the brothers will read aloud from a book—a Catholic theologian, say, or *Sayings of the Desert Fathers*. On feast days they cranked up the record player. Sometimes they played opera, other times big band music. They played all of it on vinyl, and, for the benefit of the hearing-impaired older brothers, they played it with the volume cranked high. It is a surreal experience to sit silently at a table with a group of monks, eating mushroom risotto and Caesar salad, while the *Chariots of Fire* theme blasts at full volume, listened to and appreciated without irony. Acknowledging how strange the experience must be for me, Brother Dismas turned around slowly and caught my eye, nodded his head up and down, and silently mouthed *Oh. Yeah.*

On this anniversary of Leonard's death, I'd been pondering the strange connection I had felt to that man, having suddenly been pressed into service as his pallbearer. Brother Robert smiled at me and went on his way through the kitchen door, and as he passed I thought again about the peculiar genius of the monastic way of life; how powerfully connected they were, gathering seven times a day for prayer and doing each other's dishes at mealtimes, even while being so solitary and removed from the normal flow of life.

For the past forty-some years Robert had been constructing a vast network of what he called *landings*—jetties and shacks and tree forts scattered around the abbey's 3,100 acres. Nothing spoke to me so powerfully in my week at Mepkin as the allure of those retreats, where the mystery of making intimate connection with God was as palpable and immediate as if I'd stepped back to the fourth-century Egyptian desert where the monastic flame was first kindled.

On my forays into Mepkin's vast network of trails I'd begun to find them. They were scattered around what the monks called Big Egypt and Little Egypt, the two vast tracts of land up- and downriver from the abbey. Just as the first monastics in the fourth century built their cells in the wasteland of Egypt's deserts, Robert had built his landings in the "desert" regions of Mepkin's acres, finding little eddies of quiet—up in a tree, among the reeds in an estuary—where a person could flee and be alone with God. The landings were patched-together affairs, jury-rigged jetties and tree houses made from old lawn chairs, tractor parts, and two-by-fours. They had a whimsical, childlike quality, an innocence of design reflective of their maker. One day I was scrambling around on the riverbank near the cemetery when I noticed signs of Brother Robert's handiwork: a steel cable nailed to a tree leading downhill to the Cooper River. A live oak jutted out over the river and up high in the tree, in a natural fork, Brother Robert had built one of his landings: a rusty metal lawn chair nailed to some plywood, which bridged several limbs. Just the kind of place I would have loved as a kid. When I climbed up into the fort, it looked like nobody had been there in years. Robert had arthritis, he told me, and couldn't tend to his landings anymore.

I had seen several other tree stands over the course of uncharted afternoon wanderings. They were often beside a trail, at the edge of a field, or overlooking the river. One day walking in Big Egypt, I found one that was more of a tree fort, perched nearly forty feet off the ground in a live oak several hundred years old. The tree leaned at a forty-five-degree angle out over a marsh, and the platform was rickety, made from a bunch of plywood and old tin. But the perch was magnificent. Sitting in a three-legged chair looking down on the gnarled cypress knees emerging from the swamp below, I felt a touch of childlike wonder.

On other walks I had discovered several of Robert's jetties. Built out over the old rice fields surrounding the abbey, which by now had become marshland, these prayer platforms jutted twenty or thirty feet out over the water, always with a lone, half-rotten chair at the end. I sat down on one of the landings in a large lagoon. Raccoon scat lay scattered about, and the exoskeletons of crawfish. Across the water I counted four other jetties, each well enough apart to provide solitude. I imagined a Sunday at Mepkin thirty years ago, Robert and Gregory and the other monks each posted up on a jetty, like watchmen awaiting the king's arrival.

I was eager to find more of Robert's hidden treasures, and when he returned from his dish duty in the kitchen that day at lunch, I caught his arm and asked him to show me his favorite spots. His eighty-two-year-old body wouldn't cooperate, he said, but if I met him after None, the brief prayer following lunch, he would bring the maps.

None, 12:50 P.M.

On a table in the guest dining room we leaned over and studied Robert's maps of Big and Little Egypt. Several were his own, drawn from memory, but he also brought two maps drawn by a visiting priest who happened to be an amateur cartographer. When Robert pointed to a route I might take through Little Egypt, I noticed his hands. They were like the gnarled cypress knees out in the marsh, his knuckles ballooned by arthritis. He'd spent a lifetime using those hands: mowing on the tractor, tending chickens, building crazy prayer platforms up in the trees and jutting out over old rice paddies.

Now he couldn't do much more than wash dishes, but wash dishes he did—and a lot of them—without complaining. Out in the world beyond the abbey gates, many people Robert's age were sequestered in nursing homes, senescence gradually claiming their minds and bodies. I now understood the full tragedy of why this was so: they were given no useful work. We cordon off our elderly, telling them they are no longer needed, and so their lives sputter and flicker out in loneliness and neglect; but Robert's fire still burned bright. Like Brother Gregory and Father Christian and the other elderly monks, Robert was both physically active and mentally engaged. He had to be; his brothers needed him.

As we pored over the maps and talked about the geography of Mepkin, we turned to the geography of Robert's life. For a number of years he lived at Gethsemani. Did he have any interactions with Merton? Yes, Robert knew of Father Louis, as Merton was called by his brothers. Once Robert was driving a jeep along one of the monastery's dirt roads when he came upon Merton, who was probably trying to escape the beehive of activity that Gethsemani had become as a result of his writings. When Merton stuck out his thumb, Robert picked him up and drove him up to the fire tower. In those days the practice of silence was more severe, and the two men never exchanged a word. It was their only interaction. Robert was then assigned to help start the new monastery at Mepkin. He never saw Merton again.

Each of my three visits to Mepkin had occurred in winter, yet I'd never seen Robert wear a coat or even socks. While other monks wore the cowl, the long white robe, Robert refused. It chafed his arms, he said, and so even in winter he wore only the thin black and white Trappist garb, his arms sleeveless and exposed. He giggled when he told me this, a small act of resistance to the monastery's status quo. For forty-seven years Robert was in charge of the chickens, which meant that each night he had to get up and check on them, and his sleep patterns are still erratic. He goes to bed around 9 or 9:30, gets up for a snack at 11, goes back to bed, then gets up at 2 A.M. and rides the exercise bike. Then he reads the Bible, a little bit every day. The whole book takes him about ten years, and then he starts over. "I skip all the begats, though," he said. By the time he's finished with his daily Bible reading it's 3:20 A.M., time for Vigils, and a new day. About five years ago Robert's heart developed a murmur, then arthritis kicked in and his energy level greatly decreased. When he does venture into the woods now, he doesn't go far. The old trails are overgrown, the landings in disrepair. "But if we had a bunch of young guys like you," he said, his eyes suddenly growing bright, "why we could fix them up!" Robert longs for the days when he could set off for the woods and spend the night in one of his half dozen little shacks, a man in his prime with little clothing and no possessions, carrying with him only a flashlight and the desire to go deeper into God's mercy. He was like Saint Anthony living out in the elements. Give him a cave, a stale crust of bread, and a codex and he'd be content. Along with my choir-mate Gregory, Brother Robert seemed to me one of the happiest people I'd ever met.

He told me I should look for a special overlook along the river several miles south of the monastery. It was beautiful there, and along the way I might even see an old rice boiler from the plantation days. He smiled and handed me the clutch of maps as a gift, then shook my hand like a well-wisher seeing a friend off on a long voyage. He wished he could accompany me, he said, but he was confident I could find my own way.

The way was not immediately apparent. I tried to take a shortcut behind the monastery and follow a tangled trail beside the old rice fields, but I ended up hacking through greenbrier and spiky palmetto palms. Soon I was cut up and frustrated. A barred owl hooted above me in a dead oak tree, which I took as a sign, and I turned around. Backtracking, I found the way I should have followed.

The first field I came to was named Saint Joseph's, leased to a neighboring farmer who planted it in cotton. At the edge of the field stood a massive live oak, and up in a crotch in the trunk I could see a wooden platform. Though this was not the overlook Brother Robert steered me toward, I climbed up, dropped into an old rusty lawn chair, and entered into prayer.

As a boy growing up in Montana I used to hunt from a tree stand. I would sit with bow and arrow until long after dusk, waiting for a big buck to emerge from the thicket below. It was a contemplative pursuit, a kind of active waiting. The deer may or may not emerge, but you waited with full expectation that it would until eventually the waiting became an end in itself. When I was sixteen my father, brother, and I traveled to northernmost Quebec to bow hunt. South of Ungava Bay, near the Arctic Circle, I killed two caribou. But that was different: I was hunting in a group, and there were so many caribou migrating across the lake that it would have been difficult for my arrow *not* to hit one. In all my years sitting alone in tree stands, I never shot a deer. And yet those hunts are some of my most memorable.

I understand now that I was not really after deer. Sitting high up in a stand of aspens or perched in a big maple between two alfalfa fields, my body swaying with the trees in the cold breeze of an October evening, I was like Elijah in his cave on Mount Horeb, waiting for God to pass by. God would come to me then, across the vastness of the fields, and I would suddenly be enveloped. My teenage worries would vanish, and for long stretches—fifteen minutes? forty-five?—I would lose myself. I would simply *be*. Resting in God, the monks call it. And the hunting I found most conducive to such rest was from a tree stand. Perhaps that's why Brother Robert had built so many of them in Mepkin's woods.

Scrambling back down, I took a dirt road bisecting St. Joseph's that led me through the fields of cotton. On either side of the road I began to see mushrooms, first one or two, then whole patches of them. They looked like Parasols, or perhaps the poisonous Destroying Angels. All of the mushrooms were on the side of the road, none in the tilled cotton fields. This was a conventional cotton field, and fertilizers had replaced the nutrients fungi had once supplied to the plants' ancestors. For fungi to flourish, the soil must remain undisturbed; plowing destroys mycelium. Yet all around Saint Joseph's field the undisturbed woods were undergirded and fed by the fungal web, invisible strands connecting field and forest.

I left Saint Joseph's, passed through a short stretch of pine and live oak, and emerged at Saint Anne's field, where I discovered another tree stand. This one looked too tidy to be one of Robert's; his were always cobbled together with old wire and bits of scrap wood, while this one looked almost new. I climbed up for a look, sat down, and without even meaning to, again found myself praying.

I would need to return to the abbey soon to keep my appointment with Father Kevin, my spiritual advisor for the week, but it was such a restful place that I lingered. Why rush off to talk about my prayer life when I was experiencing prayer here and now? As I sat and thought about why I'd come to Mepkin, I realized that, despite these solitary moments in the trees or beside the river, the connection with God I sought could not be sustained in retreat from the world. I did not, after all, really want to escape the messiness of human life; I wanted to embrace it. I wanted to claim my role as a co-creator with God of the earthly city. And that meant claiming my place in the human family, with all its frailties and frustrations. I was no hermit.

I didn't find the overlook Robert had recommended that day, but I discovered something else: the realization that I didn't need to escape to Mepkin to find my own little prayer landing. I had one back home.

The spiritual ecology of prayer always includes such places of withdrawal—landings, tree stands, a chair by the wood stove—unadorned places where your soul can touch down for a while and simply be. It is in such silent emptiness that God is waiting. Here there is no need to plow the air with constant chatter. Let the mind's field lie fallow, such places tell us, let the mycelial strands of prayer run in the dark and see what fruit may come. And when you leave, those same strands will follow under your feet, undergirding everything you do.

Vespers, 6 P.M.

Perhaps it was the fullness of the week, but as I sat in Vespers singing the Lord's Prayer on my last day at Mepkin, a sweetness welled in me and brought me to tears. The music, the prayers, the bowing and rising, the incense—all of it was breaking down my defenses. That's what good liturgy does. It breaks your heart open and turns you toward God. And these brothers sitting around me in choir? They were not spiritual escapists, trying to flee the world in search of purity. They knew that the biggest battle was not with an evil world, but with the waywardness of their own hearts. They had come to the abbey to turn themselves toward God. They were simply a group of very human beings coming together for a single goal: to go deeper into the Divine Mystery. This realization gave me strength, and at that moment I didn't want to leave.

Suddenly the service was over, and I lingered around the altar. Was I alone in feeling a certain fullness in the air? Others seemed to be milling about, too, not rushing off to their tasks as they normally did. There was a warmth, a welcome heaviness on my shoulders: the

Spirit's presence was among us. I walked about, unsure of my direction, as if tipsy or slightly dazed. I was not alone; we were drunk on God, woozy with the weight of glory.

In between Vespers and Compline passes an interval of roughly an hour. Mostly that time is free for the monks to engage in some kind of constructive activity. On the Feast of the Immaculate Conception, Brother Dismas and I agreed that drinking beer and reading poetry were suitably constructive activities, and ones best practiced together. He read to me from his collection, which was under consideration by a small press in Canada. There were dark poems, full of internal struggle, but the best were the poems that left angst behind and opened into something larger. My favorite was a poem about his visit to a community of handicapped people. He meets a girl with cerebral palsy, bends down and touches her cheek, and two souls make contact. The poem was called "Love Song of a Celibate Man."

Compline, 7:35 P.M.

At the end of a long day it was good to sit again next to my friend Gregory. One afternoon earlier that week we sat together in the senior wing watching a pair of nuthatches flit about the feeder outside the window.

Father Kevin had told me a story about taking Gregory to the VA hospital in Charleston. Gregory was a veteran of World War II, and on their trips to the hospital he always wore his Trappist habit. In the waiting room a little girl turned to her father, pointed a finger at Gregory, and asked "Daddy, what's *that*?"

"That is a *he*," Father Kevin said to the little girl, "and *he* is a monk." The girl's father looked perplexed. "I didn't know they still had *them*."

That afternoon while watching birds I had asked Gregory about his life. He had been the monastery's infirmarian for most of his life, but as his body aged he gave up that role and began a ministry over email. People wrote to the monastery with prayer requests and Gregory would respond, sometimes spending seven or eight hours a day in front of the computer. But he developed a urinary tract infection from so much sitting, he told me, and he no longer did much emailing.

I asked Gregory the kind of questions a young man in search of wisdom asks of an older man who possesses it, but his memory was fading. He mostly smiled and nodded, staring for long moments out the window. His membership among the brothers here was drawing to a close. Soon he would join the great cloud of witnesses. As he broke off and looked into the far distance, he seemed to be joining them even now, reluctant to return.

I had asked Gregory about Merton, but he couldn't recall much other than that he had lived across the hall from him for a few years. December 10, my last day at the monastery, was the anniversary not only of Merton joining Gethsemani, but also of his death. While attending a monastic conference in Bangkok in 1968, twenty-seven years to the day after his entrance into Gethsemani, Merton was in the bathtub when he reached to switch off an electric fan and was accidentally electrocuted. As Abbot Stan said, shaking his head in fond remembrance, "We all knew that Father Louis and machinery didn't get along."

My week at Mepkin ended all too abruptly. On the drive out I spotted a sign on the road depicting a camouflaged hunter falling from a tree with this warning: *Tree Stand Injuries—Avoid Them!*

The transition back into family life was not easy. I was distracted, thinking about the blissful silence of the monastery and my long walks among the prayer landings. Elizabeth had to remind me to help with the dishes or fix our boys' breakfast. When the boys wanted me to jump on the trampoline or read them a book, I found myself unable to focus. I became short-tempered and moody, all the peace I had accumulated the previous week suddenly vanished. I had gone to Mepkin in search of a solitude that might help me connect better with others, yet here, back with my own family, I had fallen from the tree.

"Bring the monastery home with you," Elizabeth pleaded. "You are here now. We need you. You need us." I remembered Father Kevin's words about *lectio divina:* "*Lectio* is about the word of God written in scripture. But what about the word of God written in your life? Your spouse? Your children? You must be open to the dynamic Word that continues to come." Father Kevin suggested that, once I returned home, I should set aside twenty minutes of complete silence each morning, no distractions, to be with God. During this time I should try thanking God for five things in my life. Gratitude leads to humility, Father Kevin said, which leads to praise. Which leads you to focus not on yourself but on God. Finally you must focus your attention upon those with whom you share your life—family, friends, neighbors, enemies—and give thanks for them. For it is in their faces that you will discover the image and likeness of God.

Two weeks after I came home, just two days before Christmas, Brother Gregory died. I knew him so little, yet I felt as though I'd lost a good friend. His body was placed on the same bier I had prepared for Leonard, he was waked, then removed from the bier and lowered into the ground, where the dirt was placed on him one shovelful at a time. He lies there now, on a bluff overlooking the Cooper River, awaiting the resurrection of the body.

I remembered sitting beside Gregory my last service of Compline. Our voices were strong, and outside the moon was full, the night air cold. Across the fields another life, a hidden life, went on unseen beneath the ground, supporting our life above. A mycelial web, connecting and undergirding and vivifying every living thing.

Prayer ends in darkness.

But the Light shines in the darkness. And the darkness has not overcome it.

Three months after my visit, Brother Dismas left the monastery. He reassumed his old name, Josh, and when I spoke with him on the phone about his leaving, he seemed unsure in his new secular identity. At the meeting in which he informed the brothers of his departure, he admitted to his long struggle with the vow of chastity. "I want to take a brunette out for coffee," he had told the brothers. After the meeting Brother Vincent approached him, laid a firm hand on his shoulder, and said, "For God's sake, Dismas—don't limit yourself to brunettes."

In the days and weeks following my return home, Elizabeth and my three sons helped me see what Father Kevin had been trying to tell me, that I could take some of the disciplines of prayer and rootedness of the monastery, some of its special blend of solitude and connection, and apply those to my life as a husband and a father. I could be present with them instead of letting my thoughts wander. I could do my share of the housework and allow myself to be interrupted by my children's needs. I could bring the monastery home.

As Brother Dismas's departure from Mepkin attested, most of us are not called to solitude or chastity. We are called, rather, to embrace God while also embracing one another.

In my quest to find my own way to practice the sacramental cultivation of soil and spirit, Mepkin had given me some answers.

But I was still unclear about the journey. I had come to believe, years before in a tiny Mayan village in the highlands of Chiapas, Mexico, that I had been called to feed people. Now, I realized, I had to dig deeper into the substance of that calling. I had to challenge my vocation and, I hoped, reclaim it. I had found myself in a similar unsettled state of searching during that trip to Chiapas, my life having taken a wholly unexpected turn.

CHAPTER TWO

Dwellers in the Dust

This is the way; walk in it.
—Isaiah 30

Chiapas, Mexico—Spring 2001

Before I tried my hand at planting gardens, I'd first tried to seek peace. In the winter of 2001, not long after graduating from divinity school, I signed up with a group of nonviolent Christian activists, hoping to get placed in a war zone.

When I'd first arrived in San Cristóbal the summer before, I had spent my first few days banging on the doors of nongovernmental organizations, but none was especially interested in hiring a twenty-something gringo with no experience. They wouldn't even let me volunteer. A few of them, though, directed me to the tiny office of Christian Peacemaker Teams (CPT), headquartered in Chicago with bases in Hebron, Colombia, and Chiapas. But when I knocked on the door of CPT's office in San Cristóbal and asked about working with Las Abejas, a Mayan civil society with whom CPT worked, they told me I had to first undergo their rigorous month-long training course in nonviolent activism, and that the next class would begin that coming January, in Chicago. Now here I was, a fully trained peace activist several months into my stay in

Chiapas, at the beginning of the most sacred Christian week of the year.

When the Virgin crested the hill, a man emerged from his doorway and gave a shout. Others rushed from their huts. Perched on a dais borne on the shoulders of four men dressed in leather sandals and white tunics, she descended the narrow dirt trail toward the village. Behind her, a long procession unfurled over and down the hill. Musicians marched in front, playing wooden harps and guitars and child-sized violins carved with a hatchet. A lone trumpeter announced the Virgin's arrival, his notes bearing no particular relation to the melody.

The village of Nuevo Yibeljoj (*Yee-bell-ho*) was a half hour's walk from the nearest highway, perched on the side of a steep ravine in an airy, rugged land of mountain mists and waterfalls. The villagers were members of Las Abejas, a nonviolent civil society of Mayan Catholics who had become targets of government persecution. Chiapas was the site of the 1994 Zapatista peasant revolt and since then the Mexican government has waged an ongoing struggle there against its own Mayan citizens. When I first arrived in June 2000 more than seventy thousand troops, a third of the Mexican military, were in Chiapas. To travel anywhere one had to pass through armed checkpoints. Chiapas had become a police state. The simple peasants had failed to be sufficiently grateful for the crumbs thrown to them from the master's table, and they now demanded not just a decent meal, but an equal place at the feast.

Some five thousand strong, Las Abejas—"the Bees"—had named themselves as such because they were many in number and prized the communal over the individual. They had a sting, too: *Nuestra arma es la palabra de Dios,* declared their motto. Our Weapon is the Word of God. The group was distinguished from other opposition groups in Latin America by their consistent refusal to use violence. With support from their radical bishop, Don Samuel Ruiz, they had decided to take what Jesus said literally and to stake their lives on his command to love our enemies.

Some of them lost their lives trying. In 1997 Las Abejas had been attacked by government-sponsored paramilitaries wielding guns and machetes. Descending on the village of Acteal, the attackers had killed forty-five men, women, and children.

I had read about these modern-day martyrs in my last year of divinity school and been inspired by their impossible moral response to the world's cruelties. I wanted to stand with them before the next paramilitary attack.

Almost all of the villagers of Nuevo Yibeljoj had been displaced from their homes three years earlier by paramilitary forces sponsored by the Mexican government. They had shouldered the few belongings they could carry and walked several hours to the village of X'oyep (*Sho-yep*), where they built shanties, becoming exiles in their own homeland. Then, just a few months before I arrived, they had returned, despite continuing paramilitary threats. They found their houses destroyed and their land taken by others. So they built a new village down the hill in a ravine, a "new" Yibeljoj. The Virgin was being carried toward the little wooden chapel constructed since their return, and her arrival signaled the start of Holy Week.

Seeing my Abejas friend José sitting on a hillside above the chapel, I hiked up to join him, and we watched the slow procession in silence. It was the spring of 2001 and I was nearing the end of my tour in Chiapas with Christian Peacemaker Teams. I had no idea what I would do next.

I thought about the trajectory that had landed me here the previous summer. After bumming my way around the Guatemalan highlands, I had boarded a bus bound for Chiapas and twelve hours later got off in the mountain city of San Cristóbal de las Casas. This was the heart of Graham Greene country, where groves of ancient crosses sprouted from hillsides "like trees left to seed," as Greene wrote in *The Power and the Glory*. In 1938, Greene ended a grueling three-day mule ride there, which his antihero, a nameless whiskey-besotted priest, would repeat in *The Power and the Glory*, Greene's novel about faith and doubt in the anticlerical Mexico of the 1920s. Greene would also describe the three-day mule journey in his nonfiction account *The Lawless Roads* as a journey into the "mountainous strange world of Father Las Casas, where Christianity went on its own frightening way."

Having read *The Power and the Glory* in a divinity school ethics class, I'd been hooked by its depraved characters who ached with desire for God. The priest, despite his obvious flaws, renounced everything—even his life—to save his people. What I had in mind was more a vague notion of *helping* people. But now that I needed a specific plan, I found myself at a disquieting juncture.

Should I continue my work as an international peace activist? Return to the States and apply for a Ph.D. in theology? For months I had prayed and agonized and wrote long, self-indulgent journal entries imploring God to give me a vocation. Lately I'd been dreaming of starting a fair trade coffee business. The idea had come to me after I heard José describe the difficulty the Abejas had in getting a viable price for their main cash crop.

As the Virgin drew near, a hush descended, and the villagers parted to let her pass. Her graven face appeared long and dolorous: the gaze of one who has seen much suffering.

Rumor was her statue had taken a bullet during the massacre in the nearby village of Acteal. "La Virgen de la Masacre," they called her: On December 22, 1997, more than a hundred paramilitaries descended upon the village. Fearing such an attack, the villagers had been praying for peace for three days. The chapel where they were huddled was the first building the paramilitaries attacked. Unarmed and committed to nonviolence, the Abejas fled into the surrounding woods, and for the next six hours the killers hunted them down: men, women, children. The Virgin Mary had watched her own son be put to death; that day in Acteal forty-five more of her children were slaughtered.

As a Protestant, I had always wondered why Catholics venerated Mary—adoring her, lighting candles to her, even praying to her, which seemed borderline idolatrous. In the Evangelical Free Church of my youth we didn't even have Holy Week: why dwell on the cross when Christ had already risen? But I learned in Chiapas how Holy Week acknowledges that suffering and humiliation can't be bypassed; pain must be confronted and endured. Mary bore a child destined for calamity, as had many of the Abejas. She was human, like them, but she had the most intimate contact with God, carrying him in her body. I now understood why they adored her.

The Virgin's sad, maternal gaze as she rode by seemed an assurance that God doesn't abandon his people; He suffers with them. Even in the midst of a massacre like that at Acteal, there was Mary, singing of mercy. Mary's Magnificat was also a song of revolution, as the Abejas well knew, though it was a revolution whose strength began in weakness. The tables of injustice have been overturned: *He has shown strength with his arm,* Luke's Gospel recounts. *He has scattered the proud. He has lifted up the lowly.*

The Mother of God was among us, and Holy Week had begun.

José told me of his plans to work in his field of *cafetales*—coffee trees—later that week. The field was near the homes of several known paramilitaries, he said. Would I accompany him? Perhaps

I could provide him with some small measure of protection against the paramilitaries. We decided to go in three days, on Maundy Thursday, the day of Jesus's Last Supper with his disciples. José would collect me at 6 A.M.

"Hora de Fox?" I asked, though I knew the answer. I still liked to hear his reply.

José smiled. "No. Hora de Dios."

The Abejas had named daylight savings time after Mexico's then president, Vicente Fox. *Hora de Fox* was a human invention that changed according to the whims of a capitalist economy, but out here in the villages they operated on God's time. A small act of resistance.

We CPTers weren't the only activists in the villages. There were also those called *campamentistas*—one who camps or visits. They'd come to act as human shields. Soon after the left-wing Zapatista rebels had declared war on the Mexican government in 1994, the government had responded by training paramilitary groups to attack Mayan villages. The idea behind the *campamentistas* was that, although paramilitaries might slaughter Mayan farmers by the dozens, they would be unlikely to kill a ruddy-cheeked gringo from Minnesota or Manhattan. And it largely worked. The attacks grew sparse. But as the violence decreased, the number of Western activists ballooned. Tourist guidebooks even recommended that travelers spend a week as "human rights observers" in a rural village during their trip through Mayan country. But the inescapable truth was that, other than possessing a warm body covered in white skin, we were all generally of little use to the Abejas.

Which is why I'd been thinking more and more about my fair trade coffee scheme. In recent years the market price had fallen below the cost of production. What if someone would agree to buy their beans for a sustainable price, I thought? And what if that someone was me?

I had met with Pablo, the president of the Abejas coffee collective, and had spent time at the Jesuit compound talking with Arturo, an oblate who knew a lot about the coffee business. Both Pablo and Arturo helped me formulate a plan to launch a coffee store back home. I didn't know where I would get the money, and I didn't know how to roast coffee, much less market it. But those were minor obstacles. The important thing was to learn as much as I could about growing coffee while I was there.

So when José asked me to help him in his fields, I thought of it as research. I also liked that I would be useful to him, offering not only my white skin as protection, but the simple, true work of my hands. Maundy Thursday couldn't come soon enough. A bell rang. Down the hill I could hear people gathering for afternoon Mass.

The wooden chapel wasn't large enough to hold everyone, so a crowd spilled outdoors. The Virgin was safely ensconced behind the altar, and the priest read from the scriptures in Spanish, which Sebastian the *catecista,* or lay leader, then translated into Tzotzil, the Mayan tongue. After the reading he paused, then read the entire passage again. The scripture that day was from the prophet Isaiah, that of the Suffering Servant:

> *Here is my servant, whom I*
> *uphold,*
> *my chosen, in whom my soul*
> *delights;*
> *I have put my Spirit upon him;*
> *he will bring forth justice to the*
> *nations.*

He will not grow faint or be
    crushed
until he has established justice
    in the earth;
and the coastlands wait for his
    teaching.

Christian tradition has long read that passage for its messianic fore-shadowing of the suffering Jesus would undergo, but that day I re-member being struck by the poetic mystery of the last phrase. I was standing above those coastlands, high up in the New World among an ancient people who weren't just hearing the teachings of Isaiah but were recapitulating them in their lives. They dwelt within that ancient story.

Some of them had suffered modern-day crucifixion at Acteal, and the fear that followed when the faithful scattered across the land and lived as exiles. And now their Lord had gathered them together again and spoken through Isaiah's words:

See, the former things have come
    to pass
and new things I now declare
before they spring forth,
    I tell you of them.

Mass lasted nearly two hours. Before the benediction the priest asked a little girl to come forward. No more than two years of age, she had been playing with the other children in the dirt. The priest lifted her high in the air. He then pronounced a blessing over the people, a benediction of warmth and hope and the evidence of new life, like this child. *Here is my servant, whom I uphold, my chosen in whom my soul delights.*

"And now," the priest said, "it's time to dance." A keyboard launched into a *ranchera* riff. For the next two hours the Abejas got down and boogied, Mayan style, straight-faced and stiff, arms at their sides, moving only their legs, men dancing on one side and women on the other. On a hillside ravine on the heights of the New World, hundreds of feet shuffled to a rhythm offered in praise to their Creator.

Of the things I learned from my stint as a peace activist, one of the most useful was peeing on a compost pile. Lino was CPT's resident gardener, and he tended his compost with great care in the tiny courtyard of our San Cristóbal office. The garden was small, only twenty feet long and half as wide, but big enough to grow chiles, Swiss chard, and *maíz,* the Mayan corn. There was no disputing that it was Lino's garden, even though it was located in our common courtyard, because Lino did all the work. He shared its produce at communal meals, but that's about all the interaction most of us had with the garden. It had been clear to me when I arrived in San Cristóbal that Lino and the team had an unspoken agreement: everyone would keep their distance.

"Lino" was Spanish for Lynn. In his third and final year with CPT, Lino came from a long line of Mennonite farmers in Virginia, where he had learned his horticultural skills. With a closely shaved head and the deep tan of a life lived outdoors, Lino looked like a light-skinned Abejas man. He carried the woven shoulder bag used by men in the villages, sported homemade huarache sandals, and spoke pretty decent Tzotzil. When I sat at the computer typing up another dull report of our latest protest, I would sometimes look out the window and watch Lino work in his garden, curious about what he did out there. Sometimes I would ask him and sometimes, if he was in the mood for human contact, he would teach me. One day he showed me the young *maíz* plants, knee high, which he grew from seeds given to him by an Abejas man in X'oyep. At the base of each *maíz* stalk he planted pole beans. The beans pulled nitrogen from the air, he explained, and gave it to the corn. As it grew, the corn would provide a trellis for the beans to climb. Under the corn and beans Lino planted squash seeds, whose long vines would cover the soil and retain its moisture. Corn, beans, squash: the three sisters. This trinity of crops had sustained Mesoamericans for millennia.

Lino was trying to replicate on a small scale the Mayan *milpa*. A *milpa* is a corn field but it is also much more, growing squash and beans, as well as chiles, melons, leafy greens, and animal fodder. Trees like oak, Mexican cedar, and ceiba form a canopy above the corn, some feeding nitrogen to the soil and some providing timber. The *milpa* is a man-made ecosystem, mimicking the stacked layers of the surrounding forest and creating a delicate interplay of soil, water, plants, and sunlight. While he may not have had the canopy trees, Lino was still trying to replicate that botanical dance in miniature right there in our office patio garden.

The one contribution to his efforts Lino did encourage was the offering of our liquid nutrients. Liquids only, he insisted, no solids. Each night when I slept at CPT headquarters, I walked barefoot across the cobblestones of the courtyard, passing the lush *milpa* and its stalks of *maíz* now shoulder high, and unzipped my fly. While I peed I would look up at the stars undimmed by light pollution and feel a sort of giddiness. Here at least was a small and necessary role I could play. As I contemplated the spongy, raucous community of life I was filled with awe. Millions of lives swarmed beneath my feet, transubstantiating food scraps, weeds, and urine into crumbly, black, sweet-smelling humus. One day, when Lino had deemed the compost ready, I helped him shovel it into the wheelbarrow and transport it over to the *maíz*. Picking up a handful I inhaled the fecund smell of the forest floor, the smell of life itself, marveling in the ancient law of return: that which comes from the soil must return to the soil. Ever since, I have maintained my own teeming horde of compost, and I've retained the habit of bestowing upon it my own urine. It's like giving a piece of your living body, until one day you give your whole body, like Brother Gregory, to the hungry earth.

Early on I had no interest in helping Lino, but increasingly I found myself intrigued. Perhaps gardening was something I was missing. Lino clearly loved his garden; and it seemed to keep him from slipping off the edge of some unspoken emotional precipice.

I had noticed a steady decline in morale at CPT Chiapas, like air leaving the lungs, and nobody embodied that implosion more than Lino.

Over the coming weeks I would see him less and less at meetings. He spent all his time either in his garden or out on patrol in the villages. He seemed to be burned out, to have the nonviolent activist equivalent of shell shock.

Lino had first arrived three years earlier during the glory days of CPT Chiapas, a time when there was still some risk in going out to visit the communities; when the term "human shield" actually meant something. Not that there was outright war in the villages. The low-intensity war that the Mexican government waged against its indigenous citizens, using techniques the U.S. military had developed in Vietnam, was mainly violence of the psychological kind. Soldiers harassed you when you passed through checkpoints on the way to the Abejas villages. *Amenazas de muerte,* death threats the paramilitary groups issued against the Abejas, circulated among the villages, and there were rumors of another massacre like Acteal. Lino spent a lot of time out in the communities, and perhaps he had come to internalize those threats. But his life in Chiapas wasn't always dreary. During my first weeks there I shadowed Lino out on patrol and he told me stories of CPT's salad days, back when they had pulled off some creative protests that actually seemed to have had an impact. But now the low-intensity war was winding down, and I wondered if I'd arrived in Chiapas too late to make a difference.

When I wasn't out in the villages, I would rise at six and climb the concrete rooftop of our office to pray. The roof was bare but for a water tank, a basin where we washed our clothes, and a small writing desk I had carried up. The walls were chest-high and I could hear but not see the town below. Under the canopy of a cloudless sky in the thin blue light of dawn, the roof was private yet expansive. It was just a rooftop, but at the time it seemed to me full of holy mystery, a cathedral suspended in the sky, and as cathedrals are meant to do, it directed my thoughts toward God.

When my mind wandered from my prayers, I would pick up a book and read for an hour. My daily reading was divided into two parts: the Bible, and everything else. I read voraciously in both categories and with no real direction or purpose. From the Bible I read the four Gospels, Acts, Romans, First and Second Kings, and Job. For "everything else," I read the *Collected Poems* of Wendell Berry; Tolstoy's *The Kingdom of God Is Within You;* Oscar Romero's *The Violence of Love;* and two books of Christian philosophy by Søren Kierkegaard: *Provocations,* a collection of excerpts from his writings, and *Fear and Trembling,* in which he describes following God as a decision based "on the strength of the absurd." Drawn in by the beauty of his language, I increasingly found myself reading Isaiah. I savored the prophet's lyrical voice, his ripe images of agrarian life. One morning while sitting on a hill above Nuevo Yibeljoj at dawn, I watched the villagers arise with the birds and read:

Ah, land of whirring wings
beyond the rivers of Ethiopia.

Or during Mass at Acteal I would remember Isaiah's haunting, exuberant image of the Resurrection:

Oh dwellers in the dust, awake and sing for joy! For your dew is a
radiant dew, and the earth will give birth to those long dead.

Isaiah is a beautiful book. Even now I love to read it in the early morning while I'm still waking up, immersing myself in its language. It was an important book for the Abejas, too, and they read it often during their gatherings, where I came to see their lives as somehow part of Isaiah's story. Standing above the mass grave at Acteal, where all forty-five martyrs lay buried, I imagined on the Last Day the earth giving birth to those dwellers in the dust.

In the displacement camp at X'oyep, before the village of Nuevo Yibeljoj had returned home, I'd attended a service where the priest read the second half of Isaiah 65. It took me a moment to realize that he had substituted the word "X'oyep" for "Jerusalem":

For I am about to create new heavens
and a new earth. . . .
for I am about to create X'oyep as a joy,
and its people as a delight.
I will rejoice in X'oyep
and delight in my people;
no more shall the sound of
weeping be heard in it,
or the cry of distress.

•   •   •

In late March, on the day the Abejas burned their coffee crop to protest unjust market forces, they read from the book of Isaiah. A swarm of local media came, and as the cameras rolled, a man named Vicente, wearing tattered pants and a shirt with no buttons, read in Tzotzil from Isaiah 58. I knew the passage well: Vicente's emotions echoed Isaiah's call for the Lord to "loose the bonds of injustice" that the international coffee market had placed on his people, to "undo the thongs of the yoke, and let the oppressed go free."

I had been raised to read the Bible purely for its "spiritual" message, for how it spoke to *me* and my heart. But here was Isaiah, speaking through this man, addressing an entire people. These fifty coffee farmers hadn't come down that day to invite Jesus into their hearts or to inject a little spirituality into their lives; theirs was a God who moved not only in the stirrings of one's soul but in the tangible world of unjust global markets, of daily poverty, of massacres by paramilitaries. And into such corruption and human strife, they believed God would intervene.

Vicente continued:

> *If you remove the yoke from*
>   *among you,*
> *the pointing of the finger, the*
>   *speaking of evil,*
> *if you offer your food to the*
>   *hungry*
> *and satisfy the needs of the*
>   *afflicted,*
> *then your light shall rise in*
>   *the darkness*

and your gloom be like the
  noonday.
The Lord will guide you
  continually,
and satisfy your needs in
  parched places,
    and make your bones strong;
and you shall be like a watered
  garden,
like a spring of water,
  whose waters never fail.

Before setting alight their pile of beans, the Abejas discussed the meaning of the passage: Were they doing enough to feed the hungry? To clothe people? Rather than speaking against the evil perpetrated against them, they were challenging themselves. It's quite something to watch a group of people dressed in tattered garments ask what more they can do to clothe the naked. Or to set a flame, though it was a symbolic amount, to their livelihood.

When the reading was over, José lit a match. The coffee was slow to ignite, but soon a wonderful aroma filled the village. As the symbolic pyre of coffee burned, the smoke carried the people's prayers to God, and I found myself wondering: what if I offered food to the hungry?

I knew then that I wanted to be like Isaiah's watered garden, like Vicente and José, whose faces were lit by the flames. I wanted my bones to be made strong.

I was hiking with Lino down the long ridge from X'oyep to Nuevo Yibeljoj one day when he pointed to a field of *maíz* on our left. "See those corn stalks, how they're light green?" he said. "Not getting enough nitrogen." Then he pointed at the field to our right. "Those dark green stalks are getting plenty of nutrients."

While following Lino around the Abejas villages, I discovered that I didn't just want to have been with Lino in CPT's glory days; I wanted to *be* Lino. I wanted to walk among *las indígenas,* noting their joyful surprise when I addressed them in Tzotzil, having earned their respect by outsmarting the occupying army on their own helipad. The Abejas would know that I was an old soul, young in years but ancient in wisdom, a sage of peace come to cast his lot among *los pobres.* I would be one of them.

The *maíz* in our patio garden, with its compost-fed stalks of dark green *maíz,* had tasseled and put on ears. When the ears were ripe, Lino and I bent the stalks in half, using the dull side of our machetes like the Abejas men, and left the ears to dry upside down in the sun. After a week we harvested them, pulling the husks back to expose the kernels, and stashing them in the office eaves to dry. But before we could soak the kernels in lime water, grind them into *masa,* and make *waj,* Lino was gone.

His term with CPT came to an end, and he moved back to Virginia to his parents' farm. He wanted to grow food. From peace activist to farmer. I saw a poetic logic to his journey.

A year later I heard Lino got married to another CPTer. He had met Cedar, a bulgur-eating girl from Toronto who had gone through training with me, and they'd fallen in love. They had bought a small farm in rural Ontario and were making a go of it. Lino had found a wife with whom to share his love of the land, and I envied him.

Perhaps it was partly admiration for him that made me want to do something grand in his absence. In the days following the Abejas' coffee-burning ceremony, my coffee obsession had reached a fever pitch. Not only was I going into the fair trade coffee business, I had decided; I was going to save the Abejas from penury.

None of my fellow peacemakers would learn of my secret plan. I feared they would want to help me, and why should I share the glory of saving five thousand people from abject poverty? No, the act of salvation would be mine alone. I imagined returning to Nuevo Yibeljoj two years hence, after several seasons' worth of pesos had filled the Abejas' pockets. With that newfound wealth my friends would have built houses to replace their tin-and-plastic shanties; there would be a new school, perhaps with my name over the door. I would enter the village unannounced, to avoid seeming like a Big Man who needed a royal welcome, but I would be recognized anyway, and shouts would go up. There would be a spontaneous celebration that night, and José would give a speech. I would try to stop them from making such a fuss, to explain that it was not my work that had accomplished all this, but they would refuse to hear it. Someone would hold out a newborn child. *We named him Freddy,* they would say. *Please, we want you to be the godfather.* And how could I refuse?

I'd come to Chiapas to protect the Abejas from paramilitaries; I would become, I thought, with the utter clarity of the self-deluded, their financial savior instead.

When Maundy Thursday arrived, José came as promised at 6 A.M., knocking quietly on the door of the *campamentista* hut. I left behind my warm sleeping bag, quickly dressed, and followed him into the brisk dawn air.

Nuevo Yibeljoj was just waking up. Two sleepy-eyed twin boys sat in a dirt doorway, waiting for their breakfast. The smoke of a hundred campfires rose above the ravine to mingle with low-hanging clouds. On the way to José's hut we walked past dozens of thrown-together shacks, all clinging tenaciously to the mountainside like baby spiders gripping their mother's back.

By the time we arrived at José's home, the morning fog had begun to lift. His wife, Angelina, had breakfast waiting. Her kitchen, built next to the house, was the size of my closet back home. The house itself was little more than a scrap-metal roof supported by four spindly corner posts with plastic sheeting to approximate walls. Despite its ramshackle construction, it was full of familial cheer.

Breakfast at José's was a never-ending source of pleasure. He and his clan had become my surrogate family.

The food that morning was delicious. We spoke little and ate with our hands. I folded the *waj*—the tortilla—and used it to scoop up *chenek,* the slow-cooked black beans that, along with *waj,* were a part of every meal. I watched Angelina make *waj.* Earlier she had ground the corn on an ancient mortar and pestle handed down to her from her mother, who received it from her mother, and hers before. The corn was already soft from soaking for several days in lime water. Lime releases niacin in the corn and prevents pellagra, a disease caused by niacin deficiency. From the ground and doughy *masa,* Angelina pulled off a handful, patted it flat, and slapped it down on the hot oil drum sitting above the fire grate. When air pockets formed, she picked up an edge and flipped it. When it was cooked, she placed it in a cloth to keep warm.

The more I ate *waj* and *chenek,* the more I detected subtle differences in flavor and texture. With José's direction, I even began to distinguish regional differences in the tortillas based on whether the corn was grown in *tierra caliente* (the hot lowlands) or *tierra alta* (the cooler highlands). Using Tzotzil words was as much part of the mysterious pleasure I derived from eating this food as the elements themselves, so much so that the food, the words, and the people who fed me were all becoming inseparable in my mind. To speak Tzotzil while eating *waj* and *chenek* was to partake of an ancient and unnamed liturgy. I was eating my way into mystery.

"Man's real work," writes Robert Farrar Capon in *The Supper of the Lamb,* "is to look at the things of this world and to love them for what they are. That is, after all, what God does and man was not made in God's image for nothing." If Capon is right then maybe I was doing God's work in Chiapas after all, meal by meal. I looked upon *waj* and *chenek* and loved them for what they were. But the food was not an end in itself; by imbibing the world around me over and over, I came to love the people who lived in that world.

"Jaj canto jutuk kokosh?" I asked in Tzotzil: Could I have a little more *kokosh*? It was my new favorite food: *waj* that had been thrown directly onto the coals, where it turned smoky and brittle. Angelina reached toward the fire, squinting against the smoke, and placed two *kokosh* on my plate. They were the size of dinner plates, dark brown with bits of ash still clinging to them. I broke off a piece, blew on it, then sprinkled on salt and a few pieces of diced jalapeño. It was smoky and warm and tasted like the land itself, like sun and soil and rain and the campfires of my boyhood.

Soon it would be time to go. José and I washed down our meal with a last cup of sweet, weak coffee, grown on the very *cafetales* we would soon weed, but neither of us wanted to leave. I sat for what seemed a very long time on that tiny elf stool in José's kitchen. His children murmured contentedly at our feet as their bellies filled with warmth. Here was domestic bliss of another sort, entirely pared down, stripped of extraneous goods. Here was a family utterly connected to this piece of land. It could have been a hundred years ago, or even a thousand. The food, the fire, even the air itself seemed to hum with a sense of divine approval. There was nothing beyond this moment, there was no place else I wanted to be. This clarity was what I had come to Chiapas to find.

Breakfast over, we passed through the old hamlet of Yibeljoj. Several men came to their doors and watched us. José nodded to them and said, *"Melioyot,"* the traditional greeting in Tzotzil, meaning, "Here you are," but the men only stared. Later I asked José why the men did not reply to his greeting. "Paramilitaries," he said.

We continued up a series of ridges that rose up Mount Yibeljoj's flanks, and in another twenty minutes we arrived at José's field, an acre of coffee trees. With no equipment other than machetes, we whacked the large woody weeds and laid them against the slope, where their decomposing bodies would prevent erosion and also nurse the hungry *cafetales*. Up here among José's *cafetales* my job was straightforward: scrape, pull, chop, sweep, gather, spread. This was simple work, not a grand practice of "resistance" or "protest" or even of "witness." The Abejas produced *waj* and *chenek* and *café,* which rooted them to the land in a way that was palpable and intimate and went far beyond a sentimental love of nature. That was the lure I found irresistible: in growing food they were co-creators with God.

José cared for his small plot with a knowledge that could come only from a long tenure on the place, and with the belief that his children and their children and their children's children would need this land in order to live. The Abejas embodied the Hebrew understanding of peace as *shalom*. The peace *shalom* entails is not the absence of conflict. It is a completeness, an expansive wholeness where God, people, and land dwell together in harmony. Perhaps, I began to think, I might only find *shalom* if the fields in which I toiled were not just metaphors, but were as real as this one.

But didn't following Jesus mean renouncing your own life, being willing to stand up for the oppressed in places like Palestine and Colombia? Maybe for some, though I sensed that what Jesus had in mind for me was something much less glamorous.

Instead of following Jesus I had been following abstract ideals: Activism. Social Change. These had become my idols.

Perhaps my holy calling as a peace worker was a result of having read too much Romero and Gandhi and Tolstoy. I knew at least that I couldn't sustain myself much longer without being rooted to a place, without taking up some kind of labor or art that allowed me to create, build, and plant.

José and I worked most of the day. Before we parted he handed me a bag. It was full of seeds. Beautiful, shiny yellow seeds. They were from his own *maíz*. *"Los sembras en su propio suelo,"* he said. *Plant them in your own soil.*

That Maundy Thursday night before dinner, I lay on my bunk and copied into my journal a passage from a book of essays by Wallace Stegner: "American individualism, much celebrated and cherished, has developed without its essential corrective, which is belonging."

Belonging to a place. It sounded wonderful. Early in my Chiapas tour, before working that day with José, our team had hosted a family of Canadian farmers. This couple and their four children were driving around the Americas in an old pickup with a camper strapped on top, and they spent a week tramping around Abejas villages with us. The man was particularly interested in how the Mayan farmers made compost. He became volubly excited, in fact, when describing his own method of building a pile, and I now understand that excitement. When I told him I came from North Carolina, he encouraged me to visit Sustenance Farm, a small permaculture farm in Chatham County, four hours east of my home in the western part of the state. As I listened to him describe their life in Canada—long summers spent working the fields, long winters spent reading beside the woodstove—I yearned for something similar. For the past decade in a restless search for the next plan, I had never lived in the same place for longer than a year. To continue with Christian Peacemaker Teams would mean a life of peripatetic peace tours, bouncing from Colombia, to Chiapas, to Hebron. Instead I wanted to settle, to marry and have children. But where would I plant myself, and what would I do? The answers to these questions were still mysteries.

That evening the Abejas celebrated Jesus's Last Supper with his disciples, and after the foot-washing service, we sat down to a feast. As the priest blessed the food, I thought about how food was central to Jesus's ministry. A good bit of the Gospels describes him sitting down to a meal with someone: a tax collector, say, or a group of fishermen. The church universal has long proclaimed that the Eucharist is at the heart of the Christian faith. But what about everyday meals—were they each not a tiny eucharist of their own? *Waj, chenek*. Bread, wine. I felt a sudden urge, which I might now call a priestly urge, to lift up the food. *This is my body. This is the work of human hands. Corn grown and soaked in lime and ground into* masa, *baked on an oil drum lid, broken for you.*

On Good Friday, José took me and a few *campamentistas* for a day of carefree hiking and swimming at a nearby waterfall. Back in Nuevo Yibeljoj people were making the Stations of the Cross, and here I was jumping into crystal-clear pools and eating mangoes on a sunny rock. Christ's agony couldn't have been further from my mind.

When Holy Week was over, the other CPTers and I returned to San Cristóbal. I would soon begin the next phase of my life, but I still had no idea what that would be.

And then, one morning on the concrete rooftop in San Cristóbal, I knew.

I had weighed the many options: Theology professor. Peace activist. Fair trade coffee dealer. But while reading Isaiah that morning on the rooftop, I finally began to see what might lay ahead. My reading that morning was from the thirtieth chapter:

Therefore the Lord waits to be
gracious to you;
therefore he will rise up to
show mercy to you.
For the Lord is a God of justice;
blessed are all those who wait
for him.

I had waited. Each morning on the rooftop I'd read Isaiah, waiting for a word from the Lord, until I'd begun to doubt that such a word would ever come.

The text shifted from poetry to prose, a transition which caused me to pay more attention. I sat up to straighten my bent spine, my back against the wall, and read the words I would hear again years later during Mass at Mepkin Abbey:

Though the Lord may give you the bread of adversity and the water of affliction, yet your Teacher will not hide himself anymore, but your eyes shall see your Teacher. And when you turn to the right or when you turn to the left, your ears shall hear a word behind you, saying, "This is the way; walk in it."

Yes, I thought. *This is the way; walk in it.* So simple. For months I had agonized over what I should do with my life, how I should live, when all along God had laid a path before me, inviting me to follow.

I am fascinated by the ways in which God grabs hold of people and doesn't let them go, which I suppose is why I am telling this story. It was there on that rooftop in Chiapas that God made such a capture of me. I realized that all of my life I'd tried to wrestle free, to resist being taken, but this time—weary from the struggle—I simply allowed myself to be caught; I wanted to walk in the way.

As I read further that morning on the rooftop, Isaiah went on to describe what the Lord would do for one who walked in the way:

He will give rain for the seed with which you sow the ground, and grain, the produce of the ground, which will be rich and plenteous. . . . On every lofty mountain and every high hill there will be brooks running with water.

The way would lead me to farming. Growing food. Sharing it with others, as Jesus had done. Becoming a co-creator with God by caring for soil.

That summer of 2001, after leaving Chiapas, I planted my first garden on my parents' land in Transylvania County, North Carolina, a temperate rain forest where on every lofty mountain and every high hill brooks run with water.

In October when I returned from a teaching job to harvest the last of the cabbage and winter squash, I stood in that humble garden and marveled at all the food.

The next year I would begin a farming internship at Sustenance Farm, which the Canadian farmer had recommended.

Several years later I returned to Nuevo Yibeljoj to visit José and the other Abejas, friends who had proved to be my spiritual midwives. When I arrived the village had an upbeat feeling, a sense of expectancy. A new schoolhouse had been built. Gone were the plastic-sided hovels; nearly everyone lived in a modest but comfortable wood-sided house. There had been a few threats, but no more paramilitary violence.

That afternoon I met Nina, a young Swiss woman who seemed to command constant attention in the village. Later Pablo, the coffee cooperative president, told me her story. The previous year Nina had lived for several weeks as a *campamentista* in the village, where she'd learned of the coffee farmers' plight. In an orderly Swiss fashion Nina had returned to Zurich and promptly lined up fair trade coffee buyers, who bought the year's entire crop, paid the Abejas a premium, and contracted to buy the next year's entire crop as well. That night the village would hold a celebratory dinner in Nina's honor. And, Pablo told me with a proud grin, he had named his new daughter Nina. The Swiss woman would be her godmother.

My fantasy had been usurped, but my chagrin didn't last long. Nina had not stolen my dream. She had released me from it. My calling lay elsewhere.

By the time I left Chiapas in the spring of 2001, I had a plan in place. I would follow up on the suggestion of David the Canadian and call Harvey Harmon at Sustenance Farm. Learning from one of the gurus, I would inherit Harvey's forty years of organic wisdom and would then start my own farm. It was all coming together.

When I called Harvey, though, things suddenly appeared otherwise. He was interested in having me as an apprentice, but the few openings for the year were already full. I was disappointed. What of my vocation? I was called to feed people. How could Harvey not have known this? I couldn't work on just any farm. I'm not sure why, but at the time it somehow seemed important that I work only on Harvey's farm, so myopic was my focus. While I tried to sort all this out, I was offered a teaching job at a nearby state university, and I postponed my farming plans.

But I began growing things anyway. On Holy Saturday a full year after working in José's coffee field, I planted a pair of apple trees and two black raspberry canes on my parents' farm in Transylvania County. The trees lived, the canes did not. I remembered José's kernels of *maíz* and decided to plant them, too. I walked up on one of the pastures tilted toward the sun, a hillside that reminded me of José's steep slope where we worked that day cleaning his coffee trees. The bag of seed was light in my hand, yet I knew it contained a year's worth of tortillas, should I be so fortunate to harvest a crop. I loved the portent and promise in each of those kernels of *maíz*. Using a pointed stick like José, I stabbed holes right into the sod. Little did I know that corn doesn't grow in sod, but it didn't matter; crows pecked out all the seeds before they even had a chance to sprout. Clearly if I was to learn to grow food I needed training.

A year after contacting Harvey, I called him again, and this time there was an opening. I arrived at Sustenance Farm in August, the sultry, muggy nadir of the farming year, ready to begin a three-month internship in permaculture. The heat was horrendous, but I hardly noticed. I was more than ready to learn from Harvey about the interplay of soil, sunlight, plants, and people. I was ready to begin my vocation, and I would lean into it with my entire being.

CHAPTER THREE

At Play in the Fields of the Lord

Eastertide
The Lord's Acre, North Carolina

Man is a hungry being. But he is hungry for God.
—Alexander Schmemann, *For the Life of the World*

The spring following my trip to Mepkin Abbey, I decided to visit a garden in the mountains of western North Carolina not far from home, a garden that arose from a Depression-era farming ministry and whose story would connect with my own.

On the last Saturday in February 1935, Franklin Roosevelt's secretary of agriculture, Henry Wallace, stood behind the pulpit of Asheville's Central Methodist Church and issued the following prediction: "Great spiritual power will eventually emanate from these mountains of western North Carolina, which will influence the whole of the United States."

It was the height of the Great Depression and Wallace had no qualms about applying a veneer of spiritual language over New Deal rhetoric. But he didn't stop there. Though it is difficult to imagine a secretary of agriculture today giving a public address called "The Necessity of a Socialized Spiritual Life in the Countryside," Wallace made several more claims that appear bold even for his time. People had "divorced their minds from spiritual things," he said, and the reason was capitalism. In fact, "many city churches are under capitalistic rule," Wallace declared, sounding less like a member of the cabinet and more like a member of Occupy Wall Street.

Wallace, who later became FDR's vice president, said something else of note that day. As recorded by the *Asheville Citizen Times,* he alluded to a project then only five years old called the Lord's Acre Plan. It was the brainchild of a man named James G. K. McClure, a Presbyterian minister who had relocated from Chicago to Hickory Nut Gap Farm in nearby Fairview. A proponent of the Social Gospel, McClure had seen the great need for the farmers of western North Carolina to be better organized, and so in the year 1920 he started what would become a nationally renowned farmers' cooperative called the Farmers' Federation. Which is what brought Secretary Wallace to visit. But starting a successful farmers' co-op was not enough for McClure. Being a pastor, he knew people needed not only better economic opportunities, but also a way to help their neighbor. McClure imagined a strengthened social fabric resulting from farmers planting an acre to give back to the Lord. It was the old biblical idea of a tithe, returning to God a tenth of what you grew or earned. Money was scarce, but almost everybody could raise an extra chicken or plant an extra acre of corn. The Lord's Acre Plan began in 1930 and quickly gained momentum; by 1932 one hundred churches had joined.

As Wallace said in his speech in Asheville that day in 1935, "The Lord's Acre Plan carries us back toward pre-capitalistic days, to days when we had sympathy with better things." It proved a powerful force for good during the Depression years, helping churches keep their doors open and feeding the poorest of the poor. Yet as the Depression gave way to the Second World War and the sudden American prosperity that followed, people's trust shifted away from dependence on each other and returned to the capitalism Wallace decried. The Lord's Acre Plan dwindled until by 1959 it petered out.

I came to know of these things because in 2003, some seventy-three years after James G. K. McClure founded the original Lord's Acre, I married his great-granddaughter Elizabeth. In 2008, five years after our wedding, a group of Fairview townspeople including my wife's father, Will Hamilton, revived McClure's idea. They decided to create a communal food garden, for the purpose of supplying fresh organic vegetables to the local food pantry. In honor of all those farmers during the Depression who took up McClure's vision, they named the new garden the Lord's Acre.

Over the course of several months in the spring of 2012, in the season of Eastertide, I visited this reincarnation of the Lord's Acre. Henry Wallace said that great spiritual strength would one day emanate from these mountains, and I wanted to see if his prediction had proved true. I also wanted to see for myself the garden that had begun in the same year I left Anathoth, 2009, and which had so many parallels to my experience. Like Anathoth, it was a garden started by a church, in this case several churches, with a mission of feeding the hungry; it had grown quickly from the seed of an idea to a full-blown community gathering place that produced enormous amounts of food; and it made room for people of all beliefs or no belief, offering them a place to thrive.

On the last day in March at the Lord's Acre, garden manager Susan Sides was telling me the story of the stolen watermelons. We were waiting for a tour group to arrive that Susan would be showing around the garden; I had decided that a tour would be a good initiation for me, too.

The melons started going missing the previous July. Susan and her interns had lovingly tended the melon patch. Each day they would comment on their "babies," how beautiful they were, and how they were filling out. As time went on, they began wondering if there weren't fewer melons than they had started with. At first it was just one. But over the coming weeks other melons of other varieties— Sugar Babies, Moon & Stars—disappeared. Surely everyone in this close-knit mountain community knew that the Lord's Acre grew food solely to feed the hungry. Why would anybody steal its watermelons?

Then the watermelon thief made a rookie move, leaving behind a flamboyant pink shoulder bag containing a beer and a watermelon. Susan, gentle soul that she is, left the beer and bag hanging on the shed for the thief to reclaim, though she did take back the stolen watermelon. Later that same week one of the garden interns saw a woman at the grocery store with the flamboyant pink bag. He recognized her as a neighbor one of the garden members had told them about: a woman who lived near the Lord's Acre and who struggled with illness and poverty and isolation. But the proof came in early October when Susan discovered the woman sitting at their picnic table, which was covered with freshly harvested okra the woman had just cut from the garden.

Their talk started out well. The melon/okra thief, let's call her Emma, admitted to stealing not only watermelons but other produce as well. She told Susan she was ill and needed fresh food, that her landlord was an angry man and she was appeasing him with garden produce. Sometimes Emma gave food to others in need. Susan thought: "Here's something I can work with."

But as Emma talked, it became apparent she was emotionally and mentally unwell—and embarrassed. The more Susan tried to make peace, even offering her a role at the Lord's Acre, the more Emma's shame turned to anger. She started yelling. She foamed at the mouth. Susan had never seen anyone get so angry. For an hour Susan listened to Emma's verbal abuse.

"Fifteen years ago I would have retaliated," Susan said. "I'm from Miami—I know how to retaliate. Five years ago I would have retreated. But by the sheer grace of God I was able to absorb Emma's life's rage as it poured out of her." When Susan didn't retaliate as Emma expected, she became even angrier and eventually stomped off, telling Susan she'd never see her face again.

"Of course," Susan wryly noted to me, "Emma did show her face around the garden again, just not when we were there to see it." Melons and vegetables continued to go missing. Susan was glad Emma was getting food, but she wished she could figure out some way to convince her to join the garden rather than take from it on the sly. Just then, two minivans of tourists pulled into the grassy area outside the electric deer fence, and Emma's story would need to wait. Her story represented a spirit of compassion and hospitality, of the purposeful building of community at the Lord's Acre that I would come to witness over the course of several visits that spring. As I witnessed during my years at Anathoth, I saw at the Lord's Acre how the garden's work is so much more than growing food, and how determinedly Susan sought to extend a kind of pastoral grace to even the most difficult of visitors like Emma. It was Eastertide, the time following Christ's Resurrection when his followers were in a state of awe and wonder and profligate generosity—his early followers shared their possessions in common—and these qualities Susan seemed to embody as she transformed soil and sunlight into watermelons that would be stolen, as she offered love and solace to troubled people, knowing those gestures would not be returned.

I followed Susan over to the entrance gate. The visitors were members of a fledgling project called the Generous Garden from Greenville, South Carolina. News of the Lord's Acre's success had spread widely and these folks had driven nearly two hours to hear what made it so successful. As the ten or twelve folks milled around waiting for our approach, a guy with a cane and several blurred tattoos on his forearm hobbled over to the electric fence, firmly grasped the wire, and yelled, "Is this thing on?"

"Trying to jump-start your heart, huh?" Susan laughed as she walked over to open the gate.

"Oh no, I already did that once," the man said. "Don't wanna do that again." He introduced himself as Bill. I guessed from his faded USMC tattoo that Bill was a vet, though from which war he didn't say, and he had an odd way of talking that made you think he hadn't come home unscathed.

Fortunately Susan had turned the fence off earlier. She was clearly practiced in the art of guiding tours.

The Lord's Acre is not actually an acre. It's half an acre. But that half acre last year produced eight tons of vegetables—an astounding amount of food for such a small space—and donated all of it to Food for Fairview, the food pantry located just a quarter mile down the road. About seventy-five families received food from the pantry each week, and from March through December nearly all their vegetables came from this garden.

The tour group and I followed Susan into the middle of the garden, which was divided into four quadrants. Three of those were devoted to field crops—corn, squash, watermelons—and the fourth contained raised vegetable beds. This fourth quadrant of raised beds, Susan explained, produced more food than the other three quadrants combined. Like our double-dug greenhouse beds at Anathoth, the raised beds here had greater tilth, and therefore richer soil.

A lush winter cover crop mix of rye, vetch, and clover—the same mix we used at Anathoth—stood waist high in the three field sections, awaiting harvest. In these sections they were practicing a method called "no-till." In another six weeks they would scythe the cover crop and lay it down as mulch, then transplant crops directly into the soil. The rotting rye stubble, Susan said, is like a straw; it sucks moisture and oxygen down into the ground, feeding the microbial life in the soil, which in turn feeds the roots of the growing corn, squash, and watermelons.

The Greenville group was clearly intrigued with this no-till method. Pens and notebooks appeared, and Susan patiently explained it all again. Then we moved over to the demonstration area, where different garden techniques are modeled. A square bed made of hay bales corralled several cubic yards of soil, a square-foot garden with neatly marked lines, lasagna beds shaped like a keyhole, made with layers of dirt, leaves, and compost, and a *hugelkultur* bed built with old logs, sticks, turf, and compost.

"How do you spell that last one?" somebody asked. Another chimed in, "Which one is most productive?" Then somebody in the back asked, "What is your garden's mission?" More questions followed.

Bill, who was standing a little ways off from the group, looking off into the woods, suddenly called out, "Hey." Everybody turned. Apropos of nothing Bill asked, "You got any wild boar up here?"

Susan took the barrage of questions in stride. "We all approach gardening differently," she told us, "because we're all wired differently. Some people need a grid, like this square-foot garden. Others want curvy lines, like this lasagna bed." She paused, and her gaze seemed to take in the whole garden. She must have begun thinking of the question about the garden's mission. "We grow food for the food pantry, but our work here is really about finding ways to make love visible. We begin each day by asking *What does it take for this person, this plant, this community to flourish?* And not just individual plants or people, but what does it take for them to flourish in relationship?" Susan wore a yellow T-shirt bearing the words *I Like To Play In The Dirt*. A former garden writer for *Mother Earth News,* perhaps *the* flagship organic gardening magazine when she worked there in the 1970s and 1980s, Susan has been playing in the dirt for nearly forty years. She likes to say: "I have a mustard seed and I'm not afraid to use it."

She is not only one of the most knowledgeable gardeners you will ever meet, she is also someone with an intuitive sense of people's needs and the patience to try to meet them. On her email signature she has a quote by Antoine de Saint-Exupéry: "If you want to build a ship, don't drum up people to collect wood and don't assign them tasks and work, but rather teach them to long for the endless immensity of the sea." Though she would never describe herself thus, she is a garden mystic. Soft-spoken and unassuming, it is clear from five minutes' conversation that her well is deep. Sometimes at night, she is awoken with the need to talk with God, and once, after struggling for weeks with a vision for what the Lord's Acre might become and being frustrated by not getting anywhere, she was suddenly overwhelmed by a love so beyond her yet so immediate and personal that it left her reeling. "I wonder if this is what the Trinity is like?" she wrote during one of these nighttime visions. "A love so uncontainable that it must boil over into creation, into visible matter. Is this how we, how the universe was born? Love spilling over into life?"

When Susan turns a compost pile or picks harlequin bugs off the kale or leads a garden tour making sure to pause for the oddly ebullient guy with a cane, I think of saints like Hildegard of Bingen or Catherine of Siena. Over the course of my many visits to the Lord's Acre that spring, I always found myself following on her heels like this eager tour group in hopes that I, too, might receive a blessing.

"We put a lot of emphasis here on beauty," Susan said, as we walked past a bed planted with borage, echinacea, and Black-Eyed Susans. "This is a food garden, but most people who come to work here say they come because it's beautiful. And that's a result of gardening in community. Each of us on our own couldn't have a garden

this lovely. But working together we can." Lagging behind the tour,
I took in the gentle expanse of the garden. Orderly beds each four
feet wide were growing every conceivable vegetable that could be
grown in March in western North Carolina. Light green carrot tops
contrasted with deep blue-green broccoli leaves, proof that vegetable
beds could be just as beautiful as any perennial garden. I suspected
that much of the garden's beauty was Susan's doing. As Steve Norris,
one of the garden's early founders, later told me, "To get a garden
that beautiful you have to be a magician. Or an angel."

Though it was late March the temperature had climbed into
the eighties, and after the tour we happily took seats in the shade
of a massive hickory tree. Susan asked about the Generous Garden
project, and a man in his forties named Bo spoke up. Large and
muscular with Ray-Ban shades and close-cropped hair flecked with
gel, he looked more like an F-16 fighter pilot than the founder of a
community garden ministry. But Bo had looked around him and
had seen a need—sixty thousand people in Greenville County were
food insecure—and he wanted to do something about it. By way
of describing their operation, Bo began by rattling off a list of stats:
"32,000 pounds from four acres donated to eighteen agencies . . . four
5,000-gallon tanks with tilapia . . . two 100-foot long greenhouses . . .
1,416 tomato plants . . . 90 percent heirloom organic seeds . . . ver-
micompost system . . ." The list was long and impressive and utterly
focused on all things quantifiable. At one point, when he forgot a
particular number, Bo looked it up on some app on his iPhone, then
resumed his talk. At the Generous Garden, Bo grew just about every
kind of vegetable except corn. "I'm against corn," he said. He grew
up on a big corn-and-soy farm in eastern North Carolina and had
seen enough corn. Back then he farmed conventionally with petro-
fertilizers and pesticides. But no longer.

"I used to think that organic stuff was some weird Satanic cult,"

Bo continued. "Then right before I started this garden the Lord spoke to me and said, 'Bo, I want you to go organic.' Since then the Lord's just been chippin' away at my heart. I've been learning more about organic. Even veganism."

Susan mentioned that I had once directed a community garden, and soon she, Bo, and I were comparing notes, three garden managers talking shop. We talked about the tension we all felt in the mission of these gardens between the value of simply feeding hungry people and some higher calling. The Lord's Acre began as a Christian ministry, a partnership between two churches, but it had since become a regular nonprofit with no official faith position. Some of the members like Susan worked here because of their faith, while others had motivations that couldn't be deemed religious. There was nonetheless a healthy synergy at work at the Lord's Acre between Christians and non-Christians that seemed to me a hopeful example. I explained to the group that we had started Anathoth as a ministry of a church, but now the garden operated more as a nonprofit whose connection to the church was only tangential. And the Generous Garden project? "We're a Christian organization," Bo said, "but we're not. At least, not officially. We just try to love everybody."

Just trying to love everybody is pretty much the ethos each of our gardens shared. Making loving visible through food. As Susan concluded, "Everyone who comes here hungers for something. Some hunger for food. Others hunger for community. Or beauty. But we all hunger."

The week following my first visit to the Lord's Acre was Holy Week. On Maundy Thursday, the day Jesus met his disciples in the upper room and held the Last Supper, a commemorative meal was taking place down the road at Fairview Christian Fellowship, one of the Lord's Acre's founding churches. Instead of an upper room, however, we met in the church basement. It was the one-year anniversary of the Welcome Table. The Fairview Welcome Table was founded at Susan's prompting. She had heard about the idea from a chef in Black Mountain, North Carolina, named John Crognale who started the first one at his local Episcopal church. The idea was simple: one day a week, get some people together and throw a big feast for anyone in the community who wants to come, especially the most needy. This is no dreary soup kitchen. John and his volunteers break out white tablecloths, silverware—it's Chez Panisse meets church potluck. And it's free. Guests can donate if they want, but if they can't then don't worry about it. Just come eat. Susan was so taken with this idea that she placed ads in the *Fairview Town Crier,* hoping to lure someone into taking it on. That someone was Barbara Trombatori, a longtime Fairview resident.

"I've known Susan for a hundred years," Barbara said. "I want to feed people. When I heard about the idea, I knew this was what I should do."

That Maundy Thursday, their one-year anniversary lunch consisted of homemade pizza, a fruit bowl, iced tea, and a massive spinach salad cut fresh from the Lord's Acre. The eighty-six guests (according to Barbara's head count that day) were seated at long tables, and the atmosphere felt less like that of a soup kitchen than a big family gathering. Most of the guests dropped a ticket into an offering bowl when they arrived. Tickets are given out in advance. If people are able to contribute money, too, that's great, Barbara explained, but the idea is that everybody puts something into the bowl so nobody knows who's eating for free. With small structures like these in place, Barbara was trying to remove any possible stigma attached with coming here. I tried and failed to distinguish the hungry people from those who came for the socializing.

The meal takes place every Thursday. On Sundays Barbara calls

Susan and asks what they have in the garden, and she plans her menu based on the answer. On Tuesdays Barbara does the shopping and on Wednesdays she and several volunteers do kitchen prep. On Thursday she and her kitchen crew arrive at 8 A.M., and the meal begins promptly at 11:30 A.M.

The Welcome Table feeds about seventy to eighty people each week, at a cost of only about $200. In the summer months, Barbara explained, "when the Lord's Acre is going gangbusters," they make a profit. That money gets set aside to be spent over the winter when there is less produce. Some of the summer bounty Barbara preserves. Last summer she canned fourteen and a half gallon jars of tomatoes, which she used in soups over the winter.

I asked her about her motivations for this work. She responded, "In the scriptures Jesus asks Peter three times, 'Do you love me?' And he says, 'Yes Lord.' Then Jesus tells him, 'Feed my sheep.' I decided that's what I want to do. Feed his sheep. And he lets me."

Since the Last Supper in the upper room two millennia ago, eating together, breaking bread, has been the central ritual of the Christian community. Indeed, for the early followers of Jesus, most of whom were Jews, the table was the most visible and tangible example of how their world was changing. A good bit of New Testament ink got spilled over figuring out how Gentiles could become part of the tribe, and in Paul's letter to the church in Corinth, he treated commensality—Jews eating with Gentiles—as the litmus test for full church membership. For those early Jewish Christians to give new Gentile converts a place at the table was perhaps the most profound act of hospitality they could offer. It is still the most profound act of hospitality, for all of us. When a stranger sits down at our table, she is a stranger no longer.

Yet despite the intrinsic link between Christianity and table fellowship, today's churches have little connection to their daily bread.

"In a generation and a half we've all lost our connection to the land," said Pat Stone, who was the first to suggest the idea for the Lord's Acre. Like Susan, Pat also worked at *Mother Earth News* back in the 1970s and 1980s and since then he's been publishing his own gardening magazine called *GreenPrints*. Pat has been living and breathing and talking gardening most of his adult life. "We've lost the ability to *grow* fresh food, *prepare* fresh food, and *preserve* fresh food. It's a simple life skill that's been part of humanity since Day One. I mean, it's comical we're that disconnected. So that's a really important set of skills that gardens can give people. The issues to be addressed are manifold. From obesity to lack of community to fossil fuels—food touches on them all. A garden alone won't solve them. But it pushes them."

Pat told me he wanted to start a garden for the hungry because Jesus said, *In as much as you do it unto the least of these you do it unto me*. "We talk the talk, we should walk the walk. There are all these world problems you can't solve that feel so big, but we can at least grow some fresh food for some hungry people."

But why, I wondered, was this concept of growing food in community taking off so much now? I asked him why have so many people, especially churches, started planting gardens just in the past few years.

At first, he was flummoxed. "Fine, there's the recession. There are more hungry people. Fine, there's an interest in whole foods. The obesity epidemic. Junk food. Organic is trendy. Food is trendy. All those social phenomena. But it goes deeper than that. I think people really do want to do something to solve our big problems. And this looks like a way you can do it. You're not just giving money. You're giving your time. Your labor. And the Lord's Acre is a mechanism for that."

While I found Eucharistic overtones everywhere present in the

Welcome Table and the Lord's Acre, they were not explicit. Even though it was started primarily by Christians, there were a lot of folks involved who weren't of that faith. Steve Norris was involved from the beginning, and he's a Buddhist. Still others considered themselves "spiritual but not religious." As Pat Stone lamented, "Christians tend to subdivide all the time into these denominations; we wanted to do something ecumenical. Not something that's owned by the Presbyterians or the Baptists. Which is really hard for Christians to do. They want to get credit for their church." Pat and Susan and the other board members wanted the garden to be open to people who didn't share their faith. Christians have for too long tried to draw a line between themselves and the world they claim to serve, and it turns out that a garden can go a long way toward blurring those lines.

"What can you say?" Pat concluded. "Is it more important for me to bang a Christian drum or is it more important to serve other people? In as much as you've done it unto the least of these you've done it unto me. That's the purpose. On the one hand, we're not solving big societal issues. The fact that we grow eight tons of food for the hungry each year does not solve the hunger problem. It's only a drop in the bucket." Pat paused and smiled. "But it's a *good* drop."

Wednesday evenings are workdays at the Lord's Acre, and one Wednesday evening in April, All Souls Episcopal Church from Asheville brought dinner for the crew. A band calling themselves the Bumblebee Democracy brought fiddles and guitars and drums and amps and plugged in right next to the tool shed. Until long after twilight they serenaded the garden workers with everything from John Prine's "Angel from Montgomery" and the Stones' "Dead Flowers" to scratchy fiddle tunes and Appalachian murder ballads.

A group of students from Warren Wilson College arrived, and Susan walked them out to the northeast quadrant. "This is your mission, should you choose to accept it. Mob these beds and dig up every thistle you can find." She explained that thistle grows back from the root, and any piece of root left in the ground, even one or two feet down, will resprout. Thistle is one of the hardiest, most stubborn plants in the garden. "What doesn't kill thistle only makes it stronger. Oh—and we have bees." Susan pointed out two white hives in the corner of the garden. Picking a broad leaf from a patch of weeds, she instructed, "This is plantain. If you get stung, chew this up and rub it on the sting. You'll be amazed."

I visited the Lord's Acre a number of Wednesday evenings that spring. Sometimes there were potlucks after the work, and these warm evenings reminded me of Tuesday nights at Anathoth. In the spring of 2006, my first full season at Anathoth, we began holding work hours on Tuesday evenings. I often spent my evenings at the garden, working late. Elizabeth grew tired of being alone at dinnertime, so she started bringing dinner to the garden. Interns and garden volunteers were invited to share what we had, and soon they began bringing a dish, too. What began as three or four people sharing a simple meal soon became fifteen or twenty, then thirty or forty, and when the Latinos started coming and bringing *pollo con mole* and homemade tamales, Tuesday nights became a regular throwdown. Those evening meals after working together in the garden were some of my fondest memories of Anathoth. It seemed to be the culmination of all our striving. One Wednesday evening at the Lord's Acre I experienced a similar state of grace.

On this particular Wednesday night the owner of Rosetta's Kitchen, one of Asheville's most popular vegan restaurants, brought dinner. Rosetta is something of a spiritual force. When Occupy Wall Street first cranked up, she sent a carload of food. Her father, whose name is Weasel, drove it up to Zuccotti Park, taking one of Rosetta's sons along for the ride. The Occupy movement would soon be caravanning through Asheville on a nationwide tour, and Rosetta was all set to feed them when they came through. That Wednesday night at the Lord's Acre, she rolled into the parking lot in a beat-up Suburban filled with four kids and a feast of vegan barbecued tofu, gravy, mashed potatoes, and brownies.

"I thought you said there would be twenty-five," she said to Susan as we unpacked the food. "Looks more like forty."

Susan shrugged and smiled. "People heard you were cooking tonight. I couldn't keep them away. Guess we'll just have to pray for a loaves-and-fishes miracle."

I sat down next to Rosetta and asked her what drove her to offer free dinner to places like the Lord's Acre. "Food is the physical embodiment of prayer," she answered. "Food nourishes people. It's creating justice on all the different levels. When people are fed, they are warm and relaxed. It's how you reach people." In her early years she had tried protesting, but she realized that hers was the role of nurturer. She would rather feed protesters than join them on the streets.

She had recently traveled with her family across Central America for six months, and she told me she gained new perspective there about the American relationship to food. "When I came back from Central America I was like, 'We're living in a zombie culture,' you know what I mean? You lose how to grow and prepare food, and what do you lose next? Sex? Sleep? The taste of water? Things are so out of balance. And I think places like this, where little kids work next to gray hairs"—she gestured to the workers coming in from the garden—"these places are a way of coming back."

I thought about Rosetta's words about food as the embodiment of prayer as we gathered around the table that night. Susan turned to me and asked if I would be the one to pray for a miracle. Or at least a blessing on the meal. I'm not ordained, but as someone with a divinity degree I often become the default prayer guy at public gatherings.

I used to shy away from such requests. My father was always the one who prayed before family meals, and I remember being embarrassed when, eating out at a restaurant, our family would suddenly become conspicuous as we held hands while dad said a blessing, all eyes suddenly on us. But since then I've become less self-conscious about praying in public. I've actually come to wonder if, when people see others offer thanks for a meal in public, their inward reaction is not condemnation but a certain kind of envy. Especially at a table set in a garden, where food's mystery becomes much more palpable, I think we each possess a deep human desire to offer thanks.

To say grace is not only to give thanks to God. It is to become fully human.

I was reminded of this by a moment in Michael Pollan's *The Omnivore's Dilemma,* when the author and his friends have gathered around the table for what he calls "the perfect meal." Imagine Pollan with his clan of hipster hunter-gatherers: they've gleaned, scavenged, or shot nearly every ingredient at the table. As he contemplates this in the moment before the first bite, Pollan wants to offer words commensurate with the occasion. We've reached the finale of his long journey into our food's origins; our guide is about to tell us what all this finally *means.* He commends the chanterelle pickers, praises the boar hunters. But there's an ineffable *something more,* he realizes. Confronted by food's sacred mystery, our intrepid gastronomical wordsmith finds himself speechless.

Pollan later confesses to the reader that, even as a secular person, he found himself in that moment "reaching for the words of grace." I find that admission one of the most intriguing and moving parts of the book. What had until this moment been a witty, informative story about food's origins suddenly opens up into something larger, and more profound. While Pollan's confession casts a sideways glance at food's inscrutable mystery, then quickly moves on ("I don't want to make too much of it," he writes, "it was just a meal, after all"), I found myself that night at the Lord's Acre wanting to find those words of grace.

In his slim and lovely book *For the Life of the World,* Eastern Orthodox writer Alexander Schmemann writes, "The whole creation depends on food. But the unique position of man in the universe is that he alone is to *bless* God for the food and the life he receives from Him. He alone is to respond to God's blessing with his blessing."

As the forty of us gathered around and held hands that night, the garden's fragrances mingling with the warm smells of barbecued tofu, I felt that responding to God's tangible blessings arrayed there on the table before us with a blessing of my own was the thing I most wanted to do.

Friday mornings are harvest days at the Lord's Acre, and at 7:30 one Friday in early June I teamed up with Dr. Will Hamilton to harvest kale. We each took two bushel-sized harvest tubs and a pair of garden shears and worked our way down opposite sides of the kale bed.

"What should we do about these bugs?" Will asked Susan, pointing to some brilliantly marked insects, their black and yellow colors standing in relief against the dark green kale.

"Harlequin bugs? Oh, you can squash them."

"Right," Will said. "Under General's orders, I'll kill anything."

Will is English, and he looked the part, dressed in calf-high rubber Wellies, khaki shorts, and a wool sweater vest; the quintessential British Gardener. He is also my father-in-law. His wife, Susie, my mother-in-law, is the granddaughter of James G. K. McClure, founder of the original Lord's Acre in 1930. Elizabeth and I were wed in the same apple orchard planted by James G. K. himself back in the 1920s at Hickory Nut Gap Farm.

One of the many things I find remarkable about this garden and its people is how much it seems to have followed a certain trajectory of a God-infused communal life in Fairview. It is as if James G. K. McClure had begun a spiritual legacy in this valley, one whose mantle subsequent generations could either cast off or claim as their own. An outsider who came to this valley in the 1970s, Will decided to claim it. As a young physician in London in the 1960s, he had three things on his mind: church, community, and farming. He wanted his life as a doctor to become integrated with all three. He ruminated on his life later that Friday morning as we took a break from kale harvesting to share some eggs and toast. He said he believed that, while he did have regrets like not spending more time with his kids, his life largely had integrated these three things. When he and Susie moved to Fairview, they started an informal Christian commune of sorts. Will opened a natural childbirth clinic in their house. They took strangers into their home to live with them for days, months, even years at a time. Elizabeth doesn't remember a time when she wasn't sharing a bedroom with another child who was not one of her four siblings. The Hamiltons, along with Pat and Becky Stone and several other couples, shared nightly meals together—"farm suppers," they called them—and though they weren't setting out to live a Christian socialist existence, that's pretty much what they did. The early church as described in the Acts of the Apostles was fully communitarian, holding possessions in common and sharing meals. Though the young group in Fairview didn't share bank accounts, there was a certain fluidity to their lives and how they meshed. The farm suppers were not occasional affairs; they happened five nights a week. The couples helped raise each other's children. The women even breast-fed each other's infants. There was no real organization to this, no name, no denomination or covenant or rules, it just happened, and for a time the whole experiment seemed to unfurl in a beautifully chaotic symmetry of shared lives and shared faith.

But as the children grew older the nightly farm suppers became too difficult to continue, and then, on July 4, 1981, in the Hamiltons' backyard, the group decided to formalize their faith community. They started a house church.

"It was the hardest thing I've ever done in my life," Will said.

At the instigation of a local Presbyterian minister, they joined the Presbyterian Church in America and Fairview Christian Fellowship was born. The young church thrived. Soon they had a full-time pastor and a beautiful building. When they started, most of the members, while adhering to traditional Christian doctrines, were socially liberal, but the church began to attract more conservative members. It was the beginning of the Reagan era, and the church soon began to reflect all the tensions of that time, especially the dovetailing of conservative theology with right-wing politics. Twenty years later Will found himself in a denomination where 90 percent of the church leadership had voted to keep in power a U.S. president who led his country into what Will saw as an unnecessary and destructive war in Iraq. He held on, but as the years went by his increasingly progressive theology was not meshing with the conservative theology of his church's denomination. Eventually he could no longer abide what he believed was mistaken theology. After reading theologians like Dietrich Bonhoeffer and John Howard Yoder, he became a pacifist. Also, the PCA denomination only ordains men, and his daughter Elizabeth had enrolled in divinity school. How could he support her calling in a denomination that denied that calling? After twenty-seven years he resigned as an elder and left the church. He joined an ecumenical church down the road called the Chapel Door, and in 2009 that church became the host site for the Lord's Acre.

After our breakfast we hauled four bushels of beautiful kale leaves to the washing station and hosed them down before placing them in the bed of Susan's pickup. She and her interns had meanwhile picked a bushel of carrots, several bushels of lettuce, and a half bushel each of garlic, beet tops, and radishes. Will and I munched radishes and talked about how the French ate them for breakfast.

"I used to feel guilty," Will said, "because I thought my main objective in life was to drag unbelievers across the divide. I was never very good at it. But since then my faith has broadened beyond that view. I no longer look at people around me as being on one side of the salvation line or the other. I think that line has been by far the worst aspect of Christianity. Politics have fueled it. But it's not our job to say where the line is or who's on which side of it."

Will paused. Finally he said, "I've come to realize that the threads of God's glory are intertwined not only in my own life, but in the lives of whoever I will meet today. It's very liberating."

With Susan's truck loaded, Will went looking for the threads of God's glory manifesting in the clients of Food for Fairview. They brought their hunger and an empty cardboard box. He brought a truckload full of premium organic vegetables and a hunger of his own. *Blessed are those who hunger and thirst for righteousness,* Jesus said, *for they shall be filled.*

The pantry would not officially open until 9 A.M., but already four women and one man sat in line with their boxes. As we walked past, Will held out the box of radishes. "Care for a snack? They're quite good for breakfast."

The women shook their heads. The man said, "I ain't put my teeth in yet." He laughed good-naturedly, and when I sat down next to him on the bench I learned his name was Larry. It was only his second time coming here, he said, and he was still embarrassed about it. By way of explanation, Larry listed his ailments. He had a busted knee and crooked neck from a car accident, after which he couldn't work, then he had to get surgery on his innards, which he confirmed by pulling up his shirt and showing me the scars—"seventeen stitches"—all of which was enough to earn him disability, but the check he got wasn't enough to keep him and his family fed. "I came 'cause I was tired of not having enough to eat."

Larry lived way up on the mountain. He used to eat raccoons, until he learned that they carried parasites and diseases. He also ate creasy greens and ramps, wild foods long favored by mountain folk. "I love me some vegetable stew, now. That's better than a steak." I told him he should visit the Lord's Acre, where all this food came from. "Well, anyway," he said, "there's a blessing in store for you. And that's not just a hungry man trying to get some food that's saying that. I believe it. I don't know if you're a spiritual man . . . but I believe God sees what you do."

Midday in early June I rode with Susan up a winding mountain road that climbed a long ridge behind the Lord's Acre. In the back of the truck were two five-gallon buckets full of water. We turned into a dirt driveway covered in weeds that ran up to a single wide trailer. Two cars parked in front looked like they hadn't run in years. A sagging tent was propped next to a pile of rotting garbage. The place looked abandoned. Then I saw it. Roughly six by twelve feet of lumber containing soil: a garden. It was the one thing on this property that was neatly kept. In the beds were planted lettuce, cucumbers, squash, and peppers, and two low-lying leafy plants at the end. I asked Susan if those plants were what I thought they were.

"Yep," she said, and smiled mischievously. "Watermelons." We looked at the tiny garden for a moment, and then Susan said, "Emma cried when we brought the soil over."

We had come to the home of the former watermelon thief. Susan got out and knocked on the vinyl siding. There was a noise inside, but nobody appeared. "Emma? It's Susan. I'm leaving you some water for your garden." Emma had no outdoor hose, and for that matter no spigot. Susan was carting water for her. Aside from not having easy water access Emma had lupus, which made it difficult to go out in the sun.

As we were driving up the hill to Emma's house, Susan had told me the rest of the watermelon robbery story. A few months after Emma had exploded at Susan, saying she'd never come to the Lord's Acre again, the garden had sent out a flyer to all the residents of Fairview explaining about their work. A couple of months later Emma called Susan to apologize for taking the melons. She also explained that she had lupus and that she'd been having trouble with her medications, which had since been straightened out. Emma said she had received the Lord's Acre flyer in the mail, and hadn't realized that the garden gave its food away. She said she wouldn't take food in secret anymore, and at the end of the conversation Susan asked her, "Would you like us to help you start your own garden?"

Steve Norris built the boxes and Susan and the interns brought over a truckload of soil and plants, and Emma was able to plant her first garden. It was hard for her to get out the words, Susan said. Emma said she just couldn't have imagined things would turn out this way. She lived like a hermit, she told Susan. Now she would have something to do besides go to the doctor.

"It's amazing what the love of Christ can do," Susan said to me later, reflecting on Emma's turnaround. "It's no accident that Emma called me. She approached us first, which was a really difficult gesture for her, but she did it, and that was amazing. This garden attracts people with some deep wounds. Emma was hungry for food, that much was obvious; but her deeper hungers—to be loved and heard and valued—could never be found in a box of produce or in a watermelon patch. They could only be found in community— weaving itself in and around Emma and her weaving herself in and through community."

While Susan was amazed that Emma had called to make amends, I was amazed at how Susan could turn an act of theft into an act of love, what Pat Stone described as a "judo move." What would Jesus do if Emma stole his watermelons? Maybe he would help her plant a garden in front of her single wide. Maybe that's the soil he would use to heal her wounds.

I went twice with Susan on her biweekly rounds to water Emma's garden, but neither time did Emma appear at the door. She was still a bit skittish around strangers. For all my work in communal food gardens, it was a reminder that I was still a stranger in this one. I may have been in Susan's truck, but this was Emma's community.

The week after the last of my visits to the Lord's Acre, in late June, I got an email from Susan. She told me that on the grease board at the Lord's Acre, she keeps a to-do list for herself and the interns. Next to her name Susan saw Emma's name, scribbled there as Emma's reminder to Susan to visit her and water her garden. While Susan was out one day, Emma had paid her a visit, and finding her gone, she wrote a note next to Susan's name on the grease board: "I am so blessed. Oh yeah, and happy!"

Several months later I asked Susan how it was going. She told me Emma now says things like: "Can I come over and harvest beans for the pantry?" and "How did we get here from where we started?" She asks that a lot, Susan said. Emma loves to receive visits from neighbors who now stop and ask about her garden. As this year's garden winds down, Susan said, Emma has begun reading seed catalogs. She's already planning next year's crops.

A socialized spiritual life in the countryside. I'm not sure that's the ideal the Lord's Acre represents or even wants to represent. But Henry Wallace's prediction that "Great spiritual power will eventually emanate from these mountains of western North Carolina" is proving to be true. And not only in North Carolina. This power flows from similar faith-infused gardens all over the country; it is reaching out across the forests and rivers and prairies, from the Occupy tents at Zuccotti Park to Larry's mountain abode, and I believe will eventually cover the whole land. I came to see the Lord's Acre as a frail fortress tenuously keeping the powers of despair and hunger at bay. We tend to look to Washington, or maybe our state governments, and the army of agencies and nonprofits as the sources of social support. But my visits to the Lord's Acre had renewed in me the conviction that faith-infused food gardens are like arks, built to carry us to perhaps not a land of milk and honey, but to more resilient communities, to more powerful fellowship with our neighbors. We would do well to build more of them.

My visits to the Lord's Acre were a kind of homecoming. It was the promise of just this kind of close relationship to food, community, and rootedness that had brought me to Anathoth Community Garden in the first place so many years before. Now I felt called to a different role than garden director, yet I reveled in the fellowship and connectedness I felt at the Lord's Acre, feelings I'd felt so strongly at Anathoth. It was this longing for a holistic life that led me, after my rooftop experience in Chiapas, to take the plunge into a life of feeding people, even though I possessed so few skills. I somehow knew even then that starting this journey was something I would never regret.

CHAPTER FOUR

Out of Africa, Into Babylon

Though he works and worries, the farmer
never reaches down to where the seed turns
into summer. The earth grants.
—Rainer Maria Rilke, *Sonnets to Orpheus*

Chatham County, North Carolina—August 2002

Since my stint in Chiapas I'd been tearing voraciously through Wendell Berry's books of essays, poetry, and fiction. My desire was strong, but my skills were few. If I needed to apprentice myself to a real farmer, why not go to the source? Perhaps Berry himself would teach me. From his books I learned that farming is not just a quaint hobby; farming is an art. It requires vision tempered by humility. And farming, Berry's books taught me, was not just about growing food. Farming was a form of charity. "Charity is a theological virtue," he wrote in *The Gift of Good Land,* "but it is also a practical virtue because it must be practiced. The requirements of this complex charity cannot be fulfilled by smiling in abstract beneficence on our neighbors and the scenery. It must come to acts, which must come from skills. Real charity calls for the study of agriculture, soil husbandry . . . [and] the making of pictures, songs, and stories."

I wrote a letter to Berry asking if I could learn such soil-based

charity from him, sending along with my request some poems I'd
written. I don't think he saw much in my poetry—he sent them
back marked up in red ink, saying "you indeed have much to learn
about the making of poems"—but he did encourage my farming in-
terests. Berry wasn't farming much now, he said, "just some slaughter lambs." Though he didn't say this, I suspected his main crop was
words, "the making of songs and stories." He couldn't take on an
apprentice. But he did recommend that I seek out a farm near where
I lived in North Carolina, offering to help me locate one. That
prompted me to make that second phone call to Harvey Harmon,
and this time there was an opening.

The largest of Harvey's gardens was called Africa, and my cabin lay
along the edge of its northern boundary. I remember many an August night in my little shack at the edge of Africa, lying exhausted
from the day's farm work yet unable to fall asleep in the stifling air. I
read Dante's *Inferno* by the light of a single solar-charged bulb until
eventually the battery would die, and I would drift into a restless
sleep.

The garden was aptly named; the thick air shimmering hot off
the dark soil reminded me of the bush country of Nigeria, where I'd
lived for three years as a missionary kid. The Beautiful Garden and
Utopia were the farm's other gardens, which I also worked in and
admired, but over the coming months I came to love this Africa, it
was "my" garden, an acre of soil and sun and water reminding me of
my boyhood on that distant continent.

My cabin had no running water or electricity. A three-hundred-
gallon cistern caught more than enough rainwater for bathing.
Mornings were the only relief from the late summer heat and I
rose early to enjoy the cool air, drinking coffee on my cabin steps
and watching the sun come up over Africa. There was always

something happening in this garden. In addition to the acre of garden beds, Africa had a pond—Lake Victoria in miniature. Inside the pond, circled by a broken fence, lived a pair of African geese. Each day the geese escaped and each day we caught them and put them back. I never questioned why we didn't just fix the fence. There were other pressing things that needed our attention—the carrots needed watering, the fall cover crops of rye, vetch, and clover needed to be sown—but mostly we didn't fix the fence because catching the geese was fun. And also dangerous due to their large clublike wings.

In the afternoons I read books on permaculture and sustainable living—*Gaia's Garden,* by Toby Hemenway, *A Pattern Language,* by Christopher Alexander, and Bill Mollison's *Introduction to Permaculture*—and in the evenings, when the sun dropped behind the trees, I walked the farm to look for examples of what I'd read. In my nightly solar-charged reading of Dante I read about his trek through the underworld.

> Midway in our life's journey, I went astray
> from the straight road and woke to find myself
> alone in a dark wood.

Though I was less than midway in my life's journey, I did find myself alone every night in a dark wood. It was hellishly hot in that sleeping loft there in my cabin in the woods, but I could take comfort in being surrounded by fecundity. The wood was filled with mushrooms, dark under the tall oaks, and beyond the darkness lay ponds, gardens, and cool, open fields.

"Permaculture is about relationships," Harvey said.

It was 8 A.M. on our first day of class. We four interns had gathered in the round mud hut on the back of the farm. Already it was in the low nineties outside, but inside the hut it was still cool. A wattle and daub structure, the hut featured walls with sculpted shelves and nooks where you could set your coffee mug or a vase of fresh echinacea flowers. Whimsy partnered with function. A half dozen glass cider jugs were plastered right into the walls, infusing the circular room with natural light. You feel different inside a round house, the mind freed from the tyranny of ninety-degree angles.

A contraction of both permanent agriculture and permanent culture, the word "permaculture" and the system behind it was coined in 1974 by a cranky and iconoclastic Tasmanian named Bill Mollison. Permaculture is a holistic design system for creating sustainable human habitations, but it is also more than that. It's a collection of patterns for how to work *with* rather than against nature. On one level, permaculture deals with plants, animals, and buildings. But what I learned from Mollison and Harvey is that permaculture is not about these elements themselves, but rather about the relationships between them.

To demonstrate such relationships, Harvey walked us out to the chicken coop. Years ago, right in the middle of the coop, he had planted a mulberry tree. Japanese beetles, invasive insects for which there were few natural enemies, liked to congregate on the mulberry. It was morning, and the bugs were too sluggish to fly. "Watch," Harvey said with a mischievous grin. He gave the tree a shake. Hundreds of Japanese beetles rained to the ground, and when the chickens ran over to eat them, the bugs could only loll about, waiting their turn to become breakfast. The chickens also ate any overripe mulberries that fell to the ground, Harvey explained. Rather than thinking about the chickens, the mulberry tree, or the Japanese beetles as separate, individual elements, permaculture encouraged the farmer to think about how those elements interacted, and to design for the kinds of interactions that would bring the farmer the most benefit. It was all about relationships.

I was thinking a good deal about relationships just then. Five months before arriving at Sustenance Farm, I'd begun dating Elizabeth. Though I desperately wanted to absorb as much of Harvey's knowledge as I could in my three short months with him, I found myself often distracted by thinking of *her*.

I also thought about the relationships with the others at Sustenance Farm. Sith was the most adept at farming. He was from Laos, had come to live with the Harmons as an exchange student, and though he spoke little English he was friendly and easygoing. Kia was a puppeteer who made elaborate, house-sized puppets and put on plays with them. Jean was a fiftyish medical doctor who'd come to learn self-sufficient living. Though her doctor's salary would have been in the six digits, she only accepted $11,000 a year. As a former communist and current war tax resister, staying below the poverty line was a conscious political choice.

But most intriguing to me of all the farm residents was a fellow named Armor. I had Africa in common not only with the Harmons, who spent five years in South Africa in the 1980s as development workers, but I also shared that land with Armor. He came from Zimbabwe, where he was a political dissident. He had lived with the Harmons years before as an exchange student—he still called them "Ma" and "Pa"—and had recently returned because of his opposition to Mugabe's government. Armor's life was under threat. Forced to leave his wife and children, he had chosen Sustenance Farm as his place of exile. A large, brooding man, Armor rarely spoke, but every so often he would brighten, like the morning at breakfast when he and Harvey burst into a song in Armor's native Ndebele complete with clicks and glottal stops, sounding as if Ladysmith Black Mambazo had crowded into our tiny kitchen. Mostly, though, Armor kept to himself. Rather than work in the gardens with the other four interns, he worked alone. He would leave early in the morning to work on one of Harvey's woodland projects, clearing trails with a chainsaw and swing blade, returning late in the day. He barely paused for lunch, chopping down sweet gums and young maples in the August heat as if something drove him. Armor preferred the hard jobs, and seemed to thrive on the combination of solitude and endless exertion.

On weekday mornings after Armor left for work we four interns met with Harvey for our hour-long class in permaculture. Afterward we went out to work in the gardens. We direct-seeded carrots in Utopia, making multiple passes down each bed with the EarthWay seeder; we harvested jalapeños in the Beautiful Garden, careful not to rub our eyes afterward; and we carted wheelbarrow loads of composted sheep manure into Africa to build the soil's fertility. Around 11:30 one of us would peel off and head to the kitchen to prepare lunch. At one we shared a common meal. The rest of the day was free for reading, exploring the farm, or taking naps. There was no exchange of money. For twenty-five hours' labor a week we earned our room and board. I learned much in those hours of work. But Harvey was mostly absent during that time, taking his basil to market in Raleigh or working on the large tract of land nearby he was turning into a sustainable housing development. The one hour of class each day was my most treasured time because I could grill him with questions.

One morning in class Harvey took us over to a pond. Another permaculture principle, Harvey said, was "catching and storing reez horses on your site." *Reez horses?* Was this a new way to tame wild ponies? Some esoteric equestrian lore? Then I realized it was simply Harvey's verbal tic. He meant *resources*. "Take this pond, for instance," Harvey continued. "Water is a very important *reez horse* on the farm."

There was no spring here, he told us, and he asked us how the pond was fed. The surrounding pasture was nearly flat. We all walked around the pond and, finding no feeder stream, gave up. Harvey then showed us a tiny ditch, a "swale" he called it, which he had dug on contour through the pasture. When it rained, the swale caught any water that fell on the pasture and drained it into the pond. The farm was full of swales, all feeding into ponds, and each pond had an overflow which fed into still more ponds—dozens of ponds—from which Harvey could irrigate all of his gardens. Harvey showed us cisterns placed under various buildings, which also captured rainwater. Any water that fell on this land would not easily escape.

But it wasn't just water Harvey caught; he also captured soil. All the raised garden beds in Utopia, Africa, and the Beautiful Garden were built on contours, that is, they followed the curvature of the land. Any soil that the rain tried to wash away was caught and held by the level contours. So much of our topsoil has been squandered, eroded by carelessness and ignorance. But not on Sustenance Farm. Like the Abejas of Chiapas, Harvey treated soil with the reverence due a living creature, for living it was. Soil was not a thing to let slip from your land.

On those morning walks with Harvey, the farm began to seem less like a place to grow food and more like an elaborate and beneficent web. The land captured all manner of reez horses—water, soil, people—and held them close for fear that if they set one hoof into the void just beyond the farm's boundary they might gallop away and never return.

How easy it is to lose the gifts of the land, and how little we have fought to keep them.

And yet, loss was not a given. It was possible to live a gracious life, the Harmons showed me, holding close the soil and its members, and also holding close the stragglers like me who came seeking knowledge, shelter, and community.

With a wry smile often hiding under his beard and soil caked under his long fingernails, Harvey was like a mischievous peasant. He reminded me of a character from one of Chekhov's stories, the quiet one who turns out to be the backbone of the village. Harvey rarely spoke unless addressed; yet behind his reticence lay a great accumulation of knowledge and wisdom. At nearby Central Carolina Community College, Harvey had started one of the most respected sustainable agriculture programs in the country. He was once awarded the Farmer of the Year by the Carolina Farm Stewardship Association. Until recently, when he shifted his considerable energy into land conservation, he'd managed a thriving Community Supported Agriculture business here at Sustenance Farm. No wonder there was a waiting list to become an intern.

Yet despite his local fame, Harvey never boasted about his knowledge. When I queried him about composting methods, say, or *Fusarium* wilt prevention for basil, he would invariably preface his response with something like: "Well, you might know more than me about this, but in my experience . . ." It wasn't false modesty; Harvey really believed that his interlocutor just might know more than him. He reminded me of one of the Abejas men in Nuevo Yibeljoj or perhaps a village elder in Nigeria, one who knew that the more he learned about the world and the ways of humans, the more he became aware of his ignorance. A lifetime of designing sustainable human environments had taught Harvey that you can never fully design a sustainable human environment; you can only give your spirit and mind and will to the work, laying your hands on the world with a benediction of labor, and pray that you might create something lasting and good and true.

*   *   *

When I returned from Chiapas, I knew for certain that my life needed to be *for* rather than *against*. Harvey's lifeblood flowed out of him and into the land, his creative spirit everywhere present on this farm, and it stood as a powerful witness *for*.

When I read permaculture expert Bill Mollison, I found another kindred spirit. Mollison had grown up in a small village in Tasmania, and became horrified as he saw fish stocks collapsing and large sections of forest disappear. He began to protest against the political and industrial systems that were to blame. "But," he wrote in *Introduction to Permaculture*, "I soon decided that it was no good persisting with opposition that in the end achieved nothing." For the next two years Mollison withdrew from society. When he returned he realized he did not want to oppose anything ever again and waste his time. He wanted to come back only with something positive, "something that would allow us all to exist without the wholesale collapse of biological systems."

What Mollison came back with was the beginnings of permaculture, a "whole human system." Like any system, it had its shortcomings. But it made sense to me, and it made sense that Mollison first had to go to the edge of society to discover it. Important discoveries in my own life had always happened at the margins.

Of all the permaculture advice I learned from Mollison, channeled through Harvey, this was the most important: seek out the edge. "An edge is an interface between two mediums," Mollison wrote in *Introduction to Permaculture*. "It is the surface between the water and the air; the zone around a soil particle to which water bonds . . . it is the border of the desert." Edge is not so much a place as it is a heightened transfer of energy that happens in the meeting of two distinct entities: field and forest, ocean and estuary, scrub and grassland. These interstitial zones between ecosystems are where the greatest exchanges of life take place. It is along the tree line, not in the meadow's center, where the hawk waits to peg the field mouse.

I was learning the importance of edges at Sustenance Farm in part because I lived on one. My little eight-by-twelve intern cabin was nestled in a narrow line of trees between garden and field. To the south and east lay Africa; to the west under a stand of oaks sat forty or fifty clusters of shiitake logs, stacked like miniature, roofless log cabins. After a good rain these little log cabins came to life, tasty fungi sprouting all over them. It became my job to harvest the shiitake, dry them in the kitchen's food dehydrator, and store them in large glass jars. Behind the cabin lay an open field slowly being reclaimed by sweet gum, yellow pine, and wild blackberries. As there was no toilet nearby, the field served as host site for my morning ablutions. In front of my cabin was the garden, source of my food; behind me was the field, my food's final resting place. I served as the interface between the two. My body joined garden and field, creating an edge where life could interact and thrive.

That life is richer at the edge than on either side was something I knew inherently. I'd always felt more comfortable on the margins. I never liked being in the center of anything, whether it was a cocktail party or a continent. At cozy human gatherings, I was always the one with my back to the wall watching and listening, and often the first to leave. And though I counted myself a member of the Body of Christ, that mystical body comprised of both the living and the dead, I had most times felt myself an outsider among Christians. With missionaries for parents, I had grown up in the church. My great-great-great-grandfather was a bishop in the Moravian Church during the Civil War, and my Moravian ancestors left their homeland in what is now the Czech Republic in order to seek religious freedom. Yet I've always felt a tad uneasy nestled in the church's bosom. Which I suppose is fitting, given that Jesus himself, though he grew up in the temple, did not stay within its secure confines. His was a ministry practiced out on the land. His most frequent words and miracles were directed not to those in the middle, but to those who lived on the margins, and in that Jesus was following a long line of divinely appointed edge-dwellers: Abraham the wanderer, Moses the speech-challenged leader, Jeremiah the reluctant prophet who married a prostitute as an act of street theater, then bought a field outside Jerusalem in the midst of a Babylonian invasion. God's chosen agents were nothing if not marginal oddities, and though I've never felt myself to be God's agent, I took comfort in their fringe-like example. "If change is to come, it will come from the margins," wrote Wendell Berry in *The Unsettling of America*. "It was the desert, not the temple, that gave us the prophets."

In those months at Sustenance Farm, I felt myself living on another kind of edge, one filled with possibility. My life was about to turn in a direction that would forever alter me. I was here to learn skills that I would need on the other side of this experience. Following my mentors José and Harvey and Mollison, I knew that growing food was an important step toward becoming human. But the certainty I'd reached on the rooftop in Chiapas was growing cloudy. Could I really feed people? Was that truly my calling? Before Harvey's class each morning I sat on the steps of my cabin pondering these things, drinking my coffee and dreaming of my own Africa, my own Utopia, my own beautiful gardens. I also dreamed of the woman with whom I hoped to share them.

Elizabeth and I met in Boone, North Carolina, where I was teaching. One night I went out to a bar to hear a bluegrass band. They were called the Steep Canyon Rangers, comprised of four guys and one very striking female fiddle player. I had to meet her. We talked after the show. Behind her smile I saw a sadness, a beautiful ache that yearned to be filled. Her current life was not the life she was meant to live. I, too, knew that ache.

The following Friday her band came to play in Brevard, where my parents lived. After the show we went out for a beer. We ended up talking long into the night. The next day I went to visit her at her parents' farm in Fairview, just forty-five minutes away. A warm spring rain was falling, and I remember walking for long hours through the woods, a gentle mist blocking out the world and enveloping us like a soft quilt. All that day as we walked in the rain I very much wanted to kiss her. But I was too shy.

Two weeks later we went camping together in Linville Gorge. The Gorge is a wild place, one of the more remote regions on the East Coast. Storms blow in from out of nowhere. Black bears roam freely. Along the cliff walls, peregrine falcons come to mate and build their nests. That first night we pitched my tent on the Gorge rim above the peregrines, a nest above nests, and for the first time we lay side by side.

It was then that our bodies first formed an edge. Though we only kissed, that night for me marks the moment that we were forever joined. On either side of that kiss there had been two separate beings, two kinds of longing, and now our separate desires met. "Productivity increases at the boundary between two ecologies," wrote Mollison in *Introduction to Permaculture*.

In our first kiss the greatest exchange of our lives began taking place, and I only hoped it would continue. The next morning we sat on the cliff's edge and looked down into the abyss. We were both quiet for a long time, a bit dizzy with the void opening before us. Suddenly she spoke, "I wonder what our children will be like?" I began to wonder the same. We'd only had our first kiss the night before, a chaste and electric and utterly profound moment, yet her question seemed perfectly apt, as if we were already married and were planning our lives. Then we came to our senses, looking at each other in shock. She put a hand to her cheek and shyly turned away. I was smitten.

"A landscape with a complex edge is interesting and beautiful," Mollison wrote.

Elizabeth came down to visit me several times while I was at Harvey's farm, sleeping in the house at the back of the farm where Nancy ran her midwife practice, and during her visits we began to dream of making our own homestead together, a place like Sustenance Farm where we might grow our own food and raise a family. Our three months' separation was difficult—we were four hours apart—but we knew that if we were going to farm, I needed this time of training. And then, all too soon, my internship was over. Just before Thanksgiving I moved back to the mountains, and back to Elizabeth.

In those three months at Sustenance, I learned much from Harvey, but perhaps the most important lessons were these: In farming, and in life, pay attention to relationships. Stay close to edges, for that's where you'll find the greatest energy. And whatever you do, hold on to your reez horses.

In February the following year I proposed to Elizabeth, and in May we were wed. The ceremony was held at Hickory Nut Gap Farm in the middle of her family's apple orchard, the very orchard that James G. K. McClure had planted back in the 1920s.

One of the texts we chose was the second chapter of the Gospel of John, the story of the wedding at Cana, where Jesus turned water into wine. I remembered one of my divinity school professors saying this about the miracle: "When the water saw Jesus, it blushed."

The other text read that day was Psalm 65, the one place in the Bible that describes God as a farmer:

You pay mind to the earth and soak it.
You greatly enrich it.
God's stream is filled with water.
You ready their grain, for so You ready it.

As the ancient words were read, I stood beside my new bride and looked out over the pastures of cows, the orchard full of laughing children and smiling old people, a strong, warm wind ruffling our hair and moving the orchard grass in waves. *The hills gird themselves with joy,* the Psalm reads in Robert Alter's translation. It was as if the land herself were a beautifully attired wedding guest come to give assent to our matrimony.

The pastures are clothed with flocks
and the valleys are mantled with grain.
They shout for joy, they even sing.

Two months after we wed, Elizabeth and I bought a farm in Orange County, North Carolina. Or rather, we bought a swamp. Our farm's eleven acres were mostly flood-prone lowlands overgrown with sweet gum and yellow pine. The Orange County soil map listed our soil type as "not fit for agriculture." It was dense, gray clay, and it rebuked all early attempts at reform with my digging spade. The place had one good acre of pasture, though, and a nine-hundred-square-foot house with passive solar heat. We put in a woodstove and added a screened-in porch.

In the fall Elizabeth started her first year of divinity school, and I found work there as a writing tutor. It didn't pay much, but at least we were in the same building. While she wrote papers on Augustine and Calvin, I was marking dozens of her classmates' papers with a red pen. My office was confining, a little basement nook where no light penetrated save the fluorescent bulb overhead, and by the end of the first semester I'd had enough. But I couldn't quit; we needed the money.

All I could think about was the farm. I decided to fence in the pasture, but not until I got pigs first. Most people would have done it the other way around, but in rookie fashion I decided my pigs could free range while my friend Baker and I built their fence. When I let them out of their travel cage the two piglets, each no bigger than a beagle, bolted straight for the woods. That night Baker and I donned headlamps and spent several hours searching for the feral creatures, finally discovering them under a poplar tree. The piglets had buried themselves under the leaves and were snoring away. Baker reached to grab one and they both bolted. We played that game for several hours until we finally gave up and went to bed. It was several days before they got hungry enough to return to the barn, where I had left some food.

Though our clay soils were difficult to work, I persisted. I added truckloads of compost and used Harvey's winter cover crop mix of rye, hairy vetch, and crimson clover to break up the hardpan and add nitrogen. Slowly our soil fertility began to increase. This first farm was a good place to refine our nascent skills of horticulture and husbandry. Elizabeth raised a few dairy goats. I raised several hundred broiler chickens and a few slaughter lambs. The piglets grew into hogs. We named them Chorizo (sausage) and Chuleta (pork chop). When they reached slaughter weight we had them butchered, sold half the cuts, and filled our freezer with the rest.

Within a few years I had learned to garden year-round, not only during the summer months of bounty during which we would put away tomatoes and pole beans, but during the winter months as well, which farmer-writer Eliot Coleman called "the backside of the calendar," sparking my love of winter gardening. Elizabeth and

I learned much during these early experiments in cottage farming, but the most important thing we realized was that Elizabeth was the animal lover and I was not. I used to think that if you wanted to be a real farmer, you had to love animals, and maybe that's true. I helped with the milking, but eventually I had to acknowledge a shameful truth, one that is nearly impossible to admit in polite society: I don't like animals. Dogs, cats, goats, horses, cuddly little rabbits, it doesn't matter what kind of domestic animal I encountered, I found all of them mildly distasteful, insubordinate, and generally irksome. I wanted to like animals. I love watching their wild relatives—hawks, elk, coyotes—but I can enjoy *watching* them because they don't require my care. It's domestic animals, ones you have to manage, that I find to be pretty much a pain in the ass.

Plants were easier to deal with. Plants don't die after getting their head stuck in a fence, like one of our sheep did. Plants don't attack you, as did our big tom turkey. Plants proved to be my talent, and during those early years of learning the agrarian arts I took as much pleasure in my failures at gardening as I did my successes. Sometimes I would even forget to harvest a crop, so rapt was I by the process of growing it. To this day Elizabeth is still the one who harvests food from our garden; having successfully brought a crop to maturity, I've by then lost interest and have moved on to planting a cover crop or turning the compost pile. Bucolic as our little cottage farm life was, however, Elizabeth felt isolated. We needed a community.

We found one in a new Mennonite church in nearby Chapel Hill. It had no pastor, only thirty dedicated members who shared all the responsibilities of preaching, teaching, and pastoring each other. All decisions were made by Spirit-led consensus, our ethos deriving loosely from the book of Acts: "It seemed right to us and to the Holy Spirit . . ." If one person felt strongly against the wishes of the group, they could either abstain, allowing the group to move forward, or they could block consensus. There was no tyranny of the majority. If one person blocked, the rest of us had to acknowledge that perhaps the Holy Spirit needed more time. I actually looked forward to business meetings, which were called Congregational Life Meetings. The three years we spent there had a profound impact on our understanding of community. We loved this community of believers, committed as we were to nonviolence and caring for each other. And being swept up each Sunday night by the voices around me singing four-part a cappella harmonies, I even learned to like hymns. In time, this community would send us forth as ambassadors to do the work of feeding people.

Perhaps the only drawback of our beloved Mennonite church was that we had no connection to a place. Our membership lived scattered in a thirty-mile radius between Durham and Chapel Hill and we met in a rented Quaker meetinghouse on Sunday nights. In this our church of radicals was not much different from most other churches in America since World War II. Despite our Christian convictions of nonviolence, social justice, and consensus-based decision making, it sometimes seemed like we were just another group of isolated individuals. After several years there I began to hunger for a community—and a sacramental life—rooted to a common piece of ground.

It's no accident, I think, that most of the biblical stories didn't happen in temples or churches. I think of the Lord speaking to Job out of the whirlwind; or Elijah, his face wrapped in a mantle, waiting for God to pass by his cave entrance on Mount Horeb; or John the Revelator receiving his vision on the remote island of Patmos. For the biblical writers, land was an implicit part of their relationship with God. The land itself was implicit in God's dealings with Israel in the Old Testament and in everything Jesus did in the Gospel accounts. Just as God scooped up the land to form the first Adam, Jesus scooped up the land to perform his mighty works. Jesus's healing flowed from the land into people through the media of soil, water, saliva, bread, fish. His ministry took place not in the airless confines of the Jerusalem Temple but in the open hill country of Galilee: mountaintops, olive gardens, lakes, rivers, the wilderness. Growing up in an urban church, I had been led to believe that those physical places in the Bible were simply quaint backdrops, interchangeable stage settings where the real action took place—the preaching and praying, the baptizing and converting, the healing and resurrecting—but the more I spent time on our farm the more I believed those places to be inseparable from the Story itself. The land and its goods were also part of the mystery of God assuming human flesh. The atoms and molecules of the Galilean hill country went into Jesus's flesh in the form of olives, grain, fish, and they came out of it as well. Were not the soils and watersheds that fed us part of our own salvation story?

Though I had resisted the call of organized religion for so much of my life, and had blanched at group involvement, I still yearned for a community where work, worship, friendship, and solitude were held in place *by* a place, where liturgy and land were not separate categories, but were part of the same vibrant and luminescent whole.

In the summer of 2004, while we were still members of our Mennonite church, Elizabeth began a preaching field placement at a small Methodist church in rural Cedar Grove, a one caution-light town in northern Orange County not far from our farm. Just a mile down the road from the church sat a bait and tackle store owned by a man named Bill King. One sunny June afternoon, just one month into Elizabeth's internship, Bill was closing up his shop on the corner of Mill Creek and Carr Store Road when someone walked through the door and shot him in the back of the head. It was never known if this murder was racially motivated, but Bill was white and his wife was black. What is certain is that, in the weeks and months following Bill's murder, whites and blacks began coming together in unexpected ways.

Before the Kings bought the place, the store was a haven for local crack dealers. The first thing they did when they arrived was to ask the dealers to leave. Soon parents began bringing their children to the store for ice cream; neighborhood kids rode their bikes down for a soda. When people couldn't pay, Bill would let them take food on credit. Whatever sense of safety this little farming community had enjoyed before that afternoon in June, one trigger-pull had shattered. The people of Cedar Grove were angry and afraid.

Valee Taylor, one of Bill King's friends, was just angry. Several weeks after the murder, Valee visited Pastor Grace to talk about what the community should do. It's not often that an African American man will set foot in a white church in Cedar Grove, but Valee and Pastor Grace had become friends after meeting at the post office one day. Valee wanted to put out a reward. Pastor Grace had another idea—a prayer vigil.

The town of Cedar Grove is no bigger than a church, a post office, and a stoplight, yet over one hundred people attended the vigil in the parking lot of Bill's store. Hearing Valee tell it, that afternoon was a sort of beatific experience. "The sunlight was shining down on us, the air was crisp, there was a light breeze. Here were blacks and whites together praying for peace in the community." One of those in attendance was Valee's mother, Scenobia Taylor. Mrs. Taylor's ancestors had been sharecroppers in Cedar Grove, yet her father at one time was the largest landowner in Orange County, and she had inherited some of that land. As Mrs. Taylor later recounted to Pastor Grace and me, she was moved by the prayer vigil, and a few weeks after attending the vigil, she had a dream. In the dream, God told her to give five acres of her land to the community. She felt that somehow this land would help heal the community's wounds. But to whom would she give it? And for what purpose?

The next spring, Pastor Grace initiated a series of community conversations about faith and land. She had invited people from the Methodist church she pastored as well as from the wider Cedar Grove community—farmers, retirees, the local librarian. I had visited Cedar Grove UMC when Elizabeth interned there the summer before, and knowing about my knowledge of gardening, Pastor Grace called to invite me as well.

Elizabeth urged me to go, and I had a strong feeling that I should, but I was reluctant. The people seemed nice enough, but I had little interest in this sleepy rural church and even less interest in Methodism. When the night of the first meeting came, I stayed home.

The next morning Grace called again. She excitedly told Elizabeth that several people in the group wanted the church to start a community garden. They would need somebody to manage it. They were meeting again the following Tuesday night at the parsonage. Would I come?

When the voice of God comes into your life, I have learned, it is not actually a voice. On the outside, it comes as "the hint half guessed" (T.S. Eliot) or a series of hints or even outright imperatives uttered by people around you. *You should go.* But what happens on the inside is harder to discern. A welling-up. An internal summons. A fullness that presents itself at first as a distant thought which then draws closer and which soon becomes no longer a thought but an actual Presence awaiting your acknowledgment, the Presence slowly filling your imagination until one day you wake up and realize you've been thinking of nothing else.

I really did not want to spend a Tuesday evening with a group of retirees, a rural librarian, and a Methodist pastor I barely knew. But by now the thought had become a Presence I couldn't ignore.

That night we had the kind of conversation I'd been wanting to have at the Mennonite church. Here we are, Pastor Grace said, a rural church with prime farmland all around, yet people are going hungry. She had been meditating on a certain verse in the prophet Jeremiah, "to pluck up and pull down, to build and to plant." Several years before, the building of Cedar Grove UMC had burned to the ground in a freak fire. Here we were literally building, she said. Maybe we also should literally plant? Others chimed in. The librarian wanted a place for kids to play. One man voiced interest in building a barn for a community gathering place. The excitement was palpable.

By the end of that first meeting, I knew for certain that there was nothing I would rather do than help this church start a community garden. They didn't have a place picked out, there were no funds, they had no idea how to get it going or where the food should go, but that didn't matter. The reality was that there were hungry people all around us. There was land for growing food, and Jesus's words *feed my sheep* were compelling us to act.

I've been an edge-dweller in the church universal my whole life, yet I'm always suspicious when people wheel God out to explain their own desires or ill-considered motives, all too eager to substitute theophany for thought, and so it is with great reluctance that I say this: That night driving home from the meeting, I became as certain as I'd ever been about anything: God was leading me here. I should help them start this community garden. God would work out the details. All I needed to do was give up control. Hop on the ride. Trust.

Based on that one meeting I quit my job as a writer/tutor with no replacement job lined up in the hopes that I would help a small group of people I barely knew start a community garden. It was foolish, looking back on it. But it was a holy kind of foolishness.

Right away I began applying for grants, and before long we got one that would fund the garden for the next three years. That summer our Mennonite church commissioned Elizabeth and me to go and work among the Methodists, and in August 2005 I joined the Cedar Grove UMC staff as the garden's director.

But we still needed land. Pastor Grace had heard about Scenobia Taylor's dream, and one summer afternoon the two of us paid her a visit. We told her about the garden idea. We prayed with her. And right there she declared that she would donate five acres. She gave it to the Cedar Grove UMC to act as trustee, with the stipulation that it could never be sold. It would remain a community garden in perpetuity. A black woman in the South giving land to a white church. She could have given it to her church, one of several African American churches in Cedar Grove. But she gave it to the main white church in town.

When Pastor Grace quoted that line from the book of Jeremiah—*pluck up and pull down, to build and to plant*—I reread Jeremiah and fell to thinking.

The year of Bill King's murder, 2004, was the year Jeremiah came up in the lectionary. It was also the year American forces were failing, as they would fail for another seven years, to mop up the aftereffects of the 2003 U.S. invasion of Iraq. Jeremiah knew something about invasions. At the time he was writing, the Babylonians had just sacked Jerusalem in a "shock and awe" campaign and carted off the first wave of captives. Jeremiah's people were dragged from their homes and forced to live in a strange land where they had no power, no job opportunities, and didn't speak the language. During the Babylonian siege, God told Jeremiah to buy a field at Anathoth. The known world was crumbling. Yet this little chunk of real estate became a symbol that God would restore his people, that *houses and fields and vineyards shall again be bought in this land.* This field at Anathoth, it seemed to me as I read, became a sign of hope in a war-torn world, a continuation of God's earlier message to the exiles. To those marginalized people, those who had become edge-dwellers in the midst of Babylon, God instructed them through his prophet Jeremiah: *Plant gardens and eat what they produce . . . seek the* shalom *of the city where I have sent you into exile, and pray to the Lord on its behalf, for in its* shalom *you will find your* shalom.

Shalom is not just the absence of violence; it is a state of well-being, of living in harmony with one's community and with the land, and it seemed to me that Jeremiah was the first person to link the planting of gardens with the seeking of *shalom.* They were symbiotic practices—like sowing beans with your corn or marigolds with your tomatoes—and exactly the kind of companion planting the church should be doing.

What I learned from Jeremiah is that the way to get along in this world is to skirt Babylon altogether. Don't waste time fighting the Empire, or trying to make it a little less evil; opt out. Step around it and go about your business. Grow your own food, for instance. One reason you plant gardens and eat what they produce, from Jeremiah's time until now, is that you can't trust Babylon with the food supply.

And yet reading ourselves into Jeremiah's story was in some ways anachronistic. Cedar Grove United Methodist Church was mostly a group of white middle-class landowners. We weren't the exiles; we were Babylon. Real exiles—the rural poor, migrant workers, crack addicts—lived all around us. How could we ourselves live in *shalom* when, within a five-mile radius of Cedar Grove, there were at least twenty families who lacked indoor plumbing? North Carolina had one of the fastest-growing Latino migrant worker populations in the country. Many of these people were driven from their farms in Mexico due to the pressures of falling corn and coffee prices, thanks in large part to economic trade policies like NAFTA, which were created and enforced by our own government. Welcoming these landless exiles to grow food at Anathoth seemed at least one way the church could seek the *shalom* of our community.

I found it curious that Jeremiah didn't tell the Jews to escape, or seize the reins of power, or advance the Jewish cause by lobbying Babylon's halls of power. Instead, he told them to build houses and inhabit them; plant gardens, and eat what they produce. Marry and multiply. In other words, *settle down and flourish*. Live as if you were perfectly at home. Home is no longer a territory to be defended. Home is now whichever Babylon God happens to send you. *Shalom* doesn't begin once every last Babylonian is convinced they need to get on board. It begins with a few people planting gardens in a land at war. It begins with a field.

We would take the name of Jeremiah's field—Anathoth—and we would discover our mission in Jeremiah's words to the exiles: *Plant gardens and eat what they produce and seek the peace of the city.* Cedar Grove was no city. But even in a one caution-light town, there was plenty of peace that needed seeking.

It takes a special kind of person to be against a community garden, and Cedar Grove, it turns out, had some of those special people.

A few of the naysayers included members of Scenobia Taylor's own extended family. They wanted to know why a black woman would give five acres of prime agricultural land to a white church. Why weren't they, her own family, given that land instead?

But most of the naysayers were on the receiving end of Scenobia's gift, in the very church to whom the land was given. That land sat only a quarter mile down Mill Creek Road from where Bill King was shot. What if the murderer, people asked, started coming around the garden? Within a three-mile radius of the garden were several known crack houses. Some church members worried that vegetables and tools would be stolen. "You should at least build a gate and lock it," they said. And then there was the fact that Mill Creek Road was part of the black section of town. Though no one came out and said it, they were opposed to the fact that Anathoth would be a place where blacks and whites could meet on equal ground. For some in this rural, conservative town, even in the Year of our Lord 2005, racial equity remained a threat. When Pastor Grace welcomed Sister Doris as the church's first black member several years before, a small group of people left in protest. One church member approached Pastor Grace and asked why the church was building a garden "down there," suggesting that we build it closer to the church on a lot the church owned. "The reasons you *don't* want to build the garden down there," Grace told the man, "are exactly the reasons why we *should*."

CHAPTER FIVE

A New Heaven, A New Earth

Pentecost
Tierra Nueva, Washington

All will come again into its strength:
the fields undivided, the waters undammed,
the trees towering and the walls built low.
And in the valleys, people as strong
and varied as the land.
—Rainer Maria Rilke, *The Book of Pilgrimage*

The Skagit River in Washington state is an unstoppable slurry of life. For eons it carried microbes and minerals storm-chipped and glacially melted, bore them hastily from the high Cascades down steep mountain canyons, nudged them slowly across the valley floor, and finally disgorged its load of life into Puget Sound. Before all of that life from on high was lost, however, some of it became soil. From time to time the river rose over the levees and edged outward, like a quilt spreading itself across the wide lap of the valley. For the land waiting to receive it, the influx of carbon-rich alluvia was a riparian gift; a transfer of energy whereby the mountains shared their bounty with the valley through the wonder-working power of the river. The river was the medium. A force ever present and still at work in unseen ways, the river rises while the valley sleeps, rises in spite of human attempts at its control, filling the land with life.

It is the work of rivers, and the detritus of mountains, that make civilization possible. I once visited Wes Jackson, one of the godfathers of the organic farming movement, at his home on the short-grass prairie of Kansas. "You know the pyramids weren't built by humans," he said. "They were built by the Nile." Monsoons chipped nutrients from the Ethiopian mountains, Wes explained, and sent them down the Blue Nile. The steamy jungles of Africa sent organic matter down the White Nile. Where those two rivers joined they formed the Mother River itself, which created the fertile soils of the Nile delta. Those soils provided the carbon that fed the workers who built the pyramids. An ecospheric process, Wes said, in which humans were just the unwitting agents.

The Skagit River, bearing the detritus of the Cascades, has given the Skagit Valley its silty loams, which are some of the deepest, richest soils on the continent. Since the first settlers in 1867 established a trading post in La Conner, a small town on the river mouth not far from Burlington, young men have come to this valley in hopes of bettering themselves from these soils. They are coming still.

On the afternoon of June 10, Pentecost Sunday, I arrived in Burlington at an old bank building, the headquarters of a ministry called Tierra Nueva. Founded by Bob Ekblad and his wife, Gracie, in the 1980s, Tierra Nueva began as a soil conservation movement among peasant farmers in the mountains of Honduras, where the Ekblads spent seven years. Afterward they moved to Montpellier, France, where Bob pursued a Ph.D. in biblical studies. When he finished his dissertation they made the decision to start a northern version of Tierra Nueva in Washington's lush Skagit Valley. There they began to work with a group they refer to as "people on the margins."

Some were meek and law-abiding migrant farmworkers who had been hounded by *la migra,* the immigration system; others were drug dealers or gang-bangers, recent returnees from the hinterlands of bad behavior.

If Tierra Nueva could be said to have a communal ethos it might be this: people on the margins should be on the front line of the sustainability movement. If we're going to see widespread social change in America, Bob believes, we need the former gang-bangers and ex–drug lords leading the charge. Tierra Nueva works to raise up leaders from the young violent men among whom they minister, and some of these have joined the staff. Bob describes their work as husbandry: repairing the soil of people's lives, which has become toxic from any number of poisons: drugs, broken homes, abusive upbringings, U.S. immigration policy, conventional Christianity. Before Bob had a charismatic experience in Toronto, that work of husbandry was conducted mostly through Bible studies and a kind of earnest activism through which he thought he could effect real change. But those things weren't enough, Bob discovered.

There's now a family support center for migrants, a biweekly jail Bible study led by Bob and Chris Hoke, a Tierra Nueva staff member and one of Bob's young protégés. Tierra Nueva has also recently started two social enterprise projects: the Underground Coffee Project, and New Earth Farm. The coffee project is run by Zach Joy, a six-foot-seven former meth cook whose life had been turned around in one of Bob's jail Bible studies. Zach now roasts small batch artisan coffee with organic beans bought from Tierra Nueva farmers in Honduras. The New Earth Farm is a community-supported agriculture project that employs several Oaxacan migrants and serves as a volunteer host site for juvenile offenders.

Neither of these things is particularly out of the ordinary for a progressive Christian ministry. What makes Tierra Nueva unique is their blend of social justice work and sustainable agriculture with what Saint Paul called "the gifts of the Spirit." Following a dramatic second conversion experience in Toronto where Bob received these gifts of the Spirit, he has built his ministry around one desire: to see heaven come down to earth. From what I'd read about Tierra Nueva in Bob's books, there were times when it seemed as though it had. Still, I found it hard to suppress my skepticism. I grew up in a charismatic church that my wife's British grandfather would have called "happy-clappy." We didn't have hymn books; instead we sang "off the wall," all eyes focused on grainy transparencies shown cinema-style on the back wall with an old slide projector. People raised their arms, prophesied, gave teary confessions. When the service was over they shouted Hallelujah! and then filed out the door each Sunday with praises on their lips and on Monday they went back to cutting each other down and cheating on their spouses and trying to make a killing in the stock market. I remember one lady at our church who stood up every week, unraveled a crumpled sheaf of notes ripped from a yellow legal pad, and began to read words that the Lord had given her, words that always began with "My child . . ."—the voice of the Lord addressing the woman—and always seemed to say, week in and week out for years on end, basically the same garbled gibberish. As an adult, I'd come to see such displays as falsely emotive, even hypocritical, and I wasn't eager to jump back into that world. Hypocrisy is nothing new, of course, and it's not limited to Christians. Get any group of people together for whatever reason, and you're going to have to try hard not to see them fail to live out the high ideals that they proclaim. Perhaps it's just more noticeably egregious when the pendulum swings so far toward the side of holiness on Sunday only to return so quickly to human shortcomings on Monday.

Yet I perceived that there was something different about Tierra

Nueva and Bob Ekblad. When I first spoke with Bob at the potluck prior to the Sunday night service, I sensed in him a quiet confidence, a feeling of deep peace that seemed to ooze from his pores. Years ago I had read his book *Reading the Bible with the Damned,* and was riveted by his stories about reading Genesis and Matthew and Acts of the Apostles among thieves and murderers in the Skagit County Jail. And Tierra Nueva had a fair trade coffee business and an organic farm; perhaps their charismatic ethos might not be the overwrought spiritual woo-woo of my childhood church but something I had yet to see or experience, something more authentic and trustworthy. Or so I hoped.

Bob Ekblad is one of a handful of people I've met who have crossed over into the Great Beyond and returned to tell the tale. I'd met a few others like that: alpine climbers, war veterans, the deeply religious. That Bob happened to be all three further solidified his holy aura. It wasn't so much a glow as something you saw in the eyes: crow's-feet, the thousand-yard stare, an unblinking gaze that has alighted upon distant shores and found there a pure and bottomless mercy.

Bob Ekblad: preacher, biblical scholar, former bad-ass mountain climber, survivor of Central America's dirty wars (as a noncombatant), a man who will tell you he is not super-interested in farming but who spent seven years teaching sustainable farming techniques to poor Honduran peasants because he believed it was the only way to get them out of poverty, a goofy, mild-mannered guy who is humble and unassuming and who has been given the power to cast the demons out of heroin addicts, gang-bangers, and murderers, to intercede on their behalf before the Lord of hosts.

Bob's story begins in Israel. As a young man, he traveled there pretending to be Jewish so he could work on a kibbutz. Bob wanted to study Torah, but on the kibbutz Bob was befriended by a Cuban Jew who taught him about the injustices of Central America. He was on a spiritual search and he felt that Central America was where he needed to go. After several months of riding the chicken buses around Guatemala, Bob called up his high school sweetheart, Gracie, from a phone booth in Quetzaltenango and asked her to marry him. He flew home, they married, and the couple then returned to Guatemala. It was the mid-1980s, the height of Central America's dirty wars. They spent several months learning Spanish with Guatemalan Marxists, and then began making plans to work with Salvadoran refugees. They were within one week of securing an assignment when their contact person on the border was shot. That's when they met Elías Sánchez.

Bob described Elías as a Honduran Wendell Berry. Poverty in Central America, Elías believed, could be eradicated with sustainable farming. Bob and Gracie knew nothing about the soil conservation practices Elías preached—contoured ditches, alley cropping, compost—yet they were drawn to his charisma. They studied with him on his model farm, Loma Linda, "beautiful ridge," where they learned biodynamic, permaculture, and French-intensive farming techniques, all state-of-the-art organic practices they would teach to Honduran peasants.

Elías would test his young pupils. "What do you think is really the problem?" he asked. "Soil erosion," Bob would say with certainty. "And to prevent it the soil must be protected with contoured ditches."

"No, you are not thinking," Elías would reply. "You must first stop erosion in people's minds. You must cultivate their intelligence and dig contoured drainage ditches in their hearts. You must build compost piles in their minds. If you do not change the farmer, then you will never change the land."

Bob and Gracie also watched their teacher engage Honduran farmers in various community forums where, Bob said, Elías would use "the most vile examples." Entering a community, he would say, is like entering a woman. You can't just jump on her, you have to use lots of foreplay. Elías could be raw and graphic and winsome, but he could also be pensive and philosophical. He viewed soil as life itself. And what does life need? Air, water, food, and community. Soil is made up of microorganisms that must be husbanded and cared for. Just like people.

The overriding question was, How do we help the soil to flourish, which will help people flourish? How do we create the ultimate environment for life?

After their apprenticeship Bob and Gracie soon found themselves enlisted to start a soil conservation project in Minas de Oro, a tiny Honduran village where they would live for the next six years. A Honduran peasant woman gave their new organization its name, based on Isaiah 65, where God says, "Behold I am creating a new heaven and a new earth . . ."

Tierra Nueva, "new earth," became a model farm where the Ekblads trained the trainers. Over the next six years on those steep Honduran hillsides they refined *la técnica,* the cutting-edge sustainable farming Elías had promised would lift the peasants out of poverty. They dug miles of contoured ditches, built thousands of compost piles, introduced velvet bean to inter-plant with corn, and convinced people to cease their slash and burn practices. Yields increased tenfold, so much that Tierra Nueva started grain cooperatives based on the Acts of the Apostles, where early Christians held all things in common. Tierra Nueva became a kind of Christian-Marxist collective, and within four years some two thousand families became members. Slowly people's dire poverty began to lessen, just as Elías had predicted.

But soon Bob began to see unintended consequences of their work. For one, there was never an end to improving the soil, not in a place as badly eroded as Honduras. In an unpublished book about his Honduran experiences, Bob described how the exhausted soil, never entirely suitable for corn farming in the first place, began to feel "like an insatiable god, and *la técnica* a new law with infinite demands."

Bob had come to Honduras full of ideological motivations: dismantling U.S. imperialism, ending poverty, escaping white middle-class guilt, saving the environment. As motivating forces, those couldn't sustain him. The poor people he served began to seem less pitiable and more onerous with each passing day. One Honduran's high corn yields would allow him to get drunk more often, then he would beat his wife. Another might spend several years building up his soil fertility, only to have a neighbor, jealous of his new farm, cut the man's fences at night and let cows graze the corn, destroying that year's harvest. Then there were farmers Bob trained who got really good at *la técnica* and who began to look down on their neighbors who didn't come to Tierra Nueva's courses, becoming what Bob called "evangelists of the god of wrath."

The proclivity toward fundamentalism, Bob saw, could run in the sustainable farming movement just as easily as in the Pentecostal churches all around them. These churches encouraged an otherworldly kind of faith that tended to support right-wing politics, both repugnant to Bob's sensibilities. The Pentecostals saw Bob as a communist. Yet Bob noticed that many people who had afflictions— health problems, alcohol, anger—would go to these churches and be healed. He asked himself, "How can they get free if they have such bad theology?" On top of these mounting problems, USAID showed up and started giving away free fertilizer to any farmer who would denounce Tierra Nueva and join them. The Honduran government was jealous that a nonprofit run by gringos was outperforming the efforts of their own agronomists.

After two and a half years Bob bottomed out. Every one of the people he was trying to serve, he realized, was a finite, broken human being. Each of them had their *mañas,* their idiosyncrasies that made them hard to love. Just loving one person, let alone the masses of the Honduran peasantry . . . it was too much. He and Gracie realized they were up against larger forces, spiritual forces. That's when they got recruited into reading the Bible with the poor peasants who were excluded from the church. Several years of such Bible studies were fruitful, but the Ekblads realized they needed more training. They left for France. In Montpellier, Bob enrolled in a doctoral program in the Old Testament, and began learning Greek and Hebrew. From his French professors he learned to come to scripture first of all as a respectful listener. "Biblical scholarship involves learning the arts of cross-cultural communication with a living God via a dead language." They hoped to return to Honduras after these studies and begin doing Bible studies with peasants. But along the way they decided to return to their home state of Washington, because by then the forces of oppression that kept Honduran farmers poor and oppressed were also making themselves known in *El Norte.*

Bob sees the highest priority as helping people deal with their underlying insecurities that drive them into consumption, or criminal behavior, or addictions. He sees a deep restlessness in people, a deep insecurity that never lets them be satisfied. In Central America people called it *El Fiebre del Norte,* the Fever of the North, and it drove people to leave their homes and risk their lives. "Whether you're a peasant in Honduras or a middle-class white person in the States, the problem is the same: how much is enough? A little bit more. How do we address that deep restlessness in people? How do we be content with enough? We have to learn to live within our limits and be satisfied with life on the land. That's a spiritual problem."

I asked Bob how he addresses that spiritually.

"You first have to help people recognize that they're a beloved child of God, a God who loves them and wants to provide for them. They need to step away from that insecurity. But that involves inner healing and deliverance stuff. A lot of my emphasis is on that now. Even as we keep the sustainable farming vision alive, there's just so much work to do on the spiritual front."

Which is why Bob and Chris and the others here at Tierra Nueva were going after the young violent guys. Whole underclasses of people in this country are being warehoused in prisons, and many of them, Bob believes, are highly talented young men. Bob and Chris want to mobilize them. They want these guys leading the movement for social change and sustainability. "The front line of sustainability should be working with those most wounded by the system."

But the question becomes, How do you take somebody who's out of control and wounded and bring them into a place of health?

"Husbandry," Bob said. "It takes a lot of one-on-one mentoring and love."

I mentioned a passage I'd read in Bob's unpublished book on Honduras and the spirituality of farming: "The ecology of the reign of God must elevate the weakest members of the system, standing with them before the strong in a highly unnatural way. The ecology of the reign of God will appear not of this world." I asked why it was not natural, not of this world? "Because coming alongside a violent person on the margins and trying to love them is just not something most people will want to do. It's counter to our whole understanding of security. Plus, there's no guarantee that that person will get healed up and choose life."

The only way such deep transformation can happen in a person,

Bob believes, is through an intervention of the Spirit. After nearly a decade of working alongside violent young men in the Skagit County Jail, Bob had another bottoming out. He kept seeing guys returning, unable to shed their addictions or their violent ways or the other demons that plagued them.

At the urging of his brother, Bob flew from Burlington to Toronto to visit the Toronto Airport Christian Fellowship. This particular church was well known as the place where a heavy dropping of the Holy Spirit had been occurring over and over, seven nights a week, since the early 1990s. Bob had been highly suspicious of such claims, and thought Pentecostal Christians were not much more than the Republican Party at prayer, but that night Bob felt the Spirit descend upon him. He felt tongues of fire on his palms and forehead, and he remembers being surprised by a feeling of weight, a good kind of heaviness that dropped him to the floor where he lay for about forty-five minutes.

When Bob returned to Burlington, he began to heal and cast out demons in Jesus's name. Many of the inmates at his jail Bible studies had dramatic conversions and healings. This new intensity nearly ended his ministry—his own Presbyterian church, which had supported his efforts at Tierra Nueva, distanced itself from him—but it was then that he started seeing real transformations in the violent young men he mentored and ever since that night in Toronto nothing here at Tierra Nueva has been quite the same. These charismatic gifts have spread to others at Tierra Nueva. Zach Joy, the meth-cook-turned-coffee-roaster, was now a leader in the ministry. And Chris Hoke told me of another young man named Bones, so named for his skinny physique, who now sat in a prison cell in solitary confinement. Bones had a dream about starting a farm for young homies who needed nurturing and who could heal their wounds on the land. He and Chris were already making plans for this farm, and when Bones got out in two years they would begin. Later that week Chris wanted to take me to visit Bones at the maximum security prison in Monroe.

Since Bob's welcoming of the Holy Spirit had become a regular part of Sunday worship at Tierra Nueva, it seemed an appropriate way to begin my time there by attending one of those services, on Pentecost Sunday itself.

When the day of Pentecost had come the members of Tierra Nueva were all together in one place, which happened to be the lobby of the old bank building in downtown Burlington. Suddenly, as if from heaven, there came a sound like the rush of a violent wind, and it filled the entire lobby. When I turned around I saw that wind in fact came from a white lady in a multicolored African dress standing in the back of the lobby waving two red banners over our heads.

When the Holy Spirit fell on the first Apostles, as recorded in the second chapter of Acts, *divided tongues, as of fire, appeared among them, and a tongue of fire rested on each of them.* The first apostles had gathered fifty days after Jesus's ascension into heaven, and among them, reports the Acts of the Apostles, there were *devout Jews from every nation under heaven living in Jerusalem.* When the Holy Spirit dropped they all began speaking in other languages, yet each one heard the others speaking his own native language. Parthians and Medes, Cretans and Arabs, all spoke about God's deeds of power. *All were perplexed, saying to one another, "What does this mean?" But others sneered and said, "They are filled with new wine."*

There would be no divided tongues as of fire coming to rest on us tonight, but there would be other signs and wonders.

On that first Pentecost, onlookers in Jerusalem thought the Apostles were uttering gibberish, but Acts reports that the speakers each heard the other talking in his own language, even as they were in fact speaking in other tongues. Today's charismatics also speak in tongues not their own. Later that week Chris told me about a linguist who studied different examples of glossolalia. The linguist wondered if the speakers were uttering a celestial language or just babbling nonsense but he found it was neither. They spoke actual human languages, just not ones known to the speaker. Chris told me about Heidi Baker, a charismatic preacher who lives in Mozambique. When the Holy Spirit dropped upon her, Heidi would turn her head sideways and shout, almost spit out, the words *shika baba, shika baba,* not knowing what she was saying until a man who spoke Swahili told her that those words in his tongue meant "cling to the Father." During worship that first night at Tierra Nueva, I heard the lady in the African dress muttering strange words. I strained forward to hear, but it wasn't in a language I could understand.

It was a small group that Sunday night, perhaps thirty or forty people. Chris Hoke was the normal worship leader, but he was on a flight home that night and the stand-in, a lone guy with a guitar, was struggling to generate much enthusiasm. We sang a few songs off-the-wall style, and then there was a blur of movement in the pew in front of me. Earlier at the pre-worship potluck I'd met Ricky, one of the homeless guys that come here, who was now standing directly in front of me. He was doing something I'd never seen anyone do in all my churchgoing years: karate chopping the air.

Ricky wore dark green sweat pants, a light green T-shirt, and a *Gilligan's Island* hat, which made him appear like a slightly overgrown leprechaun. His skin was covered in an alarming number of sores, scabs, and pustules. As the singing picked up and the banner lady sent forth a violent wind, Ricky began to sway. Suddenly he did something that was either an early indicator of the Holy Spirit dropping or was evidence that Ricky wasn't quite right in the head. At first he spread his legs in a fighter stance and did a series of quick one-two punches at the air. One instant he was singing and swaying to the music, and in the next he was mixing it up with gut punches and a left uppercut. Then more karate chops. Not angry karate chops. More like eyes-closed-lovingly-executed-karate-chops offered up to his Maker, and he didn't throw just one; Ricky unleashed a whole series of karate chops, which turned into a full-fledged routine, like some kind of liturgical kung fu. Maybe, I thought, this was Ricky's way of giving his personal demons an ass whupping.

In the evangelical church of my youth I'd heard a lot about demons. Junior high Sunday school classes often featured talk of spiritual warfare. There was a great spiritual battle raging all around us, we read in books like Frank E. Peretti's *This Present Darkness,* and if only we prayed enough we would help the angels defeat the demons. I had graduated from all that. I did not doubt the existence of evil, but I also believed that God granted us human agency. I'd seen too many people use Satan as a smoke screen to cover their own mistakes, and it was hard not to think about these things as I sat rigid in the pew while the violent and annoying wind of a prayer banner nipped at my neck. Whenever I'd seen people get charismatic I was not like those witnesses at the first Pentecost who were amazed and perplexed and asking "what does this mean?" I was one of those ready to sneer and say "they are filled with new wine."

After twenty minutes the music tapered off, Ricky relaxed his karate stance, and Bob Ekblad got up to preach. Bob was six-foot-two, and in his blue jeans and rumpled T-shirt he looked far more like the lithe and gangly rock climber he once was than a radical charismatic leader. The Pentecostal preachers I'd seen on TV were silver-tongued and slick, but nothing about Bob was false. He considered his words, pausing to reflect in mid-sentence. He made no unctuous appeals, no inflated promises of health, wealth, or prestige if only one would "get right with God," he didn't do anything, in other words, that would brand him as a Pentecostal as I'd understood the term, and as I listened I found myself sitting up straighter in my chair. Bob gave a short talk about "despising the shame," how when we find ourselves falsely accused, as Jesus did, we should despise not the accuser but despise the shame that accompanies the accusation. Then, because this was Pentecost Sunday, Bob suggested we welcome the Spirit's presence among us by forming a prayer tunnel.

Chairs were pulled back, and two lines were formed facing each other. One person at a time would walk down between the lines, Bob explained, and people in the line would touch the person and pray for the Spirit to fill them; like running the gauntlet, I thought, except instead of getting whacked, you got prayed for.

At that moment I very much wanted to slide into the observer part of my participant/observer role. But everybody was lining up, and I didn't want to be the lone wallflower. Peer-pressured by the Pentecostals, I dutifully got in line.

Bob walked down first, palms up to receive, wearing a big grin. Behind him came a black man with a red beret, doing a little shuffle dance as he walked, clearly enjoying himself. When the next guy came along, someone touched his shoulder and said, "Laughter." The man started laughing. Behind him came a young woman, eyes closed, who was giggling. The banner lady in the African dress walked next, and when someone touched her shoulder, she convulsed. It seemed that a visible current of energy traveled into her body and down to the floor, then back again to the hand that touched her. I wondered if she had rehearsed the move at home.

Next came Ricky the Leprechaun. Until now I had reached out a hand and touched people passing by, muttering a halfhearted blessing, but when Ricky walked up I paused. There was that festering neck, full of pockmarks, blackheads, open sores. It would be very un-Christ-like of me not to touch him, I thought. In fact this was exactly the kind of person Jesus would want to lay hands on. The shame at my hesitation won out over my revulsion and I gently laid my right hand on Ricky's back, though careful not to touch his exposed skin. I prayed silently for God to bless him, but as I prayed I wondered what kind of epidermal pestilence lurked beneath that flimsy gauze of fabric. I thought this and, even as I thought it, felt regret. Then Ricky moved on.

My turn was next. I closed my eyes and held out my hands palms up as I'd seen others do and slowly walked into the prayer tunnel. Not much happened. I got to the end unscathed, and since the line kept rotating, I went back and made another pass. On my second time through something odd happened. A hand touched my shoulder and a voice said, *Give him more of you, Lord. More of you.* My whole body tingled. I felt peaceful, yet strangely energized. Too much iced tea at dinner, perhaps? The third and last time through I got to the end of the line and Bob was there. I still had my eyes closed, but I recognized his voice. Bob put both his hands in mine, and in a very calm and normal voice he began to prophesy. I don't remember any words but these: ". . . you are deeply rooted, yet you desire more of the Lord . . ." Bob prayed over me for what seemed like a long time, praying things I don't remember, then concluded by asking "that the Lord would fill you with his Spirit." For what seemed like a long time I just stood there. That part of me that had been watching myself go through the evening, that critic on my shoulder who commented on my every thought and move, was gone. Or rather, he was there but I couldn't hear him, because I was hearing another voice. It wasn't Bob's voice. His seemed distant. I was hearing another voice, and it came from deep inside me, or beyond me, and I strained to hear it, tried to understand what was being spoken and why my internal defenses were dropping. But suddenly

I heard other voices. The prayer gauntlet was dispersing. When I opened my eyes, people were forming a circle. It was the final event of the service: The Lord's Supper. Bread and wine. Communion.

When Peter stood up to address the crowd on that first Pentecost, after the first dropping of the Holy Spirit, he tried to describe what had just happened. *Men of Judea and all who live in Jerusalem,* he said, *let this be known to you, and listen to what I say. Indeed, these are not drunk, as you suppose, for it is only nine o'clock in the morning.* Then he quoted from the prophet Joel. *In the last days it will be, God declares, that I will pour out my Spirit upon all flesh, and your sons and your daughters shall prophesy, and your young men shall see visions, and your old men shall dream dreams.*

I had come to Tierra Nueva because there were old men dreaming dreams and young men seeing visions and in this world so lacking in dreams and visions worth believing, I was eager for both. Bob was right. I was hungry for more of God. I'd felt a similar yearning in my experiences during mass at Mepkin Abbey, my rooftop epiphany in Chiapas, the certitude I'd experienced that evening in Cedar Grove which led to me working at Anathoth. In the prayer tunnel on that first night at Tierra Nueva, I'd caught a brief glimpse of something that touched those unknown depths, enough to show me how potent this charismatic approach could be. I believed the Holy Spirit could come into and infuse us. Yet I still carried an innate distrust of the emotional wildness that seemed to accompany such expressions of faith. Perhaps I wouldn't cross over to the Pentecostal way completely, but if such a faith could nurture people on the margins of society, then I wanted to give it its due. For now, I decided to immerse myself in Tierra Nueva's story and remain open to whatever weirdness—or blessing—might follow.

One thing seemed certain: young men like Chris and Zach and Bones were seeing visions, and old men like Bob were dreaming dreams. Whatever great things those visions and dreams might one day become, they began in obscurity. In a tiny field. Or a prison cell. In the fecund darkness of the underground.

On Tuesday morning, I was awakened by the smell of roasting coffee. I'd slept on the second floor of the old bank building, a vast high-ceilinged structure with long corridors, worn carpet, and drafty windows. During the night I left the windows open and now my room was frigid and damp with coastal fog, which seemed to perpetually blanket the Skagit Valley. I craved warmth and caffeine. Following the delicious nutty smell, I made my way down to the basement to Underground Coffee, where I found Chris Hoke and Zach Joy several batches into their morning roasting session. The space was cramped and warm and enveloped in a light haze of coffee bean smoke. Zach darted around, if a six-foot-seven man could be said to "dart," but paused when I came down the stairs and greeted me warmly. He wore Chuck Taylors, black jeans, and an aquamarine T-shirt sporting the logo of an obscure heavy metal band. His head was shaved. Tattoos of skulls and crosses and seductive maidens covered both arms from wrist to chin. A permanent tear fell from his left eye. But Zach's warm demeanor belied the dark, inky images.

"Welcome to the Underground Coffee Project," he said. "Our coffee is a blessing from seed to cup." Zach was brewing up the first of several pots he'd drink that morning, and his anticipation made him a tad jittery. "Man, I am so excited to drink this coffee! This is the best coffee in the world!" A selection of his favorite music played on the iPod—Tool, Alice in Chains, Temple of the Dog. The current batch of beans had just finished roasting and Zach opened the door. Steaming dark beans spilled into the cooling pan, filling the air with more haze and warmth and nutty goodness. Zach must have liked what he saw; suddenly he dropped into a crouch, spread his legs, and launched into a headbanging air guitar solo. "Tool put on one of the best shows I've ever been to, man. Those guys make love to the music."

The Underground Coffee Project is the flowering of Tierra Nueva's roots, a vertical integration of their story and values across two continents. A few years ago after being welcomed into the community, Zach had felt the call to leadership. Yet having no legal way to support himself, this was a way to help. For now his roasting work pays his rent, and the hope is that eventually it will support him. Chris explained that, with guys on the margins, the old middle-class white way of missionary fundraising—hitting up your church and family for funds—just didn't work. "So how do you sustain them when they want to become ministers and leaders?" Bob and Chris and Zach started thinking about all those Honduran farmers with whom Bob and Gracie worked who were now selling organic green coffee beans and asking for help finding a market in the espresso-rich Seattle area. They decided they could buy the beans direct from them, paying them above fair trade prices, hire Zach to roast them, and market the coffee to churches—an elegant circle of beneficence. Assisted by a revolving crew of former addicts, homies, and gangbangers, Zach roasts about thirty pounds a week, not much, but it's growing, and the smallness of the operation lets him craft each batch with care. "After wasting so much of my life, I just love having something constructive to do with my hands," he said. When each batch of beans hits the roasting pan, Zach stretches his hands over them and imparts a blessing.

As he worked, he told a few stories about the Old Zach. Before he signed up with Jesus and became a minister and coffee roaster at Tierra Nueva, Zach shot heroin. He cooked meth. He was an Aryan-pride racist. And yeah, he'd served jail time. Once he was cooking meth with a butane torch and burned his legs. The doctor and nurse in the ER hooked him up to an IV with painkillers but refused to push the button. "First tell us where the meth lab is," the doctor said. Zach remembers screaming the pain was so bad, but more than the pain he was shocked that a doctor who had sworn to the Hippocratic Oath would resort to torture. That story segues into another story from the Old Zach about how he and his friend Steve were stealing some stereo equipment from a garage to buy drugs when the homeowner came out with a shotgun. Zach thought the guy would just tell them to drop the stuff but instead he shot Steve right in the face. It was from a distance, it didn't kill him, but Steve was badly wounded. Zach's tone wasn't judgmental, he knew he himself was no saint, but he told these stories in a sort of dumbfounded amazement that upstanding citizens could be so cruel. A doctor refusing treatment in order to play interrogator. A human being shooting another human being in the face over a hundred dollars' worth of stereo equipment. What darkness lurked within us that would cause us to do these things to each other? Who are we, and where are we going?

With all the care of a maître d' in a fine restaurant, Zach went over to the percolator and made three cups of coffee, one of which was a 32 oz. Big Gulp. He handed Chris and me each a smaller cup and he took the Big Gulp. I took my first sip. It tasted good. I took another sip. It tasted *really good*.

Zach poured ten pounds of green beans into the roaster, set the temp at 350 degrees, and put the timer on sixteen minutes. Less time means a lighter roast, which translates into more caffeine; a longer roast means a darker bean with less caffeine. The Underground's specialty is a 70/30 blend. They call it *Light in the Darkness*.

A timer beeped. "There's first crack," Zach said. The temperature was now 370 degrees. Sometimes more heat is needed to get them to crack, he explained, because these beans are so dense. He laughed. "They're hardheaded beans." With eight hundred different flavor profiles, coffee is the most complex food substance on earth. Wine by comparison has only five hundred. One of the flavor profiles in these beans, Zach believes, is the taste of Honduran soil. As the bean heats up it expands. Eventually the outer coating called the chaff pops off. That's first crack. Second crack happens in the cooling pan. In between first and second crack, up in the higher temperatures between 370 and 410 degrees, that's where the magic happens. A good roaster will see just how far to push the bean to bring out its fullest flavor before backing off on the heat, which makes coffee roasting an art form. Or a spiritual discipline. "It's like when the heat of the Holy Spirit comes upon you," Zach said. "It cracks you open and makes you better."

"Yeah, that's good, Zach," Chris said. He stood up, walked around thinking, then said, "The flame is the Holy Spirit and the bean is our small, hardened hearts. And if we try to scrape the layers of chaff off on our own? We're just picking at ourselves and others, scarring each other. But when we pass through the heat of the Spirit, get folded into others who are in the heat of God's love, our hearts expand. That's like first crack. Our dense hearts break, and grow softer and larger. Then the chaff, all our tough layers of protection, that just falls off naturally." Chris drained his coffee and Zach hit us with a refill. We were like a group of college guys in the basement doing bong hits, except we were high on something else. Caffeine, certainly. But we'd also tapped into a more elemental intoxicant.

If what Chris said was true, I thought, then perhaps I hadn't roasted long enough. I left the worship service on Sunday night a bit disappointed, and I wasn't sure why. Maybe I had been looking too hard for signs and wonders instead of paying attention to the stirrings of my heart. When Bob laid hands on me and prophesied, I hadn't cracked, but I *had* felt myself expand. Perhaps I just needed more time in the fire. *More, Lord, give him more.*

Zach took a long pull from the Big Gulp and adjusted the temperature on the roaster. Chris continued to riff on the thread.

"You take the hard bean, bring it into an environment with a lot of God's love and watch it break. It's beautiful. And the beans lose 20 percent of their weight.

"Another thing is that when the bean cracks it becomes aromatic and flavorful. Like Zach was saying, every bean is distinct, the flavor comes from the soil and the roots of its origin. Like Zach and the other guys here who used to deal drugs or be in gangs, you can taste the pain of their past, as well as the really unique experiences they've had. It's not like once they get roasted in the Holy Spirit they suddenly become white, middle-class Christians. They still have their tats, their scars, the wisdom gleaned from tough environments—all the marks of their origins."

One of the marks of Zach's origins he still carries is his love of heavy metal music. He also loves Jesus. That he doesn't see these loves as mutually exclusive is part of what makes him unique. He can take Jesus to people who would never set foot in a church. But "taking Jesus" is not correct, for whenever Zach gets out of his comfort zone and visits people on society's margins, he finds Jesus already waiting there to greet him. This past year he's been getting out of his comfort zone by visiting and praying with people who are dying. Some have AIDS, some cancer, others are in the last stages of liver failure from hepatitis C, a disease he himself contracted during his seventeen years as an addict. "Jesus wears the cloak of the poor and outcast," Zach says. "He's a mighty king, but he's not going to come at you as a mighty king. He dwells with the needy and the poor. Whenever I enter a room I imagine Jesus laying hands on that person, blessing them." In addition to his hospice work Zach regularly attends heavy metal concerts. The mosh pit is one of Zach's mission fields. He knows metal culture, for one thing. "I think I'm powerful for God's kingdom because I speak a few different languages, such as swearing. I think swearing can be a really effective form of communication, actually." Wherever he goes, Zach's looks can be either a blessing or a curse, either alienating people or endearing them to him. His tats, shaved head, tongue ring, and Yeti frame all give him a fearsome visage, yet it's exactly these things that allow him to be accepted by society's outcasts. Others are repelled, and that saddens him. "All they see are my tattoos and body piercings and they want to hide from me. You know why I got all these tattoos, man? So I could cover up my compassion. I feel people's hurt so much that I had to cover myself up so I could keep them away. The thing people like me battle with most is not other people. The arrows slung from the devil don't affect us as much—we let that shit just roll right off us. The thing we battle with most is ourselves."

We drink what is now our third cup of coffee. The beans are roasting, for the moment there's nothing to do, and suddenly Zach does something he has not done since I entered the basement an hour ago: he stops moving. He's pondering something, turning inward. I find myself in awe of this man, of his struggles to embrace life after seventeen years of being mired in death. The more I talk with Zach the more I realize he is perhaps one of the gentlest souls I have ever encountered. When he tells me that people are attracted to the love that is in him, he says it without guile or pride, and I believe him.

"Jesus is a fisherman, and we're the lures, so we need to be attractive lures. Jesus uses us to hook people, then he reels them in, but not before. There's no coercion with Jesus's love. It's all attraction. That's what drew me to Tierra Nueva—the love I received. Saint Francis said, 'Preach the gospel every day, and use words when necessary.' That's my gig right there, man."

He leans over the drum on the roaster and listens, like a gentle doctor putting an ear to his patient's chest. Despite his gargantuan size he dances about the room with a natural grace and efficiency, hopping over fifty-pound coffee sacks to adjust some dial, whirling around to reach his Big Gulp while opening the door of the roasting drum. Zach's talk leaps with ease over tall fences that keep most subjects cordoned off from one another, and we travel from the Underground up to Bellingham (his home) back to the Skagit County Jail, then to the hospital and this one house where his friend Steve got shot in the face and then back to their cupping scores for the very first batch of beans, which was 85, which is really good, and then a story about cooking meth, so that present tense blends with past tense, which is all overlaid with future tense—the life he *wants* to live—and after a while I'm not sure what the subject is or the point, but it doesn't matter. We're all enjoying the ride. But no, there is a point. Jesus saved his ass, man. Jesus saved him. "I've always had the light of Christ in me," he says at one point. "I just didn't know it back in my wilder days." I could sit drinking coffee and stay high with this unlikely apostle all day long.

He heads over to check on the roaster and touches the drum. "Ow!" He laughs at himself. "That machine is nearly 400 degrees. Why do I keep doing that? That's the uncomfortable part of coming into the Holy Spirit's fire. You get burned."

Zach turns the fire up to 460 degrees. This will be a dark roast. He thinks a minute, slowly nodding his head, then says, "I think with us, though, there's not just a first or second crack that happens, but lots of cracks. We need to be cracked over and over."

Soon it would be time for me to pay a visit to New Earth Farm.

I swilled the last sip of coffee and asked Zach for a parting word of wisdom.

"Jesus is calling his lost children home, man, people on the streets. But the church doesn't see it. People like me, we have thick skin. We heal fast. That gives us a certain strength the church needs. The church needs to empower us, but the church is basically afraid of people like me. The church needs to say *we need you* to people like me. *We've been missing something and it's you. We don't want to fix you, we just need you.* That's what everybody has been waiting for all their frickin' lives, man. For someone to say *we need you*."

New Earth Farm was much smaller than I expected, roughly an acre of vegetables with a few outbuildings. In a group of black plastic trays sat various seedlings awaiting transplant: broccoli, kale, lettuce. Nearly all of them were spindly and yellowish with purple splotches, a sure sign of nutrient deficiency. Nick, the tall, tow-headed farm manager, gave me a warm welcome. Nick hastened to admit that he was still on the steep uphill climb of the learning curve. He had spent three summers working for a local organic farm before taking over New Earth Farm, but there were many kinks still to be worked out. They ran the farm as a CSA—Community Supported Agriculture, where members buy into the farm at the beginning of the season in exchange for produce—but he was a bit discouraged that they'd only sold twenty shares this year, even though they had planted enough crops for fifty. Each share costs $450 per year. That was only $9,000 a year in gross income for the whole farm, and after clearing expenses, most of that went to Salvio and Victoria, the Oaxacan couple who were also on the farm staff. Nick mostly raised his own support. In addition to the farm, he also worked part-time as a chaplain at the Skagit County Jail, which meant that despite all that needed doing, he often had to walk away.

While we talked, Nick grabbed a couple of stirrup hoes and we set to work weeding broccoli and cabbage. Around us was a palette of every imaginable shade of green: crenellated kale leaves, bushy peas, tall wispy carrot tops, lush rows of potatoes. Though the seedlings had looked a bit forlorn, the crops in the field looked vibrant and healthy, testament to both the rich soils of the Skagit Valley as well as the skills of the New Earth farmers.

We walked out to the field where Salvio and Victoria were reclaiming a long row of carrots from the invasive horsetail weed. They were Mixtec (*Meesh*-tek), an indigenous tribe from the highlands of Oaxaca. Many of the migrants who come to Skagit County are Mixtec, and for the past four years Salvio and Victoria have worked at Tierra Nueva serving their people as migrant pastors. Like Nick, they work part-time at the farm. Most of the money earned from the CSA goes to support them. It's one way Tierra Nueva helps people like Salvio and Victoria and Zach to become leaders. Before coming to Tierra Nueva, Salvio and Victoria had spent their lives working the land, first on the steep hillside *milpas* of their home and later as migrant workers here in the valley. I joined them weeding carrots.

I wanted to ask how they felt about working on a farm after doing that for so long as migrant workers. After the hardships they'd encountered, wasn't it a regression to go back to farming? Or could such work be redeemed by choosing to do it rather than being forced to do it from necessity? I wanted to ask all these things but my Spanish wasn't good enough, so I simply asked if they enjoyed the work. Salvio said that working here part-time was a nice break from his work at Tierra Nueva's family support center back in Burlington. He liked being outside. Victoria, though friendly, was more reticent, and mostly smiled and nodded at my questions. I wondered what kind of trials they had been through during the years that led them here. They were part of a tragic history that has been unfolding over the last twenty years.

Many years ago, it came to pass that the People of the Corn found they could no longer continue as they had. They had first taken the seed from the wild grasses and bred it into *maíz,* and for millennia they had grown it, yet now, because of trade agreements between our country and theirs, the *maíz* became worthless. There was nothing for them in their villages any longer, and so many of them left, some to work in huge factories along the border with the country to the north and others to cross under cover of night into that country, the cause of their woes but perhaps the answer to them as well. *El Fiebre del Norte,* the people called this disease, the Fever of the North, and it hounded them like a demon. If they succumbed to it, could they be blamed? And lo, thus began the Great Exodus from *El Sur* to *El Norte.* The people Israel wandered for forty years in the desert around Mount Sinai; the People of the Corn have been forced to wander for at least twenty. Must they continue another twenty? When will their wandering cease? Many were exported back to *El Sur* where they would begin their wandering all over again, while others lived under threat of expulsion, but even those who went unnoticed were always looking over their shoulder. Many were given the jobs that the people of *El Norte* would not do: picking fruit, tending animals, cleaning houses. And so the People of the Corn have wandered, unable to find rest. A very few of them settled down, believing that they could even make a kind of life here, and they began to have children.

They came to places with strange names like *Skagit,* where they worked stooped over like beasts of burden. They picked the blackberries and raspberries and tulips that would feed the people of *El Norte,* or at least brighten their breakfast tables. The People of the Corn did these things because there was no other way and because they had to feed their children but what they could not foresee was that the demon *El Fiebre* would not stop with them. He would want their children, too. While the parents stooped over endless rows of strawberries, *El Fiebre* approached their young ones, who ran along the rows or huddled in the shade of a fruit crate, and whispered in their ears, told them he had a better life for them. Why spend twelve hours a day, six days a week stooped like animals, he whispered, why pick the *cabrón*'s cucumbers or slop the *pendejo*'s hogs or scrub the white woman's toilet when I can give you something better? And so it was that *El Fiebre* offered a means of escape to the People of the Corn's children, who became the new casualties. *El Fiebre* sent demons of intoxication, wooing them with dark substances they smoked or injected into their bodies, causing them to forget the pain of being wanderers; *El Fiebre* sent other demons who formed the young men into gangs and the smartest of them he named *shot-callers*, his trusted agents who would issue directives about which girls to pimp and which to protect, which *carnal* to trust and which *enemigo* to maim or destroy. And so it was that within one generation, people who for a thousand generations had lived secure on their land suddenly found themselves landless. They were now at the mercy of landowners, drugs, and demons, often hard to distinguish from one another, and from whose power they found it difficult to escape.

Salvio and Victoria had escaped. They had found secure roles as pastoral leaders at Tierra Nueva, and I wondered how many more of their people they could help find a new life here in the Skagit Valley.

"One of the things we grapple with," Nick said, "is wondering whether the farm helps Tierra Nueva or is at odds with it." In a ministry whose primary work was advocacy for people on the margins, he wondered if the hard work of farming pulled valuable energy away from advocacy, or whether instead it provided a wellspring for that work. Most of the farm's labor comes from juvenile offenders or jail inmates who come to perform community service. He described a young Latino homie named Porky, who found at New Earth Farm a distraction from life in the gangs. Porky would show up at the farm in his long baggy shorts, wife beater, and tats, telling Nick that he wanted to work "because if I stay at home, I'll just get high all day." But most of these kids want to work in the coffee project with Zach. That's cool and sexy; the farm is a tougher sell. Still, Nick sees New Earth Farm as a way to give people like Porky a healthy environment where they can see something good result from the work of their own hands. Many of them do work with their hands, but either it's migrant work with low pay, or it's destructive work—cooking meth, dealing drugs, stabbing people. Here they can plant a row of potatoes and three months later harvest a beautiful crop. They can begin to learn the joys of delayed gratification.

I saw the same scenario play out during my four years at Anathoth. Early on we became a host site for Volunteers for Youth, a nonprofit that placed community service volunteers who had been charged with various minor offenses such as shoplifting, drug possession, carrying a knife to school. On an average week we hosted ten or fifteen teenagers on our Saturday workdays. When they arrived each Saturday morning, I gave them the stump speech about how our mission was to "plant gardens and eat what they produce and seek the peace of the city." I had no trouble teaching teens how to plant gardens and eat what they produced, but I struggled with the peacemaking part. My patience was stretched by youngsters like Mohammed, who enjoyed shocking himself on the electric deer fence that guarded the garden's perimeter; or the three boys who snuck off to the woods to smoke weed right in the middle of a major mulching project; or Bassie, the young man who played in a punk band called Noise Corps ("it's basically a wall of sound coming at you with offensive song titles") and who told his mother before coming to work with us, "I don't care if they're curing cancer out there—I'm not working at Anathoth!"

Coming to the Skagit Valley confirmed my belief that land-based ministries like New Earth Farm or Anathoth or the Lord's Acre, small and unassuming as they are, are capable of redeeming for people like Porky or Mohammed or Bassie what has become a broken relationship with the land. There are those for whom the taste and feel of working in the soil becomes the means for breaking into a new life.

El Fiebre was not all-powerful. Another force had been at work in the valley, quietly and powerfully challenging this dark Legion, and some did manage to escape. One of them was a shot-caller for the biggest gang in the Skagit Valley, at one time the most feared and respected criminal in the valley. Bones had not escaped entirely, for he was sitting in a seven-by-thirteen cell in solitary confinement at the maximum security prison in Monroe, Washington, two hours south. His release date was 2014. If Chris Hoke could pull the right strings, he would take me to visit Bones that Friday night. On Tuesday morning Chris put in a call to several high-ranking prison officials. As we waited for the person on the other end of the line to pick up, Chris raised his right hand and prayed that the doors of the prison would open and let me in.

It seemed unlikely that I could visit Bones; very few people can visit a prisoner in the hole. Before my trip to Burlington, Bones got my address from Chris and started writing me letters. Every few weeks I would get one, written in a bold cursive hand, and I would write him back. Thus began our unlikely friendship.

Abandoned by his father and raised by his migrant mother, Bones had grown up in the fields of Skagit's dark, loamy soils, playing among the rows while his mother picked the strawberries, blackberries, and cucumbers that would fill grocery store shelves across the land. She also sold burritos filled with cocaine. The burrito stand was a side business; when one of her special customers stopped by she would slip the tiny packet of coke into a burrito. She was sly, but when she finally did get caught she begged her son to take the rap. You could say that was the beginning of Bones's career as a criminal, but you could equally point to the times he was molested as a child, or the time when he was ten years old and a shot-caller named Smurf from a local gang was kind to him and invited him to join, but in order to get "jumped in" Bones was told he had to shoot a Norteño, a member of Smurf's rival gang, which he did: he shot the guy in the face point-blank. Ten years old. Or you could point to the time when Bones witnessed his stepfather hang himself in their home. Or the time he saw a neighbor stab his wife in the throat in front of their kitchen sink, and how he ran to the bathroom and wrapped himself in the shower curtain and rocked himself for the next ten hours. "It's like Saul's story," Chris said, referring to the street murder Saul of Tarsus witnessed as a young man, which led him to persecute Christians. Then Jesus appeared to him on the road to Damascus and Saul became Paul the Apostle. "What Bones saw as a young man," Chris told me, "he later recapitulated." You could also point to the fact that Bones's mother engaged in *brujería,* witchcraft, and how once she wrote a man's name on a piece of paper and sewed it into a cow's tongue and buried the tongue in a certain field and the next week the man got in a car accident. Or the time when Bones was older and incarcerated and his mother paid $2,000 to a *brujo* priest to get her son sprung and the next day, inexplicably, Bones walked free. "From an early age," Chris told me, "Bones's mom turned her son over to evil powers. She dealt drugs, she let men abuse him. It's not superstition. There is a spirit of death that has reigned over his life. Bones has been consciously moving toward God, but the colonizing powers of evil in the world are trying to smack him down."

At age twenty-nine, after spending nearly half of his adult life in prison, Bones was doing time in the hole when he received what can only be called a vision.

Over the years Bones had been in and out of prison. Chris had visited him many times, advocated for him in the courts, laid hands on him in prayer. Chris saw Bones as a brother, sick with a spiritual illness, perhaps, but one to whom he was bound by the Spirit and who needed his help. Bones's trust in Chris grew, until he began to call Chris *mi carnal,* a friend who is like a brother. Then he started referring to Chris as *mi pastor.* One day he called Chris from prison—collect—and spoke hurriedly in an excited voice.

"Chris, you there? Wassup babyboy. So check this out: I got to tell you about this vision I been having. I can't get it out of my head." Bones wanted to start a farm. He would call it Hope for Homies. Chris was surprised. A farm? "Yeah, I know, Chris—I fucking *hate* animals. I see a dog and I just want to kick it. But I can't get rid of this vision I have of kids and goats and chickens and shit."

Despite his dark childhood, was there some ray of light he remembered? In all those years of running up and down the cucumber rows, being out under this massive and humbling sky, were there memories which could redeem his past? Bones's childhood was horrific. Still, I wondered if his hands had retained their memory of the soil's goodness, even amidst the austerity of solitary confinement. On Friday that week Chris got word that I could visit Bones, and he drove me down just hours before my flight home.

It had been a long time since I'd been to a prison. Soon after we married, Elizabeth and I became Yokefellows, volunteers who took inmates out to dinner or to church. Orange County Correctional

Facility in Hillsborough, North Carolina, was a minimum security joint, and some inmates could leave on work-release or for church visits. Every week we spent Tuesday nights at the prison chatting with inmates. We soon became friends with a big lineman of a guy named Pharaoh. When I asked him how he got his name, he said, "Because I run things." Pharaoh was a gentle leader, though, one whose heart had not been hardened even in prison, and I especially loved his infectious belly laugh. He never finished high school—he was locked up at eighteen—but he was one of the smartest people I've ever met. He gobbled up books. Other Yokefellows, mostly Southern Baptists, would give "their" inmates copies of *The Purpose Driven Life* or the King James Bible, but I loaned Pharaoh my copies of *Invisible Man, Cry, the Beloved Country,* a two-volume history of Christianity. Pharaoh was black, but in prison he hung out with the Latino guys and learned to speak Spanish. Every Sunday evening we took him out to a Mexican restaurant where he had the waiters convinced he was Cuban. Pharaoh had been in the joint twelve years—first-degree murder, shot a rival drug dealer—and after about a year of us taking him out every week and easing his transition back into society, the state turned him loose. Pharaoh came over for dinner on several occasions, each time a new girl in tow, but another year passed and we lost touch. For a time he had a good job as a sous chef at a five-star restaurant in Greensboro, but he got fired when the head chef felt his authority being challenged. The last time I saw him he said he'd gone back to dealing. He just couldn't find anybody who would hire an ex-felon. The last time I tried calling him, his number had been disconnected. That was years ago. Where are you now, Pharaoh?

On the drive down to visit Bones I told Chris about Pharaoh. "I miss that guy," I said. Without pause Chris raised his right hand over the steering wheel and prayed. "Lord, I pray that Pharaoh would call Fred. Let Fred see his brother again."

* * *

We were late. Visiting hours began at four, but the traffic was so thick on I-5 that we didn't make it to the prison until 5:15. We only had until seven. Two wooden totem poles stood outside the gate. I looked at the totem on the right where animals were stacked on top of each other—eagles, coyotes, orca whales—all intriguing, but I was drawn most to the human figure on the bottom. His hands held both cheeks, mouth agape, as if unable to carry so much weight on his shoulders.

We cleared security with ease and walked through the general population visiting area, then down a long hall with rooms on our right, and arrived at door number 4. When we entered the small room, Bones sat waiting.

The first thing I noticed was his grin. It was the barely containable jubilance of a little boy on Christmas morning. Chris and Bones entered into a boisterous exchange, long-lost brothers filling each other in on the latest news. Bones was small, a full head shorter than my six feet, but even behind the Plexiglas barrier he had the look of coiled strength. On his right cheek were letters and numbers, secret markings of the gang life. We sat down and Bones described life in the Intensive Management Unit—solitary confinement. The hole. Here at Monroe they had a two-hundred-bed unit, essentially a prison inside a prison, where the state's most violent offenders are housed.

The first thing Bones wanted to tell us was how he "broke bread" with the other guys in IMU. In the Sureños, Bones explained, they had a code of conduct, and part of that code was sharing food with your brothers. But weren't they all isolated from each other? "No, we're connected like this," he said, and started drawing a sketch on his hand of the IMU unit, showing in detail the octagon layout.

"I get candy Fireballs and shit from the commissary, you know?" He described how he crushed them up and put the mashings into a folded-up piece of paper. He takes elastic from his underwear and makes a long string, then attaches the paper to the string. Then he swings it like a lasso. He can swing it sideways into another cell, or swing it up to the one above me. "It's like fishin' man." Not all the guys get money to buy food, so when Bones has money he buys candy at the commissary and shares it. "We're like fucking little kids when the commissary opens," he says, and laughs.

"What kinds of things do they sell in the commissary?" I asked.

Chris gave me a sideways look: "Everything you and Michael Pollan want to ban: Fireballs, Swiss rolls. Junk food is a cash cow for the prison system."

But it was still food, in a way, and whatever it lacked in substance was made up for in symbolic meaning. Aside from his weekly visits from Chris, breaking bread in the hole was Bones's only form of human contact. Chris later observed when we left the prison that even though Bones couldn't sit down with other guys to break bread, he was still finding a way. "It's like *Mission: Impossible* where every little scrap of junk food gets shared, even in the Panopticon of the IMU unit."

I had a voice recorder with me, and Chris asked if he could record Bones making a short speech for Tierra Nueva supporters. I held out the microphone and he began. "Hey this is Bones, I just want to thank you guys for your support 'n' shit. Me and my homie Chris are on a mission to start Hope for Homies, and we're gonna like . . . shit!" He stopped.

"You're doing great," Chris said. "Keep going." He started over.

"My name is Bones, I'm currently doing fifteen months in the hole. I have a vision for building a safe house on a farm where homies can live . . . shit, dog! I forgot this one word I want to say." He tried a few more times but couldn't remember the one word. "That's okay," Chris said. "We'll try again later."

Bones gave a sort of trajectory of his life as a gang-banger. It started when he was a kid. He had so much anger. When Smurf found him at age ten and told him to shoot that guy in the face, he was scared, but he needed a role model so he did it. At age fourteen when his mom got busted for selling cocaine, Bones took the rap and went to prison . . . he took karate and boxing and he and his buddies used to beat up drunk Mexican guys in the park . . . kids would make fun of him in school because he wore the same clothes multiple days in a row and didn't take showers . . . both his brothers, may they rest in peace, died from drugs and alcohol . . . then he started pimping his hynas (girls). "You ever read that book *Tattoos on the Heart*? That's my life right there, dog. I read it one night and cried the whole way through."

Along the way there were adults who saw his potential and reached out to him. His school principal, Mrs. Copper, took him out to eat and tried to get him to stop beating kids up at school. Then there was Judge Skelton. Whenever Bones would appear in court Judge Skelton would say, "Bones, approach the bench. Now I'm sick of this shit, Bones, you're smarter than this." Judge Skelton at one point told Bob that he would pay for Bones to go to college and law school, and when he graduated he would hand him his gavel.

"And then I met Bob when I was at the Skagit County Jail. Bob's cool as *fuck*, dog. He was telling us stories about Jesus 'n' shit, about this hyna who poured perfume on Jesus's feet and about Jesus telling people that the authorities can't fuckin' tell you what to do. It was cool, man, so fucking beautiful. I love Bob. I remember that one story about how those dudes wanted to cast stones at the girl accused of adultery, and Bob said that was like one of us standing in court and Jesus asking the judge and the lawyers who would like to throw the first stone."

This story reminded me of a question I'd asked Chris earlier on the drive down to the prison. I understood that Bones had a bad past and that evil may well be hovering over his life, I said, but he could make a *choice*. He had human agency. "Aren't you enabling him?" I asked.

Chris thought awhile before responding. "Jesus walked alongside the worst of sinners," he began, "but he did not stop them from sinning. He didn't use some kind of benign police force to prevent them from doing more violence. They were sick. You know that verse in Paul's letter to the Romans where he says *I do not do the thing that I want but the very thing that I hate . . . wretched man that I am! Who will rescue me from this body of death?* For guys like Bones, that's real."

"But what about the story of the woman caught in adultery," I asked. "Didn't Jesus tell her to go and sin no more?"

"Yeah, but only after he saved her ass. Jesus never excused adultery, but neither was he neutral. He always sided with the oppressed. When the Pharisees gathered to stone that woman he didn't say, 'Now to be fair, it does say in Deuteronomy that anyone caught in adultery should be stoned.' No, he knew the cards were already stacked against her. Engaging those evil powers doesn't mean excusing a person's sin. It means confronting the powers and turning them away. And notice *when* in the story he tells her to go and sin no more. It's only after he's defended her before the authorities. It's only after the accusers are gone. Only then does he have the authority. And right now I'm telling Bones to go and sin no more but it's only because I've saved his ass multiple times and he trusts me. But it goes way deeper than any imperative or command. When people commit violence they are acting out the greatest disease in the human race. Most people view sin as transgression of the law, transgression of right behavior. And they think the remedy for that is punishment, right? Correction. Reprisal. Most Christians have this skewed criminal justice understanding of sin. When the religious leaders of his day asked Jesus why he ate with tax collectors and sinners—people on the margins—he said, *Those who are well have no need of a physician, but those who are sick. I came not to call the righteous, but sinners.* Sin is sickness. If you see somebody bleeding, you shouldn't tell them they're transgressing the cleanliness law."

This kind of advocacy is what earned Bones's friendship in the first place. He was the most feared criminal in the valley; he had no reason to open his life to a white *vato* like Chris. Spiritual advocacy is mostly about defending people against their accusers and trying to love them, Chris explained. "We use our voice for the first 80 percent of the time to defend people against the court systems and the powers that be. That's what makes advocacy so powerful. We earn the right to speak into people's lives because we've fought for them. It also means that I don't have to figure out some kind of philosophical stance between tough love and forgiving love, I just need to ask, 'Where is the presence of the living God in this situation?'"

Bones tried another round with the tape recorder, but still couldn't find the word he was searching for, and I pressed pause. We got back on the subject of Bob Ekblad. What Bones liked was that Bob took all the pious balloons that conventional Christianity had blown up and he popped them, one by one. Bob introduced them to a Jesus who was the Son of God, but who preferred to hang with people like them, people on the margins, a Jesus who stood with them in defiance of the authorities and who then invited them to change their lives. By way of contrast Bones described another prison chaplain, a Vietnam vet, who used to teach Christianity like a drill sergeant, leading off by telling them they were all sinners. Bones didn't attend that class anymore.

Chris then asked the very question I had been wanting to ask the last hour in the car. "So Bones," Chris began, "you talked about how you used to be in your gang-banging days and how you want to be now, and how you want to help the little homies, and it seems like you're wanting to offer them something you didn't receive as a kid, whether it's good fathering or a safe place to call home, and both those are beautiful things. But why a farm? Where did that vision come from?"

Bones paused and took a breath. "You remember that movie *The Godfather,* when that guy was playing with his little grandson in the garden, and he picked a tomato and put it in his mouth? I always wanted that. I wanted a garden with roses and tomatoes. I want my kids to run in a garden and eat tomatoes and play in an orchard and have a tree house. I grew up without a home. When I was growing up I would look out in my backyard and see some drunk mother-fucker vomiting over there and this drug deal going down over here and that motherfucker screaming at his wife over here and some little baby crying on the sidewalk without any Pampers. I grew up picking cucumbers, raspberries, blueberries, blackberries, woke up at the crack of dawn and did everything. I wanted to get out in the fields because out there I wouldn't get abused. That's why I want a farm. Somewhere outside of the 'hood, out on the land. A place for pregnant teenage girls where they don't have to depend on a man who beats them or pimps them, a place where abandoned kids can come and be loved and also learn responsibility. I don't want to force work on them. I'm not gonna say, 'You gotta get up at 6 A.M. and go pick tomatoes *conmigo.*' No, they'll see me out there picking toma-toes and smelling roses and they'll want to do that, too. I'm pretty sure I'm not the only one with a fucked-up life, you know? I'm pretty sure there's people who had it worse, and I want to help them. I know it's gonna be hard to start this Hope for Homies plan, but I just dedicate my heart to God and trust. You know that verse, 'We walk by faith and not by sight'? That's how I pray, dog."

And that's how we prayed, too. It was nearly time to go, but Bones insisted.

As we prayed in our small conference room, I could hear kids laughing down the hall in the family visitation center. The guard gave a tap on Bones's door. Two-minute warning. Before the guards came for him Bones's face brightened. "You know that word I wanted to say during the recording? I remember it now. The word is *embrace*."

When we left the prison it was already dark. We started the long drive to the Seattle airport where I would catch a red-eye back to Asheville. Bones and I would continue our letter correspondence, and I would begin sending him books: Tobias Wolff's *This Boy's Life,* Chaim Potok's *The Chosen,* Thomas Merton's *Thoughts in Solitude.* In one letter Bones mentioned reading *The Tempest* and *Coriolanus.* "Is it true," he wrote, "that all of Shakespeare's main characters have a tragic flaw?"

On the way to the airport Chris told me to read a certain verse in the prophet Ezekiel. He said it reminded him of what Hope for Homies was really about. On the plane that night, as we climbed high over the Cascades, I read those words, which have since become for me a prayer:

> *The trees of the field shall yield their fruit,*
> *and the earth shall yield its increase.*
> *They shall be secure on their soil;*
> *and they shall know that I am the Lord,*
> *when I break the bars of their yoke,*
> *and save them from the hands of those who enslaved them.*
> *They shall no more be plunder for the nations,*
> *nor shall the animals of the land devour them;*
> *they shall live in safety,*
> *and no one shall make them afraid.*

• • •

During my last visit with Bob, he asked if he and Chris could pray for me. We sat down on a long bench, Chris on my left and Bob on my right. Bob asked if there was anything specific for which I wanted prayer. I told them about a back injury that had plagued me for months. *Who knows?* I thought. *It's worth a shot.* Bob prayed first. It was a simple prayer, spoken in a calm voice, as one talks to a friend. "I see in you a bridge builder," he began, "a pollen bringer, one who will carry news from one community to the next. I also see in you a humble spirit, one who desires to see more of God's presence. I ask God to heal your back . . ."

Bob placed his hand on my lower back. I felt something like heat. "I also see a heart with a wound, an open wound that God wants to heal." *What is my wound?* I asked myself. *An inability to open myself fully to others and to God?* "Give him more of you, Lord. Let him experience more of your love."

I found myself leaning over at the waist. There was a need to rest my chin in my hands. The need to steady myself.

Chris prayed next. As he prayed I felt my face muscles begin to twitch uncontrollably. My back had become very warm. A fullness. A peaceful fullness, a welling up of deep-down things, like a forgotten self that was meeting me as if for the first time. I was looking straight down now and the tears were falling fast, silent and unbidden and strangely joyful, onto the concrete. What is it that prevents us from experiencing this all the time, I wondered? An inability to relax the grip. A fear of letting the carapace we hold tight around ourselves crack. I felt God appearing as if from within. Here in this valley of alluvial soils and drug addicts and prison cells and prayer tunnels, I could not discount the larger forces at work. They were working on me.

It didn't occur to me until later that evening that the pain in my back was gone. It returned a few days later. But at least for that day I had been granted a reprieve. In the end I don't remember all the words Bob and Chris prayed. I mostly remember the feeling of human touch, of two strangers bringing me into the presence of God. Through their words and touch I felt I had been granted a glimpse of an overwhelming love, a love that breaks through doubts and cynicism and pride. In that moment I was granted what the early Christians called "the baptism of tears." And I was hungry for more.

CHAPTER SIX

Significant Soil

For most of us, this is the aim
Never here to be realized;
Who are only undefeated
Because we have gone on trying;
We, content at the last
If our temporal reversion nourish
The life of significant soil.
—T. S. Eliot, *The Dry Salvages*

In September of 2005, my first year at Anathoth, I called up a local farmer named Vaughn to see if I could buy chicken manure for the garden. I had never met Vaughn, but knew that he was a former member of Cedar Grove UMC. Vaughn told me they used all their manure on their tobacco fields. I thanked him anyway and was about to hang up when he said, "But even if I did have some, I wouldn't sell you any." Vaughn proceeded to berate me, an outsider, for coming into his community, "where my family has been since 1783," and "messing everything up." He said he thought the community garden was a terrible idea, that "outsiders" had taken over the church, and that as long as "you outsiders" were doing things like starting community gardens, he'd never set foot in the church again. I asked if we could talk about this in person. Why was the community garden such a bad idea? He laughed bitterly and hung up.

I was determined not to let naysayers like Vaughn deter my enthusiasm. Good things were also unfolding—a well digger put in a well for half price, a crew of carpenters volunteered to build the barn. Yet even as the garden project grew and won trust in the community, a small but vocal opposition persisted. Some church members, in all four years I served at Anathoth, refused to set foot on the place.

It certainly didn't help that I was a cultural outsider who practiced new methods of agriculture. "Organic" in this tobacco-growing county was a four-letter word. But despite my strong convictions about growing food organically, I tried to reach out to the older farmers in the congregation who farmed with conventional methods.

Mr. Rimmer lived across Mill Creek Road and was Anathoth's nearest neighbor. He wore coveralls every day except Sunday and alternated caps given to him by the Farmers' Credit Union, Brown's Feed & Supply, and John Deere. Sometimes I walked across the road to borrow a hank of rope or to ask his advice about planting dates ("you plant your peas on Ash Wednesday"). Other times he would drive up in his beat-up Chevy pickup to see what kind of strange things we *owgaanic* people were planting that day. Several years into the project we built a brick-fired pizza oven. Mr. Rimmer soon stopped by wanting to see our new "pizza hut." He'd farmed this land all his life, tobacco mostly, and as a result of much time spent around carburetors and corn pickers had lost the ends of several fingers on each hand. When he talked he massaged his stumps, as if he could feel those parts of himself he once possessed.

One day Mr. Rimmer donated a bushel basket of turnips. "Give these to your people," he said. Another day he brought over some extra sweet corn. Mr. Rimmer used pesticides and fertilizers on his crops, which were harmful to both people and the land, but I could not refuse Mr. Rimmer's vegetables. The gift of food from one human to another transcends categories like "conventional" and "organic."

I was opposed to machines in the garden. Plus, with so many teenagers coming to perform community service, we needed things for them to do; digging beds with hand tools was a great way to harness their energy. Yet despite my aversion to internal combustion, I knew that it would be a charitable gesture to ask one of the older farmers for some help with tilling, which, even with the help of teens, is a particularly backbreaking job to do by hand. I called Dwight Compton, a local sod farmer from the church, and he readily agreed to till up our entire one-acre plot, which, with his gargantuan sod tractor, took him all of fifteen minutes. I liked Dwight. He believed farming to be a high and holy calling. "I was chosen to farm," he once told me. That next summer Dwight came by the garden one day, wad of Levi Garrett tobacco in his cheek, and said, "You've got the best-looking potatoes I've ever seen."

Yet there was a divide between the new way of growing food that I represented and the old way.

Before Mr. Rimmer started donating his corn and turnips, and even before Dwight tilled the ground and we built the first raised beds in the fall of 2005, I decided to ask one of these older Cedar Grove farmers from the church to take a look at our garden site. I'd already had the soil tested. I knew it was decent, by no means superb, but certainly better than the dense clay in my home garden just down the road, where for the past two years I'd still managed to produce bountiful crops.

My late grandfather was a farmer. A gentleman farmer, who had hired men to do most of the work, but still a farmer in his soul. He owned a steel plant in Winston-Salem, North Carolina, and that's where he worked, but he was never happier than when he was out on his farm, training his border collies to herd sheep or taking that year's wool to auction. He died before he could see his love for the land pass into my hands. Perhaps that's why, before starting the biggest undertaking of my life, I sought an older farmer's approval. I imagined us standing together out in the field, this wizened old man and me, looking together at the land's potential. We would stand with hands shielding our brows, surveying the gentle roll of pasture, exchanging knowing looks and appreciative sighs. I would look over at this man my grandfather's age, silently awaiting his approval, and he would not withhold it. He would squint his eyes, slowly nod his head, and offer a few carefully chosen words of praise, noting how well the land lay and how a feller could do right nicely if he were to farm here. And then, with the blessing of my grandfather's stand-in, I would go forth into this land of milk and honey and help it bear fruit for the hungry people of Cedar Grove.

The man I chose for this task was a former tobacco farmer well into his seventies named Donny. Now that I was officially a church employee, Elizabeth and I had switched our membership from our Mennonite church to Cedar Grove UMC, and each week it was Donny who greeted us at the sanctuary entrance. He would hand us a bulletin, grunt, and nod his head. He was not unfriendly, but neither did he like to chitchat. Donny had worked the land in this part of Orange County all his life. If anybody could tell me something about this soil, it was he. One Sunday morning in late October, I asked if he would come look at our soil, hoping that he would lay his old paw on my shoulder and give me his blessing.

The next week he came out to the land. It was an overcast day, blustery and cold. Donny set out walking across the land, muttering things I couldn't quite catch.

"How's it look to you, Donny?" I asked.

Mmuhgrhdah.

This wasn't necessarily a bad sign; monosyllabic bursts were standard in Donny's lexicon. I followed him around the garden. He stopped in one spot, kicked the dirt with his heel, and grunted.

One of the books I'd been reading was *Scripture, Culture, and Agriculture: An Agrarian Reading of the Bible* by Ellen Davis, an Old Testament scholar who had a deep interest in soil. In Genesis, she said, the first command God gave to Adam was to *'avad* and *shamar* the fertile soil. Those words have mistakenly been translated as "till" and "keep." It's important that we get them right, these two verbs freighted with biblical meaning, for they outline what she called "the first human job description." The clues come from looking at how the verbs are used elsewhere in the Bible. *'Avad* connotes service, the kind a subordinate would render to a master either divine or human; God tells Pharaoh to "Let my people go, that they may *'avad* me." That kind of service, we can imply, is analogous to the kind of service due to the soil.

Donny stooped down. He grabbed a handful of soil and squeezed it, smelled it, rolled it around in his fingers. Just when I thought he might put it in his mouth and taste it, he snorted and let it fall like chaff from his hands. Then he shook his head.

Shamar means to "watch," "keep," or "preserve." The verb carries legal connotations as well, suggesting the metaphor of a binding contract. It leads us to realize something most of us have never considered: "There are divinely established rules and constraints attached to our use of the soil, and it has always been so," Davis wrote. To serve the soil is to put oneself in subordination to the land. Taken together, these philological details "give a depth to the kind of relationship that God first envisioned between the human creatures and the soil from which they were taken." That is, the land is not just a natural resource; it is a living entity worthy of our deference and servitude, our watchfulness, and our best attempts at preservation.

At that point the years I could claim service to the soil were few—only what I'd gleaned watching Harvey Harmon and reading Bill Mollison, plus the two years of hard-won experience on my own land—but as I waited for Donny's verdict and thought of how I would grow food on this field at Anathoth, I was certain of one thing: We would not grow crops here; we would grow soil. And the soil would grow our crops.

We didn't have seventy-foot-deep Kansas loam, but we didn't need it. I knew from my reading and from Harvey's stories that you could start with even the most eroded patch of ground in the Sahel and in a few years, if you paid attention to relationships and edges and applied good compost, you could have a beautiful, abundant garden. Which is why the longer Donny poked around and shook his head, the more puzzled I became. Donny believed that you had to *find* good soil to farm, but I saw it the opposite way. You start with what's at hand, and by adding compost and green manures and other soil food, you improve it. You *'avad* the soil by giving more to it than you take away. And then you *shamar* it, that is, you stand back and watch and allow yourself to be amazed at God's mystery unfolding before you.

It was with such high ideals that I arrived as garden manager at Anathoth.

"Dishears red land," Donny said, speaking from the corner of his mouth. He let the last handful of soil fall to the ground, stood up, and straightened his shoulders, looking off toward nowhere in particular. We had walked all over the open pasture, and each time we stopped Donny stooped down, scooped up a handful of soil, and smelled it. We walked uphill and down, soil sniffing in a half dozen spots around the field until finally he'd sniffed enough to reach a decision. Or maybe he'd already decided the moment he got out of the truck and was simply putting on a good show so as to humor me. I looked at him, waiting. But Donny just looked off toward the creek bottom.

Red land was what locals called clay soil. It wasn't ideal. *Sandy land* was the best, highly prized because it drained well and was easy to work. Red land, also known as "Carolina Clay," was dense, poorly drained soil that in the spring could be as hard to work as wet concrete. It did hold water, though, which sandy land did not, and that was a useful thing in a drought. My third year at Anathoth we suffered one of the worst droughts on record, and that year I learned to appreciate red land.

As red as Anathoth's soil was, the soils of the conventionally farmed fields around us were "in the red," running a nutrient deficit. The soil we would create at Anathoth in the years to come would be "in the black," that is, rich in organic matter—literally black in color—and therefore holding a surplus of nutrients from which plants could draw. To switch metaphors, the soil on the farms of our conventional farming neighbors was like a body in a coma. The only thing keeping it alive was a heavy cocktail of pesticides, herbicides, and fertilizers. An expensive life-support system for a corpse.

To stay in the black, I learned, there was really just one simple rule: you must give more to the soil than you take away. Asian farmers, until they, too, succumbed to the lures of industrial agriculture, had practiced the law of return for over forty centuries: what you take out in beets, sweet potatoes, or strawberries, you must return as compost or manure. For many Asians that also meant returning *night soil*—human manure. In rural China or Thailand or Laos farmers erect attractive latrines on roadsides bordering their fields, inviting passersby to "contribute." But not in America. Since the advent of indoor plumbing we don't see where all our waste goes, and such ignorance leads to squeamishness. As I had learned so happily in Chiapas, peeing on a compost pile, we needn't be afraid of excrement. The Czech writer Karel Čapek wrote, "A cartload of manure is most beautiful when it is brought on a frosty day, so that it steams like a sacrificial altar. When its fragrance reaches heaven, He who understands all things sniffs and says: 'Um, that's some nice manure.'"

Gene Logsdon, author of *Holy Shit: Managing Manure to Save Humankind,* writes, "Sooner or later, we must learn to live in the same world as our colons."

For a long time Donny looked off at the distant tree tops, perhaps not wanting to witness my disappointment. He was being kind, and finally in a quiet voice he might have used with a lame horse he was about to put down, he spoke.

"You don wohn fahm heah."

He shook his head in slow motion, still looking off toward the creek bottom. Finally he looked me in the eye.

"Soil's no good. Too heavy. Won't drain. You don wohn fahm heah."

I wasn't sure what to say.

Though farmers of Donny's generation once did see manure as holy, or at least worthy of spreading on their fields, the idea that you give back to the soil more than you take was an axiom farmers of his generation were not taught by their county extension agent. Since the end of World War II and the rise of industrial agriculture, Donny and other American farmers were taught to ignore such "outdated" practices as spreading manure on your fields or cover-cropping with legumes and rye instead of leaving winter fields bare. Living soil had become dirt—a convenient place to prop your crop while you fed it chemicals, and the only thing you needed to make sure of was that your soil was well drained. Anathoth's field was not sandy land, which meant to Donny that it was a lost cause. To be fair, Donny's primary frame of reference was that of a farmer who had to make a living. Thanks to being subsidized through grants, Anathoth's first years were at least free of financial pressure. And yet this land needed to produce as much food as possible for the people who really needed it, and I was responsible for ensuring that it did. But we were looking at the same field with very different eyes.

Donny studied the horizon with a worried expression, as if expecting a storm. After a long pause he said, "Get you some sandy land. If it'll grow *baaca* it'll grow your corn and squash and snap beans." Then he paused, looked at me again as if for emphasis, and said, "You need to look for land closer to the church."

Maybe he really believed that this land was no good. Or maybe, as a member of the church's old guard, Donny had an unspoken bias. I never knew.

Before Donny climbed back in his truck that day I thanked him for his advice, and then promptly ignored it. In early November I placed an order for 180 blueberry plants, twenty pounds of seed garlic, and drew out a map of our first raised beds. We couldn't get in a full garden that fall, but we could at least put in blueberries and garlic. Then we could really crank up in the year to come.

In the spring of 2006 we built more beds, and in addition to the blueberries and garlic we planted corn, potatoes, peas, peppers, and tomatoes, and a dozen other types of vegetables. Thanks to Elizabeth's prompting, we started weekly potluck meals, first one on Tuesday night, then another after our Saturday work mornings. Our membership grew quickly until we had twenty full-time member families. The following year we added a passive-solar greenhouse to extend the growing season, built a garden in the shape of a fifty-foot

Celtic cross, and added a deck to the barn. Almost immediately we began accepting community service kids from Volunteers for Youth. That steady influx of teenagers coming every weekend was our secret weapon, the force that built our garden. We also began a rotating student internship program through which future pastors from Duke Divinity School served their field placements with us. Then we started a summer apprenticeship program where young college grads could learn how to start and manage a community garden.

We also began delivering vegetables to shut-ins and widows like Mrs. Terrell. When she answered the door to receive our weekly delivery, Mrs. Terrell, well into her seventies, would sometimes appear in nothing but her unmentionables. She sprang her surprise on days when our young male interns made a delivery. When approaching Mrs. Terrell's house the interns would start to chant: *Please have clothes on, please have clothes on.*

As I think of the strange mix of people and cuisine, the mishmash of cultures that was Anathoth, I remember the warm evening in early September that Burley first paid us a visit. Normally Tuesdays were potlucks, but this time the meal was prepared by C'est si Bon!, an international cooking school for teen chefs based in Chapel Hill.

As the garlic-infused fingerling potatoes simmered on the stove and ears of corn dry-roasted on the grill, I looked out at Lonesome Road. A man was sitting on a riding lawnmower. He waved. I waved back, then walked over to him. The lawnmower idled. "I'm Burley," he said. "Whatchall got goin' on here?" I had seen him from time to time, cruising Cedar Grove's back roads on his lawnmower. "Just a little community dinner," I said. "Come join us." Burley pulled his mower into the driveway and parked. Behind the mower Burley had affixed a cart, evidently to carry extra gas. Next to the gas cans lay a pile of empty Milwaukee tall-boys. He drove great distances, he explained. It was a thirty-minute lawnmower ride down the highway just to get here. "Fella gets thirsty out on the road."

After he'd sampled the sautéed potato and sausage dish, the vinegar-infused carrot and cucumber medley, and several slices of pecan pie, Burley took a stroll through the garden.

"This place is amazing," he said. "I've driven by here but I've never stopped until now. It's wonderful . . . just wonderful."

Burley had been in a bad car wreck and was now on disability. He kept busy by mowing lawns, often for free. To get to the various lawns he mowed each week he drove there. On his lawnmower. On the highway.

"Looks like your lawn needs mowing," he said, pointing in front of the barn. "See right there? It needs to be knocked back. You want me to knock it back right now?—'cause I will."

"Sure," I said. "But it's already eight o'clock. Enjoy your dinner. Maybe another day, next time you're in the neighborhood."

Burley finished his pecan pie and looked out across the garden. "Wonderful, just wonderful. This plate of food makes me feel like mowing. You know what I'm going to do? I'm gonna knock this back right now."

And he did. But first he showed me his lawnmower. Two tiny American flags fluttered on the rear wheel wells. On each wheel well spun a pinwheel. License plates adorned both front and back of the mower, the front reading, *I'll do anything for money—except work.* The rear plate: *I fight poverty—I work.* Based on his mowing prowess, however, it was clear Burley favored the latter.

"This is the smoothest, quietest mower you've ever seen," Burley told me as he cranked it up. The mower sputtered and gulped, then settled into a dull roar.

A tiny radio was duct-taped to the mower's hood. Burley turned the dial to a country music station, adjusted his shades, and proceeded to knock back the grass. He knocked back not only the grass around the barn, but the big lawn as well. He had to stop before it got dark. With a top speed of ten miles an hour, he would need thirty minutes to make the five-mile trek down Mill Creek Road to his house. His headlights weren't the brightest.

The next morning, right at ten as promised, Burley came riding back down Mill Creek and turned onto Lonesome. He tipped his cap, took a long pull from a brown paper bag, and threw the mower into gear. Within twenty minutes he had knocked back the rest of the garden's lawns—around the greenhouse, in between the blueberries, under the perimeter fence. He knocked it all back.

It's not often that somebody showed up and offered to mow the entire lawn. Burley had saved us about three hours' work with the push mower. I invited him to become a member on the spot, and explained how members volunteer roughly two hours a week in exchange for produce.

Burley looked at me. "But I'm disabled. I can't work in the garden."

I looked at him in surprise. "You just did," I said. Burley grinned. Then he picked up his bag of potatoes, onions, and cucumbers, saddled his lawnmower, and sputtered off down Mill Creek. He had another lawn to knock back before lunch.

One midweek work morning in late September, several garden interns and I sat around a picnic table potting brassica seedlings—broccoli, kale, Napa and red cabbage—with Mack and the other members of Apogee Homes, a home for the disabled and infirm. Before the Apogee residents arrived, the interns and I had carefully set out seedling trays all meticulously labeled.

The blue Apogee minivan pulled in at 9 A.M. Bryan and Barry

jumped out first, promptly assuming their posts out on the road where they would spend the rest of the morning chain-smoking Kools. Dom got out next, followed by an enormous man in his early twenties. This young man carried an equally large leather Bible with him, and immediately he sat down at a picnic table and began to read from Deuteronomy. Mack was way in the back of the van, stuck behind Miss Marie and Miss Odell and the silent lady who heard voices and who refused to leave the minivan.

"Bertha! Jo!" Mack hollered from the backseat. "Can't one of you hurry the hell up and get me outta here? Man's got broccoli to plant." Mack was in his seventies, had only one leg, and needed assistance getting out of the vehicle. Bertha was a generously proportioned woman who possessed no demarcation line between neck and chin. It took Bertha enough energy just to maneuver her three-hundred-pound frame out of the driver's seat; she had no interest in hurrying the hell up for Mack's sake. Bertha and Jo were the beleaguered staff women of Apogee Homes. Every Tuesday and Thursday morning they grudgingly packed six or seven of their charges into the blue minivan, carted them down to the garden, unhitched them from various harnesses and safety belts, and dumped them into our hands. They were like baggage handlers, those women, and twice a week we received their lost bags.

I visited Apogee Homes several times. To get there you drove along the county's back roads with names like *Doc Corbett, Pentecost,* and *Lonesome.* It was a depressing place. A one-story brick ranch out in a field far removed from human society. Most days the residents sat all day and watched TV. But on Tuesday and Thursday mornings in the summer they came to Anathoth. The word *apogee* describes "the point in the orbit of a heavenly body, especially the moon, or of a man-made satellite at which it is farthest from the earth." In choosing this name for a group home, I think Apogee's owners were going for a kind of "reach your peak" ethos, but the word suggested darker, more vexing implications: once a satellite reaches its apogee, it still has to reenter the atmosphere. Most satellites don't make it back. Some spin off into outer space. And others are immolated in the searing heat of reentry. I asked Mack why he lived in a group home instead of a retirement home like other gentlemen his age. "Cheaper," he said under his breath. He winked at me, as if letting me in on a scam from which I might someday benefit.

Before I got them started that day, I gave Mack and Marie and the others a short lesson on planting seeds. I explained that for seedlings to germinate they needed seed-to-soil contact. It's not enough to simply lay a seed on top of the soil, I said. Some might sprout, but most would not. If they're going to thrive, seeds need a blanket of soil to protect them from too much sun and wind. I grabbed a handful of potting mix and sprinkled it gently on top of the seeds to show them. "Seed-to-soil contact, okay?" Mack rolled his eyes. The others' attention was wandering, but Marie nodded vigorously. Seeds were her little buddies. She knew they needed protection.

"You know, they lied about DDT," Mack said, gently caressing one of his cabbage plants. His gravelly voice had gone all soft and distant. He was reminiscing. "Shit, I used to spray a hundred acres a year with that stuff and I *never once* seen a dead squirrel or rabbit. But it sure killed the insects. Man, did it ever. Speaking of rabbits— you ever used rabbit manure on your plants? Now *that's* some good shit. Try it out." He used to sell vegetables at the Carrboro Farmer's Market, now one of the most well-known markets in the country for local organic produce. But "organic" was all a big conspiracy, Mack suspected. He was certain those organic farmers must have really been using fertilizers and pesticides on the sly. Hell, it's what he did.

He set down his Napa cabbage seedlings and spat a stream of

black liquid into a Styrofoam cup. Rolling over onto a hip, he then reached down and scratched his right leg, which ended at the knee. A mysterious blood clot appeared last year, and the doctors were forced to amputate.

"They lied about DDT being harmful to animals and people. I'd be out on the tractor spraying in a wind and that stuff would swirl all around me. I inhaled big lungfuls of the stuff, and I *never once* got sick. I'm fine. Hell, just look at me." Mack fixed his one good eye on me and fanned his right hand down his torso, as if to confirm—the very picture of health.

He pulled a Levi Garrett pouch from his jeans pocket, spat out the old wad, and loaded up his cheek with fresh tobacco. He nodded toward one of the interns and pointed at the tray of kale seedlings. "Gimme a nuthern, horsefly."

With all Mack's talking I hadn't been paying attention to Marie and Odell. Senility had turned ninety-two-year-old Miss Marie into a sweet and gentle three-year-old who could sit all morning working on a single tray of seeds, her little buddies. Age had not been as kind to Miss Odell. Her ninety-seven-year-old mind had also grown childlike, but in a mean kind of way. She was the type of child to whom you wish you could dole out a good spanking. For a nonagenarian, though, she was nimble and quick. By the time I looked at Miss Odell she had climbed up on the table and, one by one, was pulling the Popsicle stick labels off each newly seeded tray. Quickly I walked over and tried to usher her off the table. With a devious, childlike grin, she grabbed the skin on my upper arm between her skeletal fingers and didn't just pinch it; she pinched *and turned*. It was the worst titty-twister I'd had since fourth grade.

"Miss Odell!" Bertha hollered. "*Git* down from there!"

But Miss Odell didn't want to get down. She leapt lemurlike across the enormous young man who sat reading Deuteronomy and hopped onto another picnic table. She tried but ultimately failed to escape Bertha's bear hug. Miss Marie, meanwhile, was steadily plugging away at her tray of broccoli, a beatific smile on her lips as she dropped one seed after another into her tray. As she sprinkled soil on top of each, she muttered under her breath, "Okay little buddy. That's a good little buddy. Go right in there. Good boy." Seed-to-soil contact.

Bertha succeeded in capturing Miss Odell. Her frail little body struggled until she disappeared inside Bertha's generous embrace, then all was quiet.

"Yeah," Mack continued, his voice wistful, "that DDT was some good shit. Too bad they outlawed it. After you sprayed a field you wouldn't see nuthin. No squirrels, no bugs. I mean *nuthin*." One of our divinity student interns, a girl named Wren, came and sat down across from Mack, who looked up and said, "What's your name, honey?"

"Wren. You know, like the bird."

"Is that what people call you?" Mack fixed his good eye on her and looked her up and down.

"Yes," Wren said. "It's my name. What do people call you?"

"Well," he began, then chuckled at the answer forming itself in his mind. Styrofoam cup now full, he leaned over and spat a long thin stream of juice on the barn floor, where it left a dark stain. He massaged his stump, then whistled softly through his teeth. "I could tell you what a woman called me at the dance hall the other night— but I won't."

Another female intern sat down across from Mack.

"Dom!" Mack hollered. "I've got two women on my hands here. You got to help me handle them." Dom remained motionless, sitting at his picnic table in a lithium-induced stupor.

Mack turned toward me. "You know how you keep a woman?

You sit around and do nuthin. *Nuthin*. Take drugs. Get drunk. Treat her bad. Women eat that shit up. That's how you keep a woman." He smiled, winking his good eye at the two female interns, and spat on the dirt.

I looked down at the Popsicle sticks scattered on the dirt floor, the names of their brassica varieties written in black Magic Marker: *Arcadia, Marathon, Blue Wind, Winterbor.* While I was distracted, Miss Odell had managed to uproot every last one of them. Now we had several hundred plants without names. Until we planted them and they grew and reached maturity, each plant would remain a mystery.

In Robert Kourik's book *Roots Demystified,* which describes in loving detail the world under our feet, I came across this beautiful, haunting sentence: "Too much air in the pore space means that root hairs shrivel, die, and oxidize, as if in the slow burning of an invisible fire."

In the lives of my Apogee friends I wonder if there was too much pore space, too much emptiness in that liminal boundary where a person's need seeks another's affection, and as a result the root hairs of their personalities had been oxidized. The people of Apogee Homes came to us twice a week, and I believe in those few hours they found a degree of happiness. They were at least made to feel useful. But at the end of the morning none of them wanted to get back in that minivan. Back at the group home, their days would slowly burn down in the invisible fire of loneliness. There was too little seed-to-soil contact.

Bertha and Jo and Apogee Homes were not to blame. They were doing their job. Some days I found myself before a vast chasm of human need and I was afraid. How could I possibly give souls like Mack and Miss Odell the love they needed?

Some days I could feel in my gut those words of Saint Paul: *We know that the whole creation has been groaning in labor pains until now;*

and not only creation but we ourselves, who have the first fruits of the Spirit, groan inwardly while we wait for the adoption, the redemption of our bodies.

We cannot return to the garden.

During my years at Anathoth Community Garden, I could say that there were conflicts, that no matter how hard we tried to return to the garden and walk with the Lord in the cool of the day, the flaming sword still barred our entrance. I could say that we produced an abundance of food, growing vegetables for hungry people twelve months out of the year. I could say that I sometimes found plants easier to work with than people.

Yet when I think of those years, it's not the bounty of our garden that I recall most. What I find myself remembering are those naked moments when we were allowed past the flaming sword, when we were granted undeserved entrance into that First Garden. But no, that's not right. We were given a glimpse of the Last Garden, the heavenly city described in the book of Isaiah or Revelation, the New Heaven that surrounds the tree of life and which will one day descend to a redeemed earth. I remember how God's *shalom* would appear suddenly in our midst, like a gentle creature who lifts its head with a tender gaze. I remember the Saturday mornings we celebrated the Eucharist right out among the garden beds. And the times Sister Doris would arrive in a bustle of cheer with her big car and her big self and everyone would forget themselves and laugh. And the one October morning I sat on the deck with Clarence.

It was a Saturday workday in the fall. During a break I sat next to Clarence, the son of garden members Meti and Sam, on one of the wooden benches on our barn's deck. Clarence was perhaps in his late twenties or early thirties, and was severely disabled. It was warm that day, and Clarence's mother had propped him in the sun where he could watch his parents mulching strawberry beds. I don't know what level of mental disability Clarence had, but he couldn't talk, could only moan and smile and roll his eyes. He could communicate through these gestures, and although I had spent little time in his presence, I found myself drawn to him. Using an old broom handle, I was making a measuring stick to use as a planting guide for kale, and I asked if he wanted to help me. He rolled his head toward me, and I took his right hand in mine and put the marker in it. Then I closed my hand firmly around his. Together we marked the lines every foot, down the length of the stick. He laughed. We were making something, it was fun, and then suddenly he lolled his head over and rested it gently on my shoulder. For the next little while we just sat together, Clarence's head on my shoulder, and my heart at peace.

At the potluck that day, Adela, one of our most faithful garden members, brought homemade tamales. A widow from Michoacán who lived in a single wide trailer and who came every Saturday to work, Adela's hands were bleached white, whether from birth or accident I never learned. She spoke no English, but everyone adored the woman. When we planted our first spring crops before we had a well, it was Adela who helped me haul five-gallon buckets of water from the creek to irrigate. There was something elemental about irrigating by hand. It connected us to those farmers around the world who didn't have electricity, who had watered their crops by hand for centuries.

In addition to the tamales for the potluck, Adela had made a jalapeño salsa. "Muy hot," Sister Doris said. She was the sole black member at Cedar Grove United Methodist, and another one of my favorite garden volunteers. "Sí," Adela replied, "muy caliente." She and Adela were friends, though neither spoke the other's language.

Sister Doris was sporting a green velour pantsuit, one of her outfits she hadn't worn since the 1970s, but her weight was coming off and she modeled her wardrobe like a beauty queen. One day she announced that, since joining Anathoth, she had lost seventy-five pounds. "And," she beamed, "I plan to lose another hundred." Doris set out on the potluck table a large bowl of ramen noodles drowned in soy sauce. "Hey everybody—I brought spaghetti!"

I remember something Adela said one day when we hauled water together. On our thirtieth or fortieth trip up the hill when my back was sore and my knees feeling strained, I put down my buckets and watched Adela come toward me up the hill. I was ready to quit and said as much to her. But we weren't finished. She wanted to keep going.

El trabajo es bien duro, no? I asked. The work is hard, isn't it?

Sí, pero el trabajo es bonito. Yes, she said, but the work is beautiful.

Give back to the soil more than you take. An addendum to this credo might be this: goodness in people, like goodness in soil, must be preserved and nurtured. Give people more than you take.

This, I learned, was an essential part of our daily transactions at Anathoth. The times I worked well were times I knew I'd given more than I took. I fed the soil with rich compost and didn't overly tax it with too many heavy-feeding crops in a row; I sat beside Clarence, even though I had a million and one things to get done in the garden. These were the days when I wanted to work there for the rest of my life, to be in that place, with those people.

Give back more than you take, I needed reminding, just as the bread and wine give far more than we take into our bodies through the lifted elements of Communion. Tend not just the soil, but the soil people. *'Avad* and *shamar* them, working and watching, serving and preserving them as if your own life depended on it. Which, of course, it does. Our role in creation is to offer everything back to God.

In the early days I used to think how absurd it was for people like Vaughn to be against the idea of a community garden. That's like being against school lunch programs or improved health care. I had the same flummoxed reaction when the other naysayers had argued that we shouldn't build a garden Down There. But then I began to wonder if Vaughn's vitriol over what seemed like a fairly innocuous thing meant that it wasn't so innocuous after all.

Maybe a communal garden is actually a threat to life as we know it.

Of course, what Vaughn and others like him didn't know was that the result of this barrier breaking was not anarchy or bedlam. What I learned in those years is that when strangers grow and share food together, the Other ceases to be so threatening. The ones who were once an abstract category—the Poor Folks, the Rich Folks, the Black Folks, the White Folks, the Illegal Aliens—cease to be categories. They become instead the people they've always been: Mack, Donny, Vaughn, Emma, Bones, Zach.

From the perspective of the garden, I began to see the trajectory my life had followed. Its arc traced a pattern only a hand larger than mine could have writ.

Toward the end of my time at Anathoth, I remember a particular Eucharist service in the garden. At some point just before lunch on a Saturday workday in October, the work stopped, the tools were set aside, and the chalice and paten laid on a picnic table right out among the kale and collards. It was a beautiful fall day, the air crisp, a slight breeze gliding through the barn bringing smells of basil and thyme from the garden beyond.

When I went forward to receive, I dipped the bread into the cup

and brought it to my own lips. Hymns were sung, the service continued, and soon each of us would go back to our lives and the hunger
that propels us, but in that moment I was full. For a long time I
could not chew. I could only hold the supple Host in my mouth as a
lioness holds her cub, gumming the tender life, the fragile body.

CHAPTER SEVEN

Surpassing Civilization

Sukkot
Adamah Farm, Connecticut

There is a great longing in the world.
—Abraham Joshua Heschel, *The Sabbath*

11 Tishri

In the year 5772, on the 11th day of the month of Tishri—which I knew as October 9, 2011—I sat at the table of my host, Mr. Shamu Fenyvesi Sadeh, and contemplated a forkful of goat. The meal before me was certainly a feast: fresh cut lettuce and arugula tossed lightly in tamari and olive oil, homemade bread, and the main course, a clay pot filled with steaming mounds of sweet potatoes, bitter herbs, and goat meat. Everything was fresh, savory, and aromatic. Still, I hesitated about the goat.

Earlier that afternoon I had stepped off the platform at Wassaic, Connecticut, end of the Metro-North Harlem Line from New York City, where Shamu was waiting for me. Shamu directs the Adamah farming program at Isabella Freedman Jewish Retreat Center in nearby Falls Village, where I would spend the next week. The farm's name was a nod to Genesis, when God created the *adam* from the *adamah,* human from humus. Those words, Shamu said, share the root *dam,* which means "blood." There is a sense of living matter that connects blood, humans, and soil.

Shamu's garb bore the same markings as my own work attire back home: old T-shirt, worn Carhartt pants with holes in the knees, Croc clogs. He greeted me with a bear hug. Much like Anathoth Community Garden, Adamah combines organic gardening and faith practice. In Shamu I had found my Jewish counterpart.

As we drove across the broad expanses of the western Berkshires in Shamu's Prius, I learned that their main field, which they call the Sadeh and was planted in four acres of organic vegetables, had flooded the month before during Hurricane Irene. This had been a real loss, and I sensed that Shamu was still reeling from the shock.

The leaves were in peak color and the panorama of the Berkshires was an ocean of red, yellow, and brown with houses floating here and there on the surface like peaceful white boats.

As we entered the driveway of Isabella Freedman, a sign read: "It's time to slow down." I was to find that, indeed, time would slow down this week, and not only slow but shift in small but perceptible ways. "Judaism is a religion of time aiming at the sanctification of time," wrote Abraham Joshua Heschel, perhaps the most famous Jewish theologian and philosopher of the twentieth century. In preparation for my trip, I'd been rereading Heschel's book *The Sabbath*. The book is a long essay, really, a meditation on the Sabbath day. It's also a meditation on time. Jewish ritual, Heschel believed, is about constructing an "architecture of time." Judaism, he writes, teaches a person to be "attached to the holiness in time, to be attached to sacred events to learn how to consecrate sanctuaries that emerge from the magnificent stream of a year. The Sabbaths are our great cathedrals."

I was to find that not only had I entered a different time zone, I had also entered a different physical space. A line of string formed a perimeter around Isabella Freedman, called the *eruv,* Shamu explained. It's a symbolic enclosure of space separating its occupants from the world.

We parked the car and walked up a trail through the woods, crossed a stream, and arrived at a collection of cabins in the woods above Lake Miriam. The cabins were called Kfar, "village," and here I would sleep. We tried first one then another cabin and found them full of debris; they'd sat unused all summer. The third cabin wasn't too bad. A few mice had made a nest of old socks on one of the beds, and the mattresses on the bunks were a bit moldy. All the other rooms were full for the week, and this was my only free option. "Come over for dinner in an hour," Shamu said, and left me to get settled.

I was arriving in mid-October, just in time for the conclusion of the Jewish High Holidays, known as the Days of Awe. These linked holidays begin with Rosh Hashanah, the Jewish new year, and culminate with Sukkot, known as the "Season of Our Joy," the fall harvest festival. Yom Kippur, perhaps the most solemn and revered day in the Jewish calendar, falls in between. On that day Jews look back on the year and take stock and atone. Until the Romans destroyed Jerusalem's Second Temple in 70 CE, one of the priests on this day would symbolically transfer the sins of the Jewish people onto a goat. According to the book of Leviticus, the goat was then sent to Azazel, a desert place. A separate goat was brought to the altar to be sacrificed, the proverbial scapegoat. None of this was part of Yom Kippur for modern Jews, Shamu said. "But we're a farming community. We get to play around with that tribalistic stuff."

During our conversation in the Prius, Shamu mentioned slaughtering a goat, but I wasn't clear if this was the same goat that was sent to Azazel or a different one. Given that they played around with tribalistic stuff, I assumed it was the same one. The one which now sat on my plate. *But surely they don't eat the . . . ?* Maybe this was a part of Jewish tradition I had missed.

Sitting around the dinner table with Shamu and Jaime, I now had an inkling of how Jews must feel eating with Gentiles. As a boy growing up in Nigeria, I was fond of the goat curry we had for lunch every Sunday, but I was uneasy about eating a sacrificial goat. When later I asked Shamu again about the goat's connection with Yom Kippur and if a rabbi had performed their ceremony, he explained that Adamah is a nonrabbinic community. "It's nothing against rabbis," he said. "It's just that when a rabbi is present, people don't step up as much. We're a community that's all about empowerment, whether teaching people how to grow their own food or say their own blessing or lead a Shabbat—Sabbath—service on Friday night. Like the ritual goat slaughter which will happen in a few weeks, we'll do that ourselves, just like we did the Yom Kippur ceremony ourselves."

"Wait," I said. "I thought the ritual slaughter happened right after you put the sins on the goat during Yom Kippur."

"No, no," Shamu said. "Those are two very different events. We wouldn't want to connect them. That would be really confusing for folks." He laughed, seeing my confusion. "No. The goat we're eating has been in our freezer since last year."

Right.

"Would you like some more goat?" Jaime asked, a big serving spoon laden moving toward my plate.

"Sure," I said, "love some."

12 Tishri

Like a kid at summer camp, I wanted to do everything at once. I was especially eager for Friday night to arrive at the end of the week, when I could step inside the great cathedral of the Jewish Shabbat.

At 6:15 the next morning, Monday, there was a knock on my cabin door. I dressed in the dark, then I remembered I had a head-lamp. I left Kfar, walked down a path next to a stream, and skirted the western shore of Lake Miriam. When I arrived at the Red Yurt, the Adamah fellows and staff were already inside, seated in the darkness on meditation cushions.

Workdays at Adamah are divided into three parts, each being a different form of *avodah,* a word that can mean "work," "service," or "worship." The day begins with Avodat Lev, the service of the heart. The morning is spent in Avodat Sadeh, service of the field, and in the afternoon it's Avodat Bayit, service of the house. Each day begins with davening, "prayer."

Adonai s'fatai teef'tach oofee yageed t'heelatechah, we sang, "God, open my lips and my mouth will speak Your glory." This was the same line from Psalm 51 I'd recited with the monks of Mepkin Abbey during their daily 3:20 A.M. Vigils.

The group began each song in unison, with different voices breaking off into harmony on the second and third rounds. One young man sang louder than the others, his eyes closed, gently rock-ing himself on the meditation cushion. As they sang several more songs from Torah or the Psalms, the group seemed to enter a kind of trance. I let myself be drawn up into the spiral of voices, which rose upward out of the yurt's clear dome into the dawn sky. The worship music was very different from the staid European hymns or saccha-rine teen-pop-ballads-for-Jesus music of many Christian churches. This Jewish praise felt much more tribal, physical, and urgent. The singers put their entire bodies into the songs, and as I joined them I felt the words rising from the ground up through my spine and out of my mouth. I, too, began to sway.

Hebrew is known among Jews as "the holy tongue." Words in Hebrew almost take on a life of their own. *Davar* means "word" but it also means "thing." Unlike the Greek notion of a word being simply a placeholder for the thing it represents, there is a sense in Judaism that the words one speaks, especially words of Torah, have a force and agency in themselves. They are generative, alive, something loosed into the world, and as such they have great power to destroy or create, wound or heal.

I let myself be borne up by these words and strange melodies, and after a half hour of vigorous davening, the group paused. A woman named Glenn, the assistant goatherd, read a long passage from *Anna Karenina:* the part where the main character, Levin, goes out scything with his peasants, one of my favorite passages in all literature. Prayer and Tolstoy; why couldn't every day begin like this?

The blend of Jewish spirituality and organic agriculture is happening not just here at Adamah Farm. Nigel Savage told me later that week that a growing number of Jews all over the country are reconnecting with land and food. Nigel is a British Jew who lives in New York and considers Israel his true home. The founding director of Hazon, the country's largest Jewish environmental organization, Nigel calls himself "a very classically literate, intellectual, verbal Jew," not exactly the earthy type. In 2002 he founded Hazon, meaning "vision," because it became clear to him that we're burning up the planet and we need a new vision to act. Perhaps the biggest focus of Hazon's work is reconnecting Jews with the sources of their food. "It's exciting them, it's inspiring them, it's transforming their lives. The Jewish Food Movement is an extraordinary driver of social change all over the place." Hazon runs the largest faith-based Community Supported Agriculture program in the country, with nearly ten thousand members spending $2 million a year at three dozen local organic farms, "which, by the way," Nigel told me, "only a handful of whom are Jewish." In 2005 Hazon started a blog called "The Jew and the Carrot," and in 2007 held the first annual Jewish Food Conference at Isabella Freedman. Since then the movement has grown at an astounding pace. Nigel describes it as amorphous, with no central leadership. The Adamah program has played a central role, along with Hazon, "but what you've basically got is a thousand little pieces of wool all rolled up together. Pick up any one thread and it will lead you to all the others."

All this prompts the question: why now? Nigel sees the movement as a response to the disconnection of modern life. "Modernity privatized Jewish life and flattened it," he said. Modernity came along and said "technology is better than the old ways." Along came modern architecture with big concrete blocks. Formula replaced breast milk. Modern science replaced traditional forms of knowledge. Modern individualism replaced community. A growing number of Jews are now trying to reclaim what Nigel calls "organic Jewish life," the life Jews once lived in *shtetls,* the self-contained villages of Europe where spirituality and food and music and gossip and architecture were all bound up together in a communal life, with a common sense of Jewish time, Jewish ritual, Jewish identity. Which is what makes a place like Isabella Freedman so powerful. "What we have here," Nigel said to me, "is a postmodern Jewish *shtetl.*"

After davening in the Red Yurt that Monday morning it was time for breakfast and chores. Some of the Adamahniks went to milk the goats, others to feed the chickens, and some went back to Beit Adamah, the intern house, to make breakfast. The main dining hall was closed until the beginning of Sukkot, so I stopped by Shamu's house where I was offered steel-cut oats with all the fixings: organic Grade B maple syrup, sorghum molasses, and yoghurt. Across the road from Shamu's house was the Kaplan

Farm, a fifteen-acre upland field with a permaculture Garden of Eden food forest, berry rows, a compost area, and a male goat pasture called Boyz Town. A group of Adamahniks led by Janna Berger, the farm manager, were beginning Avodat Sadeh, the Service of the Field. With long knives they sliced handfuls of arugula in cut-and-come-again style, slicing an inch above the soil so the plants could regrow and be harvested again in a few weeks. Up the hill stood rows of beautiful brassicas—broccoli, cabbage, collards, kale—all dark green and turgid in the morning light. The sun was already coming over the hills. It was going to be a beautiful day.

After harvesting, I hitched a ride with one of the Adamahniks in a black Ford F-150 powered by used veggie oil. She dropped me off at the Picklearium, which Shamu calls the Center for Cultural Proliferation. Here Sam Plotkin, the Pickle Apprentice, was cutting up vegetables from the farm and, aided by lactobacillus bacteria, fermenting them into live foods. When I arrived he was chopping garlic and dumping it into a blue fifty-five-gallon drum. The goal was to put down two batches of kimchi before Wednesday at 3 P.M., when Sukkot would begin, and there was still much to do. Sam was tall and lanky and amiable. He wore a yellow tank top and black Leninesque cap. Rap music played in the background.

I laid my own hat down on a stainless steel table and offered to help chop garlic. "Oh, you'd better hang that up on the rack," Sam said. "You know, kosher and all that." Would my hat de-kosher the kimchi Sam was making? "Probably. Kosher is so fucking complicated, man. It's both a noun and a verb."

In between chopping garlic Sam checked on a batch of apple butter he was making on the stove. When the sauce had sufficiently reduced and cooled, he brought it over to the table and began putting it in jars. I asked how he got each batch the same.

"I don't," he said. Then he smiled. "It's ar*tis*anal, man. I'm all about some artisanal production."

Sam grew up with a nominal Catholic mother and a Conservative Jewish father, and they attended a Reform synagogue so Sam's mother could participate. "Reform is like a really casual way to be Jewish. My upbringing was pretty much bereft of spirituality."

Raised in the suburbs of Detroit, Sam had absolutely no interest in agriculture. Then, during his sophomore year at Michigan State, his campus Hillel president sent him to the organic Oz Farm, in Point Arena, California, for spring break. The trip was sponsored by the Jewish Farm School. After a few days, something clicked. Like here at Adamah, each day started with davening. Then, during morning farm work, they discussed things like why the agribusiness company Monsanto was the modern equivalent of Pharaoh's Egypt, in control of the food supply. "I started learning how fucked up our food system is. Seeing how animals are treated, learning that my Cheerios came from processed number two corn, then filtering all that through a Jewish lens." Sam and his cohort were asked to imagine what would happen if they practiced *shmita,* the Sabbath year that Jews were commanded to observe every seventh year and leave their fields fallow. "We learned the social justice implications behind ancient Jewish food laws. I realized religion could exist in a field, planting potatoes, and I could suddenly relate to it. All along I'd been searching for a secular Jewish community, but what I found at the Jewish Farm School was divinity, awe, the source of life. And it came to me in a way that was palpable. Are you hungry?"

Sam walked over to the walk-in cooler and pulled out jars of dilly beans, kimchi, and Adamah's specialty, spicy lemon pickles. It was late morning and I was starved; I sampled a generous helping of each. Every bite was cold, delicious, and, as I knew from my own experiments with fermented foods, very much alive.

Sam returned to Michigan State fired up about farming. He specialized in Sustainable Agriculture and Food Systems, and founded a "Judaism and the Garden" program at his Hillel. That eventually led him to the Adamah program at Isabella Freedman, "the biggest earth-Jew place in the country."

It was here that he was challenged to think deeply about his relationship with God, yet not in a way that was forced or cheesy. Here such conversations seem utterly natural. "It happens out in the field, or when you're peeling garlic for four hours. Mundane but meditative tasks actually lead to talk of God."

Now it was 11:25 A.M.—time for *tachliss,* Sam told me—and the kimchi batch would have to wait.

"What's *tachliss?*" I asked.

"Brass tacks. It basically means 'getting shit done.'" We walked over to Lake Miriam and joined the other Adamahniks.

The shit that needed getting done that week mostly amounted to preparation for Sukkot. There were upward of two hundred guests expected by Wednesday, and the Adamah crew, all fifteen of them, needed to hustle. Rain was expected during the festival, which meant lots of wet meals in the sukkah, the makeshift tent in which we would eat that week. But everyone was taking the bad weather report in stride, and the mood was light and full of good-humored banter. Shamu made a few announcements, then Aitan, the head goatherd, registered a small complaint: "It seems that tools are wandering off. They need to wander back home. The hammer likes his home in the tool shed. Please help him get back there." A large man with a black bushy beard and sun-darkened cheeks, Aitan looked like he'd just returned from summering with the goats on some high mountain pasture.

One of the Adamahniks asked about the terrorists.

"The terrorists are gone," Aitan said. Everyone cheered.

The terrorists, it turned out, were a pair of boy goats named for their ornery ways. They'd been turned into goat meat. *I'd rather eat a terrorist than a scapegoat,* I thought.

Sam had mentioned *shmita,* the enigmatic Year of Release. I wanted to learn more about this ancient Jewish agricultural law. It seemed to offer a pattern that might transform the way we grow our food. Later that week I met Nati Passow, the founder of the Jewish Farm School, who explained it to me. Sporting long dreadlocks and a wool cap, Nati is one of the young leaders of the Jewish agricultural renaissance.

"There's a profound connection between our agricultural health and our spiritual health," he said. Israel was utterly dependent on God to provide rain. They didn't have irrigation like Egypt, so farming in Israel was always tenuous. Throughout the Torah God tells the Israelites over and over, "Follow my laws and do good and you'll have rain and your harvest will be plentiful, but if you don't follow my laws then you won't have those things." Nati interprets the admonition to mean that it's not that God would punish them if they disobeyed, it's that God would allow them to experience the repercussions of their actions, a pattern we are seeing today. "We're messing with natural cycles in a very serious way; God is not punishing us for that, we're simply seeing the consequences of our own actions in our poisoned soil and water, our warming climate."

One of Nati's teaching points is the idea that Judaism is an indigenous religion; it's connected to a very specific piece of land. "So many of our rituals and prayers are focused on the land of Israel. Despite being exiled from our land, we've somehow been able to retain our land consciousness for two thousand years without actually being there. I don't know of any other indigenous culture that's been able to do that. When other cultures have been separated from their land, they've disappeared."

Until I met Nati, I'd never met anyone who spoke excitedly about the book of Leviticus. He gets especially fired up about the Torah's agricultural laws. Like the command to leave a corner of your field for the hungry, or to donate a tenth of what you grow to the poor. These laws are rooted in justice and "are designed to remind us that food really doesn't belong to us." They are also a series of checks that prevent us from becoming solely focused on production and consumption. One of those checks is the Sabbath day. Here at Adamah, the goats are milked, but the milk is given away or fed back to the animals. All work stops. People rest. Animals rest. The land rests.

The other check is the Sabbath year, *shmita*. The *shmita* was one thing that caught Sam Plotkin's attention during his studies at the Jewish Farm School, and as Nati Passow described it to me I found this to be one of the most powerful ideas I had ever heard. The first reference to *shmita* in Torah is in the book of Exodus: *For six years you shall sow your land and gather in its yield; but the seventh year you shall let it rest and lie fallow; so that the poor of your people may eat; and what they leave the wild animals may eat. You shall do the same with your vineyard, and with your olive orchard.*

Of special import, Nati said, is the phrase *so that.* At first it's counterintuitive that a cessation of farming for a whole year would result in the poor being fed, but the important part is not stopping to farm; it's releasing your ownership. Your field is not really yours in any ultimate sense. You are its caretaker, not its owner. And when every seventh year you release the claim you thought you had on your field, you can't help but remember just whose land it really is. *The earth is the Lord's, and the fullness thereof,* wrote the Psalmist.

During the Year of Release no planting is allowed, nor is food to be sold. All gates are to be left open so that the poor and the wild animals can freely harvest the field's fruit or grain. All debts must be forgiven. And every fiftieth year, after seven cycles of *shmita*, Jews are commanded to observe *yovel,* the Year of Jubilee. In that year something nearly inconceivable happens: all land that had been sold in the preceding forty-nine years must revert to its original owner.

It's questionable how much Jews in ancient Israel observed *shmita,* much less *yovel*. These laws are only legally binding for Jews today in the state of Israel, and even there most Jewish farmers sell their land for the year to get around the rigors of *shmita* observance. But Nati and Nigel are less interested in historical precedents or letter-of-the-law observance than they are in the spirit of the law. They see in the idea of *shmita* the power to change our destructive agricultural practices and recover the link between organic agriculture and social justice. These laws were intended not only to give the land a rest, but as a way of preventing disparities of wealth from spiraling out of control. There was an ancient recognition that healthy societies are inextricably dependent upon healthy ecosystems; to seek the health of both people and land we must also seek justice for the most needy among us. These laws set clearly defined limits. They recognized that the health of land and people could not be left to invisible hands or the whims of rulers or the benevolence of the wealthy. "*Shmita* is not communism or socialism," Nati said. "It's not saying everybody is equal all the time. These laws recognize certain human tendencies for competition to play out, but they keep those tendencies in check. If we don't have self-imposed limits, we know what happens: civil wars, dictatorships, ruined ecosystems. These laws are in place to prevent that."

Several years ago Nigel and Nati started a website called "The *Shmita* Project." The next *shmita* will begin on Rosh Hashanah in September 2014, and the project's goal is not to call for *shmita*'s strict observance, but rather to use the idea as a springboard for talking about agricultural reform and to help people learn to observe ecological limits in the way they eat.

As Nati looked ahead to September 2014, he described ways they were already preparing at the nearby Eden Village Farm. For starters, they were planting lots of perennials—fruit and nut trees, berry bushes—things they won't have to replant but can still be harvested. During the summer leading up to *shmita* they will focus on preserving the harvest: pickles, sauerkraut, jam, tomatoes. He's not sure if they can survive on just perennials and preserves, so they may still plant a few crops, and they will inevitably eat out some, too. Still, the *shmita* vision is larger than one's ability to observe all its nuances. "We're excited about leaving our gates open. We spend so much mental energy keeping out groundhogs, and so we're just going to say to them 'welcome.' Whatever happens, happens." One of *shmita*'s requirements is that you cannot sell food, and selling food to students is part of how the Jewish Farm School earns its keep. So to prepare for that they are experimenting with a self-imposed tax each year, a kind of *shmita* fund, which will allow them to give food away during the Year of Release.

"It will be a year of nonattachment, a year of letting things go," Nati said. "What would it look like if every seven years the richest and poorest in your society sat at the same table and had access to the same resources—what would that do in the other six years?"

"Take Monopoly," he said. "The game ends when one person gets all the property and wealth. But in real life that person is not a winner. They've just destroyed their community. One of the goals of Judaism is to create a society that can keep on going. It's sustainability on all levels. The Sabbath day, the Sabbath year, and the Jubilee—God gave us those laws to make sure that happens."

After lunch that first day I wandered over to the main lodge next to the lake where four Adamahniks—Simone, Erika, Jordan, and Chavi—were building a giant sukkah. There were many sukkahs dotting the grounds of Isabella Freedman, but judging from its size this was the mothership. On Wednesday night, the beginning of Sukkot, it would hold up to 150 guests.

Erika was decorating the sukkah's canvas walls. She hung vines of Virginia creeper woven into Hebrew letters on the wall to the left of the main entrance. *Bruchim Ha'Baim,* it read, Blessed Are All Who Enter. On the right wall she had hung a Star of David woven from garlic stalks and celosia. Normally they also decorate with pumpkins, gourds, and other fall crops, but because of Hurricane Irene there was none this year. Inside the sukkah I met Danny Raphael, a British rapper who was now a rabbinical student in the Bronx. He was standing on a ladder adjusting the *schach,* the flat thatched roof. To be a kosher sukkah, the *schach* must be made with organic material, like branches or twigs. In Israel the *schach* was traditionally made with palm fronds, but here Danny was using *Phragmites australis,* a common reed harvested from a marsh below Lake Miriam.

The sukkah itself was a replica of the kind of tents the Israelites used during their forty-year sojourn in the Sinai desert after their exodus from Egypt. The huts also called to mind the makeshift shelters Israelite farmers used out in the fields during the fall harvest. For this reason Sukkot (which is the plural of sukkah) is also known as the Feast of Booths. During the seven days of the festival, Jews are expected to eat all their meals in these tents and even sleep in them. But that was only one layer of Sukkot. Indeed, there would be ongoing classes during the festival teasing out all the myriad facets of this festival. As with other Jewish holidays, the layers of meaning quickly accrue.

Timed when both the moon and sun are at the zenith of their cycles, Sukkot marks a period of completion and redemption in the Jewish year. The moon is full. The sun has ripened summer crops to their fullness. Every agrarian society has its harvest festivals, and ancient Israel was no exception. Three times a year during Pesach (Passover), Shavuot (Pentecost), and Sukkot, Israelite farmers would have traveled from the hinterlands to Jerusalem, bringing their grain offerings to the temple. But Sukkot in ancient Israel was not simply a celebration of the fall harvest. Israel's pagan neighbors held harvest festivals with orgies that paid homage to their fertility gods. But for the people of Israel the fall harvest was not about sex or nature worship. As Heschel writes in *The Sabbath,* "To Israel the unique events of historic time were spiritually more significant than the repetitive processes in the cycle of nature. . . . While the deities of other peoples were associated with places or things, the God of Israel was the God of events: the Redeemer from slavery, the Revealer of the Torah."

Sukkot marks both the forty years of desert wandering, reminding Jews of their utter dependence on God for their daily bread, as well as a fall harvest. According to Rabbi Jill Hammer, a teacher at Isabella Freedman that week, Sukkot was the pinnacle of the holiday season in ancient Israel. It was a time of joy, of bounty, of bringing the best of one's harvest as an offering to the Lord. What was my offering to be? What was the fruit of this year's harvest from my visits to Mepkin Abbey, the Lord's Acre, and Tierra Nueva? From my journey into memory?

The origin of Sukkot is found in the Torah. It was during the feast of Sukkot when King Solomon chose to dedicate his famous temple in Jerusalem. Though the account in the book of Kings doesn't say why, Rabbi Arthur Waskow writes in *Seasons of Our Joy,* "Perhaps [Solomon] saw some analogy between the fragile sukkah—open to sky, to wind, to wanderers—and the house that he knew could not contain the God of earth and heaven." Solomon would have been following the commands in Exodus and Leviticus, when God told Israel to observe "the Feast of Ingathering," yet another name for Sukkot. The most detailed command comes from this passage in Deuteronomy 16:

> *After the ingathering from your threshing floor and your vat, you shall hold the Feast of Huts for seven days. You shall rejoice in your festival, with your son and daughter, your male and female slave, the Levite, the stranger, the orphan, and the widow in your communities . . . for the Lord your God will bless you in all your income and all your handiwork, and you shall be fully joyful.*

That last part was intriguing. Sukkot is the one festival in the year in which Jews are commanded to be joyful. Being here at Isabella Freedman, Danny said, adjusting the *schach* above his head, it wasn't hard to be joyful. "For me the agrarian setting is key. I can't get this in the city. We eat in the sukkah. We sleep in it. The sukkah helps us bring a feeling of joy and holiness back to our ordinary days."

I was also drawn to Deuteronomy's insistence that the sukkah club isn't exclusively Jewish; everybody gets invited under the big tent. Isabella Freedman places special emphasis on welcoming not just all streams of Judaism—their motto is "All Streams! One Source!"—but also the *ger,* the stranger like me. Already I was experiencing such welcome. Danny was one of several people that week who assumed the role of host, coaching me through the *siddur* (prayer book) during davening, inviting me to his table during the grand Sukkot feasts, answering my questions.

"Give me a hand with those?" Danny pointed toward a pile of *Phragmites* in the corner. I handed reeds up the ladder while he chatted amiably about his rabbinical studies, the joy he felt during Sukkot, and his rap music. Later that night over at the Red Yurt, he taught the Adamahniks how to write their own Jewish rap song.

Despite Danny's warmth, it was hard to forget my sense of being a stranger. I was in Connecticut but felt like an exile in my own land. Once inside the *eruv* separating Isabella Freedman from the outside world, I had entered another country. A foreign land full of wonderful people, but foreign nonetheless. Standing under the sukkah talking with a Jew sporting a British accent who lived in New York and sang music first invented by African Americans, I began to sense the dislocation of exile and blended identities that, for Jews, is simply part of life. Inside the *eruv* I was separated from everything I knew. The questions *who am I? where is home? where am I going?* suddenly became urgent. And yet my feelings of dislocation were also presenting themselves as a new source of spiritual strength, embodied in the transitory nature of the sukkah itself. This all could pass, will pass, and I cannot cling to any of it. The sukkah was also a healthy reminder to trust in God as my source of shelter, food, and life.

Late that afternoon I grabbed Heschel's *The Sabbath* and walked out on the dock of Lake Miriam. I looked across the water to the Red Yurt where I davened earlier that morning. The oblique rays of the setting sun warmed my bones and I opened Heschel's pages.

"The faith of the Jew," Heschel began, "is not a way out of this world, but a way of being within and above this world; not to reject but to surpass civilization. The Sabbath is the day on which we learn the art of surpassing civilization." Civilization was not something to be abandoned or reformed or protested against. No, Heschel said, you must be in this world, but also above it. You must transcend it. One of the many ways Heschel chose to surpass civilization was to march in Selma alongside Martin Luther King Jr. Yet it seemed that Jews were surpassing civilization every week in their practice of Sabbath. I was eager to celebrate my first Shabbat that Friday night, which seemed like a long way off.

Soon the sun dipped behind the mountains to the west, and late afternoon shadows slid across the dock, chilling my arms. Time for supper. I walked over to the lodge and hopped on a bike that one of the Adamahniks had loaned me, and rode a mile or so down to Beit Adamah. Literally "House of Soil," Beit Adamah was a fitting name for this abode of young farmers. That night three of those young farmers had cooked up a feast from the land's bounty: sautéed kale, challah, couscous with fresh carrots, vegetarian lasagna, and some mysterious fried balls that looked like falafel. Most of the Adamahniks present that night were girls, and the double entendres were running high. "Could you pass the balls?" one girl asked. "Oh, I'm so pleased you like my balls," another replied. Giggles. I sat down next to Chavi, whom I'd met earlier that afternoon at the sukkah. She reminded me of my younger sister: open, friendly, earnest. Chavi grew up in a strict Orthodox home in upstate New York. She asked if I had any questions about Judaism she could answer, and I asked her to translate some of the new words I'd learned that day: *daven,* pray; *shul,* synagogue. I told her how much I liked the different Hebrew names for God: YHWH ("I Am That I Am"); Adonai ("Lord"); Shekhinah (the feminine presence of God); Hashem ("The Name"). Then I asked about a strange sight I'd seen earlier on the lake dock, a curtain hanging suspended from a horizontal pole. "That's for the *mikvah,*" she said. "It's a ritual bath." Though men sometimes participate in a *mikvah* before Shabbat or a big holiday or other significant events, traditionally a *mikvah* is the ritual bath a woman takes after her period. It's the culmination of a long process of purification, Chavi explained, during which she cannot lie with her husband. The *mikvah* usually happens about the time a woman would be ovulating, she continued, "and after a long hiatus, her desire for her husband will be very strong." Chavi explained all this in a slightly detached sociological tone, as if there were nothing odd about a married man and a single young woman discussing such things. Here at the House of Soil, menstrual cycles and *mikvahs* and the procreative acts that followed were perfectly legitimate topics for dinnertime conversation. It all came back to fertility.

Stanley Hauerwas, one of my teachers at divinity school, liked to quote a Jewish theologian friend who said, "Any religion that doesn't tell you what to do with your pots 'n' pans and your genitals just isn't worth a damn."

Amen. Please pass the balls.

13 Tishri

On the morning of my second day I stopped to check on Sam's progress at the Center for Cultural Proliferation. When I walked in Sam was shoveling big handfuls of chopped garlic into one of the blue barrels half full of cabbage. I knew kimchi to be a delicate balance between garlic, cabbage, carrots, cayenne peppers, daikon radishes, onions, and salt, so I asked Sam how he got his proportions right. "Trade secret, my man. It's ar*tis*anal. Nice hat."

Since seeing him yesterday I'd bought a new cap in the gift shop, azure blue with the Hebrew letter aleph on the front. I asked Sam about the significance of the aleph. "I don't know, some kinda mystical shit. You hungry?" Sam got out jars of dilly beans and spicy lemon pickles, and we had another mid-morning snack.

After chopping cabbage with Sam, I stopped by one of the cabins for a quick shower, my first in three days, and put on clean clothes. Then, after a tasty lunch in the dining hall—fresh mesclun mix, eggplant parmesan, and challah—I ducked in the men's room for a quick pee, where I found myself side by side with Danny the Rabbinical Rapper. We made small talk as men do who are trying to pretend they aren't inches apart while performing an intimate bodily function, and then I remembered something a teacher in seminary once told me.

"Isn't there a blessing for going to the bathroom?" I asked in mid-stream ("All Streams! One Source!").

"Yeah," Danny said. "It's called the *asher yatzar*. It's attributed to Abayei, a fourth-century Babylonian rabbi."

"Do you say it?"

"Sure. All observant Jews say it. It's sort of like thanking God that everything is working properly down there. In English it could be translated like this: *Blessed is the One who has formed man in wisdom and created in him many orifices and many cavities. It is obvious and known before Your throne of glory that if one of them were to be ruptured or one of them blocked, it would be impossible for a man to survive and stand before You. Blessed are You that heals all flesh and does wonders.*"

"That's beautiful," I said.

I vowed on the spot to start praying it every time I urinated or voided my bowels. We had no such prayer in Christianity. The gnostic heresy had a strong hold on the Christian mind, the idea that we must somehow escape our bodies to achieve transcendence, or that our bodies will be "left behind" while our souls fly off to some distant heaven, a distinctly un-biblical belief by any measure, but like all heresies the body/soul dualism dies hard. In addition to dualistic temptations we Christians were often guilty of spiritual greediness. We were always busy asking God for big important stuff. Why bother with such a trifling thing as a properly functioning set of bowels? But what Abayei and all observant Jews since have wisely understood is that the workings of one's body are not trifling matters. My own father twice underwent back surgery. For months afterward he had to thread a catheter up his urethra just to urinate. Healthy plumbing can't be taken for granted. Nigel Savage put it this way: "Jewish tradition is interested in every aspect of my behavior. I don't mean to denigrate Christianity, but it's not quite as simple as asking What Would Jesus Do?"

Perhaps it was more like asking What Would Judaism Do?

Halakah, the word for Jewish law, is a verb that means "to walk." Judaism is a way, a path to follow, one carefully designed to lead you closer to God. In Christianity's early days, before it mistakenly distanced itself from Judaism, the faith was known by its adherents as "the way." Like many mortals before me who had the same daily problems, I wanted to follow on the path that led to God. Perhaps blessings like this one could help me on the journey.

In Judaism, washing your hands before a meal or performing your morning ablutions weren't just annoying bodily processes to rush through and be done with, as if those things were somehow separate from one's spirituality. A few simple words, and the act of taking a piss could suddenly become elevated into a song of praise.

Our nethers in good working order, Danny and I zipped up, washed our hands, and bid farewell. Setting off to find Shamu, with whom I had a meeting, I looked over my shoulder. Danny had paused just outside the bathroom door. His head was bowed and his lips were already forming the consonants and vowels of the holy tongue. He was offering praise to the Maker, giving thanks that all his orifices and cavities were blessedly free of obstruction. Amen.

I found Shamu on the lower field prepping future raspberry beds. Later he wanted to put in gooseberries and currants. He was trying to plant a lot more perennials up here on the upland field, which would be more resistant to the increasing floods and weather fluctuations expected with climate change. Shamu was especially worried about the Sadeh, their main field, which had flooded during Hurricane Irene. With the risk of future floods they could no longer depend on it. The surrounding neighbors—too wealthy to be bothered—wouldn't lease their fields. I could feel the weight of Shamu's dilemma. There were no easy answers, and the responsibility was his to bear. I knew the feeling.

Later that week I was chatting with an Adamah alumnus, who confirmed what I already suspected about Shamu. "He's really the wise man who holds this place together. This is his habitat. The way he teaches is technically savvy using real science, but all the time he infuses his teaching with a really potent mystery and reverence. And those things aren't in conflict. You can study the biological structure of a leaf and still feel complete surrender to the Divine."

As Shamu and I headed back to the dining hall in the big biodiesel farm truck, he looked in the rearview mirror and said, "Oh no."

"What?"

"Look behind us." Sauntering down the road was a very large black goat named Solomon, like the king, who did have a regal air about him as he pranced toward us across the blacktop. He also had a funky air—the creature stank. Solomon had departed the Boyz Town temple and was looking for action—grain, tender young leaves, a tender young doe in heat—and he'd brought his royal entourage, ten little boy goats, in tow. Almost half of Boyz Town had broken free. Suddenly we were surrounded by stinky male goats, and for the next twenty minutes Shamu and I engaged in what can only be called "goat roping." I manned the gate while Shamu rode herd and rounded everybody up. Solomon wouldn't stay inside the gate. This was one tough old goat. Facing him sideways, and pushing my chest against Solomon's left flank, I gave his royal ass a shove and slammed the gate. My clean clothes now reeked with Solomon's funk. I followed Shamu back to the truck, reminded once again why I so disliked farm animals. I needed a *mikvah*.

Goats, I learned later from Shamu, were a significant part of Israel's history. Shamu told me how the word "flocks" in the Bible was a mistranslation. In English, "flock" designates sheep, but the word in Hebrew is *tzon,* referring to a mixed herd of sheep and goats. It's an important distinction, because goats are very different from sheep. Sheep have a herd mentality, whereas goats are individuals. They are headstrong, even cantankerous, and they don't respect boundaries. They jump fences. They push back. Shamu sees the Jewish community as a *tzon,* a mixed flock. Some are passive followers, some are headstrong leaders, and like goats, the Hebrews have always been boundary crossers. Abraham was the first *ivri,* the first border crosser, leaving not only his homeland but leaving the idea of a pagan world and its multiple gods and clinging fast to the One God. A big crossing. After Abraham's descendants escaped from Egypt and crossed the Red Sea they were called *ivrim,* which means "those who have crossed over." But the boundary crossing had another sense, Shamu said. In a fit of divine frustration while speaking to Moses, God had called the Israelites "a stiff-necked people." They pushed back against God. I remembered a line from Jewish poet Richard Chess's *Third Temple,* where he describes himself as a "descendant of a fickle, querulous, ragtag crew from Sinai."

It was almost a cliché in my early days of Sunday school, how the Israelites were headstrong and stubborn. We Christians were taught to be meek, like sheep. But my own stubborn nature inwardly rebelled. I learned early on that much of what Christians call "meek" was merely a pious smoke screen to cover their own passive-aggressive behavior. I admire stubbornness. It shows that a person is forthright, engaged, has deep convictions.

The Israelites *struggled* with their God. Jacob even wrestled with God and won a temporary victory, though he limped away from the match with an injured hip. Thereafter God called Jacob *Yisrael*—the

God wrestler—and Jacob's descendants have continued the struggle. It's clearly been a lovers' quarrel. I admired such spiritual tenacity. Thinking back to the impassioned davening of the previous morning, I wished I could pray with such abandon.

14 Tishri

On the afternoon of my third day, only two hours before the closing ceremony that would move us from work time to holy time, I stopped by the Center for Cultural Proliferation where I found Sam Plotkin frenziedly putting down the last batch of kimchi. Along with Sam, three others scurried around the small room, washing scallions, chopping garlic, grating ginger. Adam, the crew boss, was back. All week Adam had been on vacation, and the mood at the center had been chill. Adam's absence meant that Sam could hone his fermenting skills at a more leisurely pace, one more conducive to artisanal production. But this morning Adam was back, and shit needed to get done, which meant that Sam needed to start busting his ass. Adam approached lacto-fermentation with all the gravitas of a trained chef, which he was, his diploma was there on the wall to prove it, and given his short stature and military demeanor, I began to think of Adam as a kimchi drill sergeant. When I arrived to help out, the tension in the air was palpable.

For starters, Adam said, the barrel should not already have garlic in it. When Sam was chopping garlic on Monday and Tuesday, he'd just shoveled it right into the barrel along with the cabbage, ditto when he chopped the onions, and Adam was worried that he'd potentially flubbed the whole batch. "You don't mix the garlic until the *end,* dude." Sam looked concerned. "Sorry, man." On top of that they had to quit by 3 P.M. The next day was

Sukkot and the next was Shabbat, which meant no work until next Monday, which meant they had two hours to make a hundred gallons of kimchi.

All was forgiven now, and soon the tension was replaced by a shared feeling of solidarity. There was a clear goal—make kimchi—and we settled into an easy groove. I helped Sam scoop out the garlic and onions, which we transferred to a smaller container. We then scooped out all the cabbage from the fifty-five-gallon barrel, our torsos disappearing inside the barrel to get to the bottom. Starting again from scratch, Adam instructed us in layering: first Napa cabbage, then scallions, then daikon radishes, a few cups of sea salt, then the garlic-ginger-cayenne combo. Repeat. Adam added the salt, which seemed like a lot, but I didn't question his expertise.

Adam needed a masher so I volunteered. After each layer, I pounded the kimchi mix with a three-foot-long wooden mallet. After all the sitting I'd done the past few days it felt good to pound vegetables. When I pulled the mallet out after each strike, it made a wet, sucking sound. Pounding cabbage felt visceral, ancient, necessary. I have always had deep peasant yearnings. Sometimes I imagined myself as Tolstoy's Levin, swinging a scythe on my vast estate, mowing through the morning until the sun was directly overhead. I would stop for black bread, *kvass,* maybe a short nap, then back to the fields to mow that upland meadow before sunset . . . But now, with the rain coming down outside, I was happy to be a cabbage-pounding peasant in the Center for Cultural Proliferation. I would have made a good kraut masher back in the *shtetl.*

Late that afternoon I planned to ride with farm manager Janna Berger down to the flooded Sadeh. Before that, however, the Adamahniks held a ceremony taking us from Work Time into

Sukkot Time. We gathered at three near the cob oven, and Janna gave everyone a handful of hard winter wheat. Each of us symbolically sowed the seeds in rows of newly turned soil, a way of linking Sukkot to Shavuot, the feast of Pentecost next June when the wheat would be harvested. As a light rain started, we recited the *shehecheyanu,* the prayer said upon reaching an auspicious moment, and Shamu gave a short *drash* (interpretive teaching). This is the time in Israel, he said, when Jewish farmers would have brought their grain offering to the temple for Sukkot, an offering of gratitude to the Lord. It's also a time to bring our own offerings and to give thanks for our year's bounty. Shamu continued, "Normally, I'm grateful for all the winter squash and kale and broccoli coming out of the Sadeh, but this year we lost all that, which makes me realize just how grateful I am for this crop of Adamahniks—you guys."

During our conversation in the truck several days before, I had asked Shamu what revived him spiritually. "Gratitude and awe," he said. The way he fostered those feelings, and taught the Adamahniks to foster them, was to make time for rituals in his everyday life. "In Judaism we have a lot of these daily reminders, whether it's blessings over meals or the mezuzah on the door post. The point is to pause. Pay attention. Get out of your head for a moment. Give thanks."

The drizzle was turning into heavier drops. After everyone sowed their wheat we gathered in a half circle around the tilled patch of ground and sang a song in Hebrew. It was a short ceremony, nothing grand, but powerful in its simplicity. An invocation, a priestly gesture, a way to mark this liminal moment and recognize our dependence on God. "Holiness in space, in nature, was known in other religions," wrote Heschel in *The Sabbath*. "New in the teaching of Judaism was that the idea of holiness was gradually shifted from space to time, from the realm of nature to the realm of history, from things to events. The physical world became divested of any inherent sanctity. To be sacred, a thing had to be consecrated by a conscious act of man. The quality of holiness is not in the grain of matter. It is a preciousness bestowed upon things by an act of consecration and persisting in relation to God." But what of God creating the world in Genesis and calling it "very good"? What about Blake's famous dictum, "Everything that lives is Holy"? My friend Norman Wirzba, an agrarian theologian, says that "creation is holy because it is God's love made fragrant, delectable, visible. Our problem is that we are too blind to sense it, and thus fail to offer it to God and others as the only appropriate response." Those kernels of wheat *were* inherently holy, simply because they were created by God; our role was to bear witness to their holiness by offering them back. Our act that afternoon in the rain was to raise up to God the potential of life bound up in those tiny grains of wheat. They had been waiting for our priestly act, which meant that we had a more exalted role in creation than we'd like to think. God gave us dominion over the earth not to rule over things, but to lift them up. To hallow them with the work of our hands.

On Friday, August 26, 2011, the day before Hurricane Irene arrived, the Sadeh was at its peak of summer bounty. There were so many different kinds of vegetables that when Janna took me on a tour of the field she had to list them in families. She named them lovingly, as if they *were* family: *alliums, brassicas, chenopods, cucurbits, solanaceae, umbellifers.*

They had begun planting in April, and though a few crops had been harvested, most were still in the field. These vegetables would supply Adamah's customers: CSA members, the pickle business, and the people gathered this year for Sukkot. Those four acres normally produced 30 percent of their yearly income.

As we sat in the black Ford pickup looking out over the Sadeh, I imagined what a glorious field it had been that day in August. Janna said, "It was a farm in full swing."

On Saturday, August 27, Hurricane Irene arrived. The Hollenbeck River surrounds the Sadeh on three sides like a giant horseshoe, and when the rains came, the river began to rise. On Friday, knowing what was coming, Janna harvested onions, wishing as she did that the rest of the crops could just get up and walk to safety.

When she arrived on the morning of Monday, August 29, the Sadeh was under four feet of water.

"Actually, it was kind of beautiful. I mean, it was hard to look at—I was crying—but I was also just awed by the beauty. It was thrilling. It was so surreal. This field in which I'd been so comfortable, where I'd done so many hours of planning and thinking and working, just seeing it totally overtaken by water . . . it was very humbling."

Janna grew quiet, and we both looked out across the desolate, flat expanse that was ringed on three sides by a row of trees. After a time she said, "There's always this weird optimism you have in extreme circumstances like this. Maybe the water will go down and everything will be okay and it will dry out. But that's not really what happened at all."

What did happen is that fish swam among the carrot tops, crawdads scuttled under kale, and after a few days the Sadeh was no longer a field but a pond. Shamu and Jaime and their kids brought down their canoe and they took turns paddling.

Ten days later Hurricane Lee brought more water, bringing the total up to ten inches. When the waters receded, most of the crops had died and rotted, or were swept away like much of the field's topsoil, which the river replaced with sand. Losing topsoil was the worst. It would take them many years of diligent cover-cropping to restore the lost fertility. Janna had found their crop of winter squash and pumpkins downstream from the Sadeh in a copse of woods, and she and the Adamahniks had harvested them. I imagined them there like little people come to gather groundfall apples from the land of giants.

Despite the loss of a whole season and the hard work of finding a new field or repairing the old one, Janna kept perspective. "There are always farmers who win or lose on any given year, and meanwhile most of the population is moving along without any idea, so this flood has really brought home to me the fragility of farming. In organic agriculture we say we're not lords over the land. The flood showed me how I had approached the land with too much control. People have farmed floodplains forever. Maybe we just need to learn how to be more resilient."

We got out of the farm truck and walked over to harvest the few crops that made it through the floods. I sensed Janna needed some space, so I left her to pick flowers on her own for the table that night while I went to harvest cabbage. There were a few heads that weren't rotten, and since I didn't have a harvest knife I twisted them off, a violent act that in that moment was oddly satisfying. Out in the middle of the field, standing tall in defiance of two hurricanes, stood a lone row of leeks. I grabbed a plastic tub from the pickup bed and filled it.

On the drive back Janna described the Sadeh as "a vulnerable space." I now understood what she meant. It was vulnerable because it was a marginal space, an ecotone residing between land and water. It could be claimed by either, and without warning. Janna reflected on how this wasn't just a personal tragedy; 180 Adamahniks have farmed that field. Thousands of people over the years have eaten from it.

As I thought about the flooding of the Sadeh, it was hard not to think about Ecclesiastes. Known to Jews as Kohelet, Ecclesiastes is recited aloud on Shabbat during the week of Sukkot, the one book in the Bible that almost gleefully describes the futility of all human striving. We are not in control, Kohelet reminds us. Sukkot may be called "The Season of Our Joy," but the rabbis were wise to cast a textual shadow across the merrymaking. Joy becomes all the sweeter when you remember that it's fleeting.

Kohelet, the eponymous author of the book whose name means Teacher, is famous for leveling human vanity, but "vanity," biblical scholar Ellen Davis said, is actually mistranslated. A better translation of *hevel* would be mist, vapor, breath. All is not vanity; rather, all is ephemeral, passing before our eyes like breath. Even the ground we walk on or the topsoil that feeds us cannot be relied upon in any ultimate sense. This is not cause for despair, however, for as Kohelet reminds us to relax our grip, he points us back to the Author of life, often in quite lyrical terms. Toward the end of the book, after deflating our very human strivings, the Teacher says, *Just as you do not know how the breath comes to the bones in the mother's womb, so you do not know the work of God, who makes everything.* "Kohelet teaches, more concretely than any other biblical book, about humility," Davis says in *Proverbs, Ecclesiastes, and the Song of Songs.* "And the core of his teaching is this: life can never be mastered or shaped in conformity with our desire."

Kohelet uses the word *adam* (humankind) fifty times, which makes me think that despite his cranky insistence on the fleeting nature of our lives, Kohelet shows profound concern for human life. Davis continues, "The *hevel*-life we all share is ephemeral but not empty of meaning." Kohelet's is no disembodied, otherworldly faith. The life he describes is lived "under the sun" in all its joy and troubles. Kohelet depicts our lives in realistic, even seemingly fatalistic, terms. *What do people gain from all the toil at which they toil under the sun? A generation goes, and a generation comes, but the earth remains forever.* But Kohelet's realism is not fatalism. It is tempered by a God he can't quite disavow, a God who *has made everything beautiful for its time.*

The rituals and prayers and stories I heard that week were all ways of marking the beauty of each act, each person, each *davar* (word) by situating it in its God-given time. Each prayer was a small stone one built into a cathedral of time. Heschel: "The higher goal of spiritual living, is not to amass a wealth of information, but to face sacred moments." Such moments, if faced over a lifetime, were small investments against despair, so that when you lost your crops or your topsoil or a loved one, for we all lose something important to us eventually, then you would have enough beauty stored up to keep you buoyed. You would have built a house sturdy with hope, and from there you could emerge and begin the necessary work of repair. God has made everything beautiful for its time, even the act of rebuilding from calamity. But it takes training through prayer to see it.

One of the effects of climate change in the northeastern United States, scientists predict, will be an increase in the intensity and frequency of storms like Irene, Lee, and Sandy. On Shabbat that week, Janna gave a talk for the Sukkot visitors about the events she described to me that afternoon in the Sadeh. The title of her talk was a summary of the growing season, but it struck me as a prescription for life in the twenty-first century, at least in this part of the world: "Farming Humbly Through Floods and Feasts."

On Wednesday night, the start of Sukkot, everyone gathered to find a seat for dinner in the mothership sukkah. On my right sat Sarah Chandler, Adamah's associate director; to my left was Garth Silberstein, a hirsute Adamahnik from California. The expected rain began earlier that afternoon, but just before dinner it let up and the kitchen staff hurriedly dried tables and chairs, set out white tablecloths and candles, and welcomed us into the sukkah. I looked around at all the beautiful faces smiling in the candlelight. As the wine was poured we prayed the *shehecheyanu,* to mark this auspicious moment. The long shadows on the tent's canvas walls were like benevolent ancestors who had arrived to wish us well. Someone said *ķiddush,* the blessing of the wine, recited to sanctify time. We each raised a glass.

I found myself unexpectedly emotional. Waskow described the feeling: "We walk into the sukkah—the fragile field hut, open to the light of moon and stars, that our forebears lived in while they gathered in the grain . . . and we feel the joy that for a moment life is so safe, the world so loving, that we can live in these open-ended huts without fear."

Seeing all the laughing faces lit up by candlelight, lifting my wineglass beside theirs—*l'chaim!*—I felt myself among long-lost cousins whom I'd never met, but who welcomed me like one of their own. It was a glorious moment. But it was also a moment full of melancholy. I was still a stranger in a strange land. Here amidst all the familial cheer and elbow-rubbing jostle of a big feast I suddenly missed my wife and sons, missed them with an intensity and longing that until then I'd been too busy to notice. But the pain went deeper still. It was hard not to feel the weltschmerz of history, especially the pain of Jewish history, standing just beyond the sukkah's warm glow. Inside the sukkah, life was so safe, the world so loving, that all could gather without fear. And yet, it had not always been so. In a post-Shoah world, Waskow's words seemed laden with pathos. Was that not the overriding desire of every person and tribe, to live in their huts without fear? To worship God unhindered? To be joyful? This was the promise of the prophet Micah, who spoke of a time when all would be able to sit under their own vines and fig trees, "and no one shall make them afraid." I thought of other exiles in distant lands like my friend José in Chiapas, who spent years of his life living in a shelter not unlike this open-ended sukkah yet unable to live without fear of paramilitary violence; or the exiles in my own land like Bones, who at that moment was sitting alone in a prison cell three thousand miles to the west, or my friend Pharaoh, whether dead or alive I knew not; and what of those who suffered the exile of mistrust and anger whose pain made them hurt others, and kept them from fully being themselves? We were all exiled from our true home, some of us just more visibly than others.

But this was the *z'man simchateinu,* the season of our joy, and sadness had no place here. I remembered the words of the prophet Amos, who foretold a time when sorrow would disappear and all could live in their huts without fear. *I will plant them upon their soil and they shall never again be plucked up out of the soil that I have given them, says the Lord your God.*

In his delightful book *The Jew in the Lotus,* Rodger Kamenetz recounts a Hasidic teaching, that before every human being walks a retinue of angels, announcing, "Make way for an image of the Holy One, Blessed be He." We are each created *btselem elohim*—in the image of God—all of us exiled from our Maker and longing for home. "How rarely," Kamenetz writes, "do we see in another human being's eyes an image of everything we hold most dear."

Sarah broke off a piece of challah and passed it to me to dip in a bowl of honey, symbolizing the sweetness of Sukkot. I did the same for Garth, sitting next to me, as he did for his neighbor, and on down the table. "People say this Jewish farming interest is a new trend," Sarah told me between bites of challah, "but actually it's an old trend. Once we were connected with the land and the flow of seasons. We're known as the People of the Book, but once we were also the People of the Land. Because of exile, and because Jews weren't allowed to own land in Europe, we grew disconnected from the land. Now we're rerooting ourselves, which makes our faith that much more powerful."

After dinner the festivities picked up. David Weisberg, Isabella Freedman's director, walked around the sukkah with a bottle of expensive Polish vodka, dispensing shots like a benevolent king doling out medicine to his loyal subjects. Like the others, I gratefully held up a glass to receive my grog. I had a long, intense discussion with a guy named Matisyahu. Not the famous Hasidic reggae beat-box singer Matisyahu, but a musician nonetheless. He had grown up the son of a Methodist preacher, then converted to Eastern Orthodox Christianity, then became a Sufi, and after marrying a Jewish woman had finally found his home as an Orthodox Jew. I wanted to hear more about his mystical journey, but suddenly he was called upon to sing. By the light of a hundred candles, Matisyahu and his wife stood and performed a lovely duet. Perhaps it was the Polish vodka or the feeling of suddenly wanting to be held by my own wife or my unfulfilled spiritual longings, but as they sang I felt a deep and painful ache. The song was one the couple had composed from the Song of Songs, perhaps the most mystical book in the Bible. I remember one of the lines: *You have ravished my heart, oh my sister, oh my bride. You have ravished my heart, with one glance of your eyes.*

On the way back to my little cabin at Kfar, the moon broke through the clouds, and as I walked the shore of Lake Miriam a lone kayaker paddled slowly between pools of moonlight. The moon has great significance in Jewish spirituality. In the days of the messiah, the moon will be as big and bright as the sun, ending the moon's cycle of waxing and waning. Just as the moon is renewed each month, so the Jewish people hope to be renewed. In the days of the messiah, the story goes, the moon will be bright as the sun, and Jews will see an end to cycles of spiritual and physical exile.

Just as the moon reflects the sun's light, I thought, so the messiah reflects the light of God.

The moon was partially obscured now as I entered the woods, but behind the clouds I knew it was almost full. Its light was bright enough that I didn't need a headlamp to find my way up the trail. I looked back across the lake. On the opposite shore I could see revelers who would sing and dance until the wee hours. The moonlight was soft and supple, bathing everything in a warm embrace. The woods and lake, sukkah and sukkah people—all were illumined by the gentle, reflected light, and it seemed to cover the whole world.

15 Tishri

Early Thursday morning I awoke distraught. It had rained all night and would continue raining the rest of the day. Though it was dawn, the wooded glade of Kfar was dark with downpour. I had been dreaming.

I stood in a crowd among the people of Israel. We were all gathered on a high place, waiting. I stood with them, though slightly apart. As I looked around I saw other Gentiles slowly making their way up the mountain. We had reached the end of days, but my chest was heavy. Something was wrong. I should have been rejoicing like the rest of the nations who were streaming to Jerusalem, drawn by the light of the Lord's glory shining from Mount Zion, but though I wanted to speak, I could not open my mouth. We were awaiting the messiah's arrival. Was he coming for the first or second time? I needed to tell the people Israel of my pain, to tell them that though we stood side by side, a great gulf separated us. How I longed for unity between Jews and Gentiles . . . but neither of us could change our expectations. It seemed that this messiah was an obstacle so great that even here at the end of days we would forever remain separated, and this thought made me mute with sorrow. Then I awoke. Tears ran hot and silent down my face. I lay there as if a great weight pressed me to the bed. But instead of drying my tears and shaking off the dream, I returned to it.

As sleep returned, I now saw that those gathered were one great mass, no longer the people Israel at the center and others on the periphery, but a mixed flock, a *tzon* of both Jew and Gentile. Standing before us was a figure dressed in white. It was not the messiah. We were still awaiting his arrival, but my earlier worries had been resolved. The person in white was one of the people from the numberless crowd. I recognized her as Elizabeth—my wife, lover, friend—and now she began to sing. She sang the words of Psalm 34, perhaps my favorite of all the songs she sings, and her voice then, as always, was beautiful, angelic. She sang the entire psalm. *Magnify the Lord with me,* she sang, and we all sang with her. Our voices grew in strength and number until we became a continuous field of song, a summer meadow in which you could roam, a spacious and holy field with wildflowers and gentle breezes where all of us, Jew and Gentile, magnified the Lord together. The last thought I had before I awoke was the certainty that the sun would never set on this grassy Sadeh of Song, that our one desire all along had been to arrive here at this field and magnify the Lord together, and that this song of songs would never end.

16 Tishri

"There is a great longing in the world," wrote Abraham Joshua Heschel in *The Sabbath.*

Heschel's own longing was for consummating his union with

God, a foretaste of which could be experienced on the Sabbath. "Judaism tries to foster the vision of life as a pilgrimage to the seventh day; the longing for the Sabbath all days of the week which is a form of longing for the eternal Sabbath all the days of our lives." Sabbath is not just a day of rest but a day of spiritual harmony, a window into the world to come, not an interlude in living, Heschel wrote, but living's fulfillment. "The idea that a seventh part of our lives may be experienced as paradise is a scandal to the pagans and a revelation to the Jews . . . eternal life does not grow away from us; it is planted within us, growing beyond us."

Although Shabbat would not begin until sundown, there was a palpable anticipation throughout the day of its, or rather "her," arrival. Jews personified Shabbat as a queen, and all afternoon people were preparing themselves to give her a royal welcome. They congregated in groups of twos and threes, engaging in friendly talk, singing, studying Torah. In the main lodge a young man began a sentence in English, "This summer when I was in Vilna . . ." and finished it in Yiddish. On a bench overlooking the lake, a girl sat with her legs thrown over her boyfriend's lap, reading to him from Martin Buber's *Tales of the Hasidim.* I saw Danny Raphael, who was on his way to the lake. A group of men were about to *mikvah,* he said. Did I want to join them? I declined, content to wander and watch.

There is a Kabbalistic belief, Nati told me, that the world is an upside-down tree. The roots are in heaven, and the branches and fruits are here on earth. Whenever we take from this earth, whether it's a pear or a sunflower, we should say a blessing. Our prayer sends the divine sparks of life back to their source, feeding the roots of the tree of life. If we don't give thanks, we block the cycle. For that reason, when Jews eat they often say, Now what are we going to do with this energy? Are we going to do good things in the world and keep the flow going? As I pondered this image of union between heaven and earth, between this world and the next, it seemed fitting. For Shabbat is that reunion reenacted every Friday night, and it was about to begin.

17 Tishri—Shabbat

After three days of rain, Shabbat dawned clear and windy, as if something new had blown over the mountains and down into our little valley. The Sabbath is not just a day; it is an aura, a spiritual force that infuses everything with the gentle and feminine light of *Shekhinah.* "The seventh day is like a palace in time with a kingdom for all," Heschel wrote. "It is not a date but an atmosphere . . . the Sabbath sends out its presence over the fields, into our homes, into our hearts. It is a moment of resurrection of the dormant spirit in our souls."

Maybe it was just my imagination, but this day did feel different from the rest. I had cherished the joyful celebrations of Sukkot, yet as a Christian I wasn't going to start observing that holiday at home; it was particular enough to Judaism that it didn't travel well. The Sabbath, however, was portable. God gave Sabbath to the Jews, and the Jews gave Sabbath to the world, yet the world did not receive it.

Most of the Christian world has taken up a loose approximation of Sabbath, but compared to the richness of expression it finds in Judaism, the Christian Sunday looks either overly strict or overly lax. Most non-Jews think of Sabbath, if they think of it at all, as just a day off. It helps us return to our workweek more rested, more prepared to work. But that makes Sabbath a subset of the human economy, where rest is simply a means to prepare yourself for work. In

God's Sabbath economy Heschel describes, rest is an end in itself. In Genesis, the seventh day is the culmination of all God's creative acts.

The Romans held Jews in contempt because they completely stopped work one day a week. What impudence! Who would keep this great empire running if people practice such frivolity? "Two things the people of Rome anxiously desired—bread and circus games," Heschel said. But bread feeds only for a short time and we are once again hungry. Circuses provide only momentary diversion. "Man does not live by bread and circus games alone. Who will teach him how to desire anxiously the spirit of a sacred day?" And we moderns, in our similarly ceaseless craving for productivity and entertainment, don't we, too, genuflect before the altar of the Endless Economy? How we fail to recognize this insatiable beast that is devouring the world, and devouring our souls as we bow. What if, from sundown to sundown one day a week, we simply stopped— everything? And not just rested *so that* we could be more efficient workers in the Empire come Monday, but turned away from it altogether. What if resting in God became our life's goal? Heschel: "The Sabbath is not for the sake of the weekdays; the weekdays are for the sake of Sabbath. It is not an interlude but the climax of living."

I spent the morning strolling around the lake and, like an excited young anthropologist who has been living among a remote Amazonian tribe, was eager to try out my new words with the natives. "Shabbat shalom," I said to every person who was within earshot. *Sabbath peace.* I had a long, lingering midday meal in the sukkah with Nigel and his wife, who said, "I just want everyone to stop and look at the lake." We did stop. We turned around. We gazed on the loveliness of the water and the cool blue air and the trees behind the lake, full of ocher and sienna. There was time for that today, world enough and time. Indeed, we had entered a different world where time was altered. Time had not ceased; it had been remade, molded into something more amenable to rest and wonder. The architecture of time. After lunch, Nigel and I continued our Sabbath conversation.

"The world needs Shabbat," he said, fingering the fringes of his tallis. "The Torah teaches that rest for a person and rest for the land are connected to each other; to do one, we have to do the other. In both cases, we do not merely *allow* the land or the person to rest; we require it."

Nigel wants Jews to be more evangelical. There is much wisdom to be plumbed in Jewish tradition, both ecological and spiritual, and the world needs to hear it. Like practicing Sabbath. "Planet Earth right now needs Shabbat. I don't care whether you keep it on Friday or Sunday or Tuesday, but just think if seven billion people set aside one day a week to *just stop*." Nigel tells a story about being on a Jewish wilderness retreat for a month in the mountains of North Carolina. They observed Shabbat each week, and at the end of the month one of the retreat staff said that what he would take away from that trip was practicing Sabbath. He was Jamaican, a Christian, but he loved how Nigel and his colleagues set aside the Sabbath day. They made better food. They slowed down. They ate meals with a sense of ritual and celebration. They sang. "That," Nigel said, "is the kind of evangelizing of Jewish tradition I want to do. On a planetary scale."

Most Jews, however, are "completely freaked out about being perceived as arrogant. We don't want to push our stuff on anybody. But Judaism is an amazing, miraculous part of the ecosystem of Planet Earth, and we Jews need to share it more widely."

The other practice Nigel wants to evangelize is keeping kosher. The literal meaning of kosher is "fitting," or "right." It's the notion of asking "Is this fit for me to eat?" The larger context is to ask what is fitting or right for the earth, what is becoming known among Jews as *eco-ḳashrut,* because if it's fitting or right for the earth, then it's going to be fitting or right for our bodies. "That's a question everybody alive on this planet needs to ask." There are perhaps one or two billion people who are so hungry they don't have a choice, Nigel said, but the other five billion need to ask that question. How was the land treated that produced this food? How were the animals treated? The workers? How much sugar is in this? What is this doing chemically to my body, to my children's bodies? Is this fit for me to eat? For Jews, keeping kosher falls under the larger idea of *tikḳun olam,* repair of the world. "There is a place in Jewish tradition," Nigel said, "where perfecting the world is not about the world to come, it's not about heaven and hell, it's about how can we incrementally make the world a better place now."

On Saturday night we all gathered in the sukkah for Havdalah, the beautiful service bidding farewell to the Sabbath Queen. Bowls of spices were passed, an aromatic reminder of the day's holy fragrance. In the middle of the sukkah, Matisyahu lit a lone candle whose two wicks were braided together in white and blue wax. The other lights were extinguished. Matisyahu began to chant in the holy tongue. After three days of rain, the sukkah was getting soggy; to avoid the mud I stood on a chair at the sukkah's edge, ducking my head under the *schach* to better see the light. Havdalah is an experiential service calling on all five senses. You hear the blessings, taste the wine after *ḳiddush,* smell the spices, behold the flame of the candle, and feel its warmth. Matisyahu held up the candle, and as we sang we all reached our hands toward the light. We looked at our fingertips, watching for how the light pushed back the darkness. We were once again at a threshold, a liminal moment, whose essence was captured by the Havdalah blessing:

Blessed are You, Adonai our God, Ruler of the universe, who makes a distinction between sacred and secular, between light and darkness, between Israel and the other nations, between the seventh day and the six working days. Blessed are You, Adonai, who makes a distinction between the sacred and the secular.

The cantor held up the *kiddush* wine and into the glass he inserted the lit candle. The light went out. All was quiet. Then everyone erupted in singing. Other candles were lit, and we danced outside the sukkah where a large group of Adamahniks and other young folk gathered to sing. An amazing young saxophone player jammed beside Matisyahu on guitar. A bongo player emerged, and soon fifty people danced in a rotating circle around the musicians. They started slow with Leonard Cohen's "Hallelujah," then picked up tempo with some snappy klezmer tunes.

As I stood watching the merriment, I thought how so many of us have impoverished identities. We look for our identity in football teams, TV shows, brands. And then there are the Jews, a people with such a strong identity it could choke you. But standing at the edge of the sukkah during Havdalah, and now seeing the dancers move and sing with abandon, I saw how that identity was also an incredible source of life and vitality. Nowhere was this identity more exemplified than in Saturday night's talent show.

I'd never been to a talent show that wasn't hokey and completely lacking in, well, talent. Until I went to Sukkahfest 5772. Danny Raphael was the MC. He leaped onstage and did a free-style rap song. The young saxophone player played a jazz tune accompanied by a woman who sounded like Ella Fitzgerald; Sarah Chandler did a stand-up comedy routine; another young woman played flute and tap-danced in a kind of Jethro Tull tribal rain dance; Matisyahu and Rachel sang the Bride Song . . . *you have ravished my heart*. All of these people had ravished my heart. I loved them all, these brothers and sisters from my long-lost tribe, laying aside irony and embarrassment and postmodern angst and just being themselves. Such confidence, such grace and dignity. There was even a non-Jewish fiddle player from the Appalachians—me—who got up to play his tune. I feared performing solo, so I brought up the house band—the sax player and Matisyahu—and we played the one klezmer tune I knew, called "Itzikel," named after the prophet Ezekiel, a trancelike melody in the key of D minor that always makes me feel like a Gypsy.

"I think I'm the lone Gentile at this gathering," I said after taking the stage. All two hundred people cheered.

"All Streams!" I shouted.

"One Source!" came the reply.

All week, I told them, I drank deeply from those different streams which flowed so beautifully from Hashem ("The Name") through all of them. People are thirsty, they need the living water that only Hashem can give, I said. My hope was that they would not keep this life-giving water to themselves. I asked that they would share it with the world.

18 Tishri

On Sunday morning I boarded the train at Wassaic and traveled to Manhattan. In a few days I would catch a flight home. The day was cold but lovely and full of sun. Still, my heart was heavy. I missed Elizabeth and the boys. What was the word for this ache? After a week with the Jews, my Christian community back home now seemed like thin gruel. I had found a tribe of people I wanted to join, to whom I wanted to introduce my family. It wasn't a feeling of wanting to abandon my Christian beliefs. Despite my beatific vision that morning in Kfar, the pain over our differences had no easy balm.

Toward the end of the talent show the previous night, I was standing alone toward the back, and Chavi approached me. She asked if she could pray with me. "Yes," I said, slightly taken aback. I thought only evangelical Christians engaged in spontaneous prayer. But Chavi, an Orthodox Jew, was an evangelical in her own tradition, one for whom spontaneous prayer seemed natural. She laid her hands on my shoulders like a priestess ready to bestow a blessing, and then, with the confidence of a daughter of Moses who had led his people forth from slavery and lived forty years in a sukkah and encountered YHWH on the mountaintop, she prayed. It was simple, short, and heartfelt: safe travels, a blessing on my wife and sons, that my book would inspire many people and bring them back to God. Amen.

When I arrived in New York I decided to walk off my anxiety. That afternoon I was walking down on Canal Street when I passed a strange sight. A group of men in black coats and black hats, whom I recognized as Hasids from the Lubavitcher sect, were standing around a big Ford F-150 pickup with dually tires. On the back sat a makeshift sukkah. Some klezmer music blared from a stereo. They invited people to shake the *lulav,* a bundle of palm and willow branches that are traditionally used during Sukkot. I chatted with Pinchas, a man about my age who sported a red beard and a Yiddish accent. He told me that in the days of the Messiah, who will usher in the world to come, all seventy nations will gather on the Temple Mount in Jerusalem. Drawn to God's light streaming from Mount Zion, they will gather to worship in unity, he said. All this will come to pass during the festival of Sukkot. I remembered a line in Rabbi Waskow's *Seasons of Our Joy:* "Sukkot is the moment when God's Name will become One to all who live on earth." I was reminded, with startling prescience, of my dream that morning in Kfar.

I told Pinchas that I, a Gentile, had visited Isabella Freedman, and how much it made me envy the Jews. "Maybe that's a sign," I said. Just like he said, Gentiles were being drawn in. It was the beginning of the end. The world to come was upon us. "Yes! Yes!" He laughed and pumped my hand and seemed very pleased. Then he told me about an all-night block party in Brooklyn each night during Sukkot, from 10 P.M. until 6 A.M., and encouraged me to come. "I guarantee—you never see bigger party." The chance to throw down with the Lubavitchers was enticing, but I politely declined. I was all sukkahed out.

Before I flew home, I spent the next several days walking the streets of Manhattan, and now I noticed sukkahs everywhere: a skinny one-man sukkah on the back of a bike, a giant house-sized sukkah next to the farmers' market at Union Square, and beside each one a group of friendly Lubavitchers trying to hustle people inside, like ushers seating concertgoers for the Show of All Shows.

My pilgrimage was drawing to a close. Time to return to the hinterlands. Back to my family, my garden, my life. I thought about something I'd read in Rodger Kamenetz's *The Jew in the Lotus*: "As Jews we do not have to choose between family life and the monastery—we have a blueprint for combining both, if only we will follow it." That was what I needed, a way of combining the monastic disciplines of prayer and solitude and humility with the joyful messiness of family life on the land. After this visit I would not be lacking in good examples.

One final memory:

It's Saturday night. Everyone is gathered for Havdalah. We hold our hands out to the candle, watching the light through translucent fingers, as if absorbing its goodness into our pores. A glass of wine appears. Someone turns the candle upside down and plunges it into the wine.

The light goes out. Suddenly, the world grows dark.

But the darkness is not complete. I'm still on the edge of the sukkah, standing on a chair with my shoulders brushing the *schach,* but when I duck my head outside I can see light falling softly on my shoulders. The light illumines all the sukkah people, the lake, this big Sukkah called Earth. It is a gentle, reflected light and it shines on us all, the light of a full and expectant moon.

Epilogue

He who works with the earth from whence he came and to which
he will return gets healed of his wounds. In a strange way he is
somehow deeply reconciled with God again and walks at eventide
with Him while they both look over the creation of their hands.
—Catherine Doherty, *Apostolic Farming*

When we left Cedar Grove in 2009, Elizabeth and I sold our little
farm near Anathoth Community Garden and we moved to my parents' farm up in the mountains. We now live in a house overlooking
a steep pasture in which we've planted a permaculture orchard and
double-dug vegetable beds on a series of terraces. It's winter now. A
year has passed since my visit to Mepkin Abbey. Lately on these cold
mornings while I write, a rafter of wild turkeys bob and weave their
way up through the orchard, scratching through layers of frozen
leaves and clover, searching for the soil's secret riches. The turkeys
seem to like our hillside orchard. It's the same hillside where I once
unwittingly fed the local crow population with José's *maíz*.

I think often of Chiapas, and of that vision on the rooftop as I
began to dream then of a life on the land. In my journal one day in
Nuevo Yibeljoj, I wrote down my ideal daily schedule on my future
farm ten years hence. I didn't know then what one actually *did* on a
piece of land. My farming verbs then were vague, even cliché: *tilling,*

sowing, reaping. But I surmised that it would require a good bit of work, and about that much, at least, I was right. In my journal I imagined how my days would unfold:

> Get up around six A.M., write for four hours, eat lunch (something I will have grown), read for an hour, then perform manual labor all afternoon until dinnertime. At five I will come in sweaty and tired. My wife, a lovely lass, and I will share a glass of wine. We will chat amiably about our day, then have a nice relaxing meal one of us has cooked (we will take turns). After dinner we will read. Around 9 P.M. we will make our way to the bedroom and fall into each other's arms, expending ourselves in passion, and be asleep by 9:30 P.M. I can do a day like this over and over for years. Of course, soon will come little grapplers running around, and I will be around the house to help look after them. This will allow my lovely wife to work elsewhere if she wants, though preferably she, too, will work on The Land. We will have a cottage industry.

Such were my visions of domestic bliss.

I recently uncovered that journal from Chiapas, and for a season of my life it was striking just how prophetic my words proved to be. Those first few years after I left Anathoth, I made my living as a writer. My days were not far removed from how I once envisioned them eleven years ago in José's village in Chiapas. I got up around 6 A.M., wrote all morning, ate lunch, usually something from our garden. I read for an hour, drank tea, and if it wasn't too hot I would work in the garden most afternoons. Around five I came in sweaty and tired, jumped on the trampoline with our three boys, then wandered inside. But now I've recently begun a new job directing a Food & Faith program for a divinity school. It's worthwhile work and I'm grateful for it, but there are days when the main light I see is that coming from the white screen in front of me, and in that I'm no different from many of us, I suppose. With the garden so close, though, I can slip out for a half hour of digging here, twenty minutes of planting there. The garden keeps me sane.

As does cocktail hour with my wife. Elizabeth and I like to have a glass of wine together. Back in B.C. days (Before Children), we used to chat amiably about our day as we sipped our Pinot, but now that we have three boys we gulp our juice down and try to keep the chaos at a containable level until suppertime. After supper we read to the kids: *Goodnight Moon, Ox-Cart Man, The Jack Tales*. Around nine we make our way to the bedroom and fall into bed. The passion I'd hoped for is there in abundance, but now that we have kids, all we have energy for most nights is reading. As I imagined my life that day in Nuevo Yibeljoj, I told myself I could do a day like this over and over for years, and that's proved to be true. We have a cottage industry, Elizabeth and I, though I wouldn't say it's a financially viable operation. We're subsistence gardeners. We harvest fresh vegetables from our garden every month of the year, grow a dozen different kinds of fruit, ferment our own kimchi and sauerkraut. We cook most of our own meals, which, all boasting aside, are much fresher and tastier than restaurant food. Lettuce doesn't get more local than the backyard. Through Elizabeth's music gigs and my writing and teaching our income is modest, but our life feels indescribably rich, abundant, blessed.

One of those blessings is that I'm back in touch with my old friend Pharaoh. Chris Hoke's steering wheel prayer that day on the drive to the prison has been answered. At 7:30 one morning I got a call from Pharaoh. He'd just woken up from a dream and somehow found my number again. In his dream the two of us were walking side by side in a field, we were laughing, and when he awoke he knew he had to find me again. He has a wife and two sweet little kids, a boy and a girl. When we met again, our children played together. Recently Pharaoh learned that he has an enlarged heart. He doesn't know how much longer he will live. He may live out a normal life, or he may not wake up tomorrow. Which is true for all of us, I suppose, but my friend Pharaoh has become more acutely aware of this truth than most of us. "I always knew you had a big heart," I tell him, or "God hardened the heart of the first Pharaoh, but he enlarged yours." We don't let the proximity of death get in the way of having a good time. In a recent letter he wrote, "So here I am, thirty-seven years old, and the only thought on my mind is to keep sharing my love of life."

It's a good life, friends like Pharaoh teach me, a blessed life. As Father Kevin predicted, the more I give thanks for my blessings, the more I see how everything I have and everything I am is all gift. That's one thing I've learned from the monks, at least.

The brothers of Mepkin have inspired me to begin cultivating mushrooms. I've learned that my part of western North Carolina is on par with the Northwest as one of the best places in the country for growing fungi. I bought four books on how to identify the wild mushrooms, and learned which ones can kill you—Destroying Angels and Death Caps—and which ones offer the tastiest of meals—lion's mane, maitake, bolete. But despite the excitement of hiking through the woods and finding a clutch of bright orange chanterelles growing beside the path, such finds are rare.

In both the active and contemplative life, you cannot rely on serendipity; both require cultivation.

I grow shiitakes and oysters, like the monks, though I grow mine outside on logs, and don't tend them as carefully as they do. But I enjoy looking out my office window at the stacks of shiitake logs in the woods behind my house, and as I do I think about the mycelium running through the logs and into the earth, connecting dead wood with living soil. It's a reciprocal relationship, one that gives me, on occasion, a harvest.

I am also cultivating a prayer life. I still rise early, but the times of sinking into a stupor beside the woodstove are slowly being replaced with something else. How to describe it? A kindling of the heart as it warms to the Divine heat? If it is fire, then it is still a small one, and sometimes it goes out. But each morning I strike another match. I do my best to be vigilant and guard the flame, for this inner heat is a refiner's fire, helping me become more fully the person God created me to be. I read a Psalm, or a chapter from the Gospels, and I pray the ancient prayers, especially this one: I beg you, God, make me truly alive.

The vision of *shalom* at work in Anathoth continues, both there and in the other faith communities described in this book. Since leaving Anathoth in 2009, I've visited or spoken with dozens of similar faith-infused garden projects, even as far away as the city of Curitiba, Brazil. What each of these projects has in common, I've learned, is this: a desire to deepen one's faith through connection to both a piece of land and to a community.

In each faith community I visited or spoke with, I asked what motivated their work with the soil. The answers varied, but they all came back to the hunger of which Susan spoke. The hunger not only for good food, but also for friendship, conviviality, communion. Coffee shops are touted as our cultural commons, but very few people in coffee shops actually interact with strangers; everyone just stares at their screen. A communal food garden is really one of the few places in our society where you can go and meet someone outside your ethnic or class boundary. "In a garden there's no hierarchy," Susan

Sides from the Lord's Acre told me. "I know that's true intellectually, but still, every time I see it I'm blown away." Perhaps that's why
so many of the gardens I've visited are more like small collective
farms than community gardens. Gone are the individual plots for
each family, where you could work your own soil and not necessarily
have to interact with others. At Anathoth, we worked common land
and shared the produce according to each family's need. It's a model
that seems to be increasingly popular. When we started Anathoth in
2005, there were very few such projects. Now they are popping up
like volunteer tomatoes.

The radical "eco-nuns" of Genesis Farm in Blairstown, New
Jersey, began practicing Green Christianity long before it was hip.
Thirty years ago the Sisters of Saint Dominic started the farm as a
response to the ecological crisis and since then, through both a Community Supported Agriculture program and an eco-literacy program,
Genesis Farm has become a thriving model. The nuns there are
rooted in a belief that "the Universe, Earth, and all reality are perme-
ated by the presence and power of that ultimate Holy Mystery that
has been so deeply and richly expressed in the world's spiritual tradi-
tions." One way they are practicing this belief is through Transition
Town trainings. The Transition Town movement, started in the U.K.
in 2006, is a community-based response to peak oil, looking for low-
tech ways we can wean ourselves from fossil fuels and still thrive.

Other gardens are serving to foster racial reconciliation. One of
the most intriguing of these is the London Ferrell Community Garden in Lexington, Kentucky. London Ferrell was a black minister in
the early 1800s in Lexington. When a cholera epidemic broke out,
Ferrell was one of only three ministers who remained in Lexington to bury the dead. He became a hero, and years later was buried
in the local white Episcopal cemetery. Fast forward to the 1960s.
When the Episcopal church put a fence up around the graveyard,

they unintentionally fenced out London Ferrell's grave. The local African Americans in the neighborhood thought it was one more slight in a long list of slights. Thirty years later in 2008, when a new community garden was planted next to the cemetery, a parishioner researched London Ferrell and the history was revealed. The church placed a new gravestone for London Ferrell inside the church sanctuary. The garden is managed now by Seedleaf, a collective of community gardens serving poor neighborhoods in Lexington, and through participation in it, whites and blacks are beginning to reconcile their troubled past.

Even the bikers are going back to the land. The year before I visited the Lord's Acre, I learned that Crossfire United Methodist Church, a biker church in nearby North Wilkesboro, North Carolina, ran several intriguing food ministries: the Giving Table and God's Garden Community. I called up Dwight "Bubba" Smith, one of three pastors at Crossfire, who managed the church's feeding ministries, and Bubba invited me up for their big "Jesus Rocks" motorcycle rally.

On the first Saturday in May I got out my old black leather jacket, the one I had back when I owned a motorcycle in divinity school, pulled on my leather boots, and, in a sad attempt to earn myself some street cred with the bikers, asked my six-year-old son to paste a dinosaur tattoo on my left bicep. Crossfire UMC is located in what once was an old refrigerated trucking terminal. On the phone Bubba described the building's defining features: big warehouse, industrial, chain link fence topped by razor wire. "Come to think of it," he said, "it looks kinda like a jail."

Which is oddly apropos. On a Sunday morning visit to Crossfire I met a guy who told me he'd just been released from prison. He had gold pirate hoops hanging from both ears, and a giant bowie knife strapped to his right boot. During the service the congregation gave him a prodigal's welcome, with cheering and rounds of applause.

Since its inception eight years ago, Crossfire has become known for welcoming not only bikers, but former convicts and ex–gang members, recovering drug addicts and alcoholics. Not exactly the kind of folks you'd expect to start a church. Or a garden ministry. Most have left behind their wild past, or are trying to do so in Crossfire's rehab program, Celebrate Recovery. Ask any one of them and they'll tell you that the transformation they've experienced at Crossfire—spiritual, physical, emotional—is real. One way they share that new life is to help their hungry neighbors. Feeding people is part of their calling.

Pastor Duncan Overrein, who started God's Garden Community, told me about his desire to feed those whom society overlooks. With his big beard, long gray ponytail, and tattoos, Duncan can relate to those who've been ostracized because of their past or the way they look. One Thanksgiving a few years ago he and his wife invited sixty people to their single wide trailer, folks he met on the street who had no place to go. "We invited people who are rejected, who most people consider worthless. People who've been kicked around, moved from state to state. I had all kinds of scriptures going through my head that day. Like the parable of the banquet where the master goes out and finds all the unworthy to come and feast."

North Carolina ties with Arkansas for sixth place among states with the greatest food insecurity. Among North Carolina counties, Wilkes County is designated as Tier One, marking it among the poorest in the state. Hunger even among parishioners at Crossfire is a real issue. Of the 120 regular attendees, at least thirty are unemployed.

Crossfire's mission to feed people has assumed a variety of forms. Every Wednesday through their food pantry the church provides up to fifty families with enough food to last them the entire week. Three of the congregants put in a total of fifty hours a week, with others helping distribute the food. For the past several years, with help from six or seven other Crossfire members, Pastor Duncan has organized an acre-sized community garden and donated the produce to the needy. Partnering with Wilkes County, they received a grant to build a greenhouse on the former county landfill. Methane gas produced by the landfill will be captured and used to power the greenhouse, which will produce pesticide-free vegetables. Those vegetables will be stored in Wesley's Storehouse, the church's non-profit entity that rents the building's seventeen thousand feet of cold storage space. They'll then be distributed to those in need. As Pastor Duncan told me, "Man, all this time, bikers just want people to know that we're people, too. We just want to feed people."

I said before that soil is a portal to another world, but I've since learned that it's not just one world. Working with the soil opens us inward where we find a God eager to lavish upon us God's mercy and compassion and love. Soil also opens us outward, where we learn to receive the fruits of this good earth, and where we also discover that ours is not the only hunger. Soil work reveals the joyful messiness of human life where we find others who need us, and whom we need in return. How we hunger is who we are. We are each one part pain and one part desire, and we should not be ashamed that our ache to be filled is so great, so overwhelming. God gave us this hunger, and we should not squander it on lighter fare. As a stream will run downward until it joins the immensity of the sea, so will our soul seek the level Ground of our being. It is our desire, after all, that makes us most like God.

As I travel and speak about what I've learned, I'm sometimes asked how to start a project like Anathoth. Here's an attempt at an answer:

- *Find land*. Not the best land or even good land, because you can create the kind of soil you will need to feed people. But you need land of some kind. Even an abandoned piece of asphalt that can be covered in topsoil. Don't be lured by technological wizardry promised by the latest gimcrack product of the Industrial Mind. Get your hands in the soil.

- *Water*. Dig a well or pipe it in. Buy drip irrigation. Through swales or ponds or cisterns, catch and hold as much water on your site as you can. Water is an important reez horse.

- *Borders*. Don't lock your garden. Don't build a fence to keep people out. If someone takes your broccoli or watermelons, let them. If you are worried about liability, start an insurance company. Leave the work of growing food to those who maintain a porous sense of edges and ownership.

- *Tools*. Buy only the best digging forks and spades, for these get the most use. A good scythe, with an Austrian hand-forged blade and aluminum snathe. Hefty rakes with one-piece heads. Right-angle trowels for transplanting. Wooden flats, preferably cedar or redwood, for starting seeds. A hand-cranked broadcast seeder. A U-bar broadfork, welded by your friendly neighborhood arc-welder and for which he will overcharge you but for which you will gladly pay, because a good U-bar will last several lifetimes and will save you the trouble of repeated double-digging.

- *Machines*. Use them if you must, but distrust them. They compact the soil, stultify the brain, and substitute power for knowledge. Machines are smelly. They break down. The time and money you spent purchasing, using, maintaining, and fussing over them could be better spent in a hundred different ways. To get your garden work done, encourage a different kind of internal combustion: the combined beating of a dozen human hearts.

- *Plants*. Buy the best organic seed, grow that seed in compost-fed soil, and you will have the best plants.

- *Pests*. When people ask how you deal with pests, crouch down and scoop up a handful of soil. Lovingly describe for them how plants grown in healthy soil are seldom bothered by pests, just as people who eat healthy plants are seldom bothered by disease. Tell them pests are your teachers, for the damage they do teaches you about what you still have to learn.

- *People*. Choose, if you are given a choice, the strays. Invite to your community garden the rejects, the riff raff, the outliers from the bounds of respectability. You'll also want the hard workers, the responsible adults, the morally upright, for growing food is hard work, and it takes people willing to lean in. These people, too, will be changed, and perhaps humbled. But the garden you are creating is first of all for the widow who comes to the door in her negligee, the migrant worker who works three jobs and comes to the garden to unwind, the senile old coot with one leg who lives at the local halfway house and who keeps telling you about that damned rabbit manure while making unwelcome advances on your garden's female interns—these are your treasures, these are the ones who will receive exalted status. Go out into the streets, drive along your county's back roads with names like *Doc Corbett, Pentecost,* and *Lonesome,* bring with you bags of free sweet potatoes and collard greens and invite these people to the feast. Keep a special eye out for those troubled of mind, like the young man who startles other garden members with grand schemes of starting his own harem, the same anguished soul who comes to church with you one Sunday morning and spends the entire service making a homemade tattoo of a cross on his wrist with a needle and your broke-open Bic pen, and when it's time for Prayers of the People raises his hand and asks for prayer for his two-year-old daughter who is dying in the hospital, which is touching and sweet except that he doesn't have a daughter, and when the pastor prays for this little girl who doesn't exist, you realize this is why you haven't left the church, because where else can people bring their shadowed fears, their unnamed sorrows, and give them voice? Where else but on the altar of mercy can you lay your burdens down?

On garden workdays, pay attention to the people who when you ask them to do a job will do it either halfheartedly or half-assed or not at all, those who wander among the cabbage beds muttering to themselves, those who are so fat they can't bend over to tie their own shoes much less weed a bed of Jericho lettuce, the ones who when you hand them a pen with the New Members form to fill out will pause, an embarrassed smile shadowing their face, and hand the form back to you saying *could you just do it for me*. Find these people, the meek and lowly and poor in spirit. Love them. They are your garden's prize crop.

For theirs is the kingdom of heaven.

With them did the Son of Man go eating and drinking.

It is they who will inherit the earth.

Acknowledgments

Soil and Sacrament was a seed that lay dormant in the ground for many years, so many years that I wondered if the seed would ever germinate. But sprout it did, and from the emergence of those first cotyledons, the book's life has been tended by a number of trustworthy caretakers. It's often said that writing is a lonely pursuit, and it most certainly is; but from the beginning of this journey I have been supported by so many wonderful souls that the long hours at my desk have felt less lonely.

First, I'm grateful to those who trusted me to write about their lives. Not only did people welcome me into their gardens and share their stories, but some of them were gracious enough to read their parts of the manuscript, correct my mistakes, and make suggestions for improvement, not all of which I followed. For their charity as host, reader, or both, I thank:

The brothers of Mepkin Abbey, especially Abbot Stan, Father Kevin, Father Guerric, Brother Gregory (RIP), Brother Robert, Brother Theophilus, Brother Anthony-Maria, and Josh Warner (formerly Brother Dismas). The members of the Lord's Acre, especially Susan Sides, Will Hamilton, Steve Norris, and Pat Stone. The Tierra Nueva family, especially Bob Ekblad, Chris Hoke, Bones, Zach Joy, and Nick Bryant. The staff, students, and visitors I met at Adamah Farm, especially Shamu Sadeh, Janna Berger, Sarah Chandler, Daniel Raphael Silverstein, Nigel Savage, Nati Passow, and Sam Plotkin. To all of you, my deep respect.

Special thanks to my fellow writers for reading and commenting on the entire manuscript: Chris Hoke, Jonathan Wilson-Hartgrove, Ragan Sutterfield, Kim Meyer, and Norman Wirzba.

Several key writing grants sustained our family during the research and writing: a Kellogg Food & Community fellowship at the Institute for Agriculture and Trade Policy, a Louisville Institute Sabbatical Project grant, and a North Carolina Artist Fellowship in creative nonfiction. To these fine institutions I offer my gratitude.

I wish to thank the editors at *The Sun* and *World Ark,* where early parts of the book initially appeared.

At Wake Forest University School of Divinity I wish to thank Dean Gail O'Day, who hired me to direct the Food, Faith, and Religious Leadership Initiative, and to the staff and faculty at the School of Divinity for being such pleasant and supportive colleagues.

Thanks to the intrepid Wendy Sherman, the book's agent, for her steady encouragement and for connecting me with just the right editors at just the right publishing house. The first editor was Emily Loose, who saw the promise in the seed and who nurtured the manuscript through its early and middle stages. Michael Szczerban helped the book find its final form. Servants of the word both, Emily and Michael were my ideal team, and I'm grateful for the depth of attention and empathy they each brought to the work. I'm also grateful to others on my team at Simon & Schuster, especially Meg Cassidy, Marie Kent, Fred Chase, and Gypsy da Silva.

To the Bahnson and Hamilton clans, thank you for your love, for feeding me, and for suffering a writer in the family.

My love, my deepest gratitude, and on many days my dumbfounded awe, goes to Elizabeth. First and best reader, trusted advisor, she adopted this book into our family like some orphan child in need of her care. Through the years of honing my craft, Elizabeth has given me the greatest gift a writer can receive: her belief. This book is as much hers as it is mine.

Recommended Reading

It would be impossible to list all the books that influenced the making of this one. Below are the books from which I quoted directly and others that were often in mind as I wrote. To this list I've added others to which the reader might turn if he or she wishes to continue the journey.

Soil

Ager, John. *We Plow God's Fields.* Boone: Appalachian Consortium Press, 1991.

Berry, Wendell. *The Art of the Commonplace.* Berkeley: Counterpoint, 2012.

——. *The Unsettling of America.* San Francisco: Sierra Club Books, 1996.

——. *The Gift of Good Land.* Berkeley: Counterpoint, 2009.

Harrison, Robert Pogue. *Gardens: An Essay on the Human Condition.* Chicago: University of Chicago Press, 2009.

Hemenway, Toby. *Gaia's Garden: A Guide to Home-Scale Permaculture.* 2nd ed. White River Junction, VT: Chelsea Green, 2009.

Howard, Sir Albert. *The Soil and Health: A Study of Organic Agriculture.* Lexington: University Press of Kentucky, 2007.

Jackson, Wes. *Becoming Native to This Place.* Lexington: University Press of Kentucky, 1994.

Jeavons, John. *How to Grow More Vegetables.* 8th ed. New York: Ten Speed Press, 2012.

Kourik, Robert. *Roots Demystified: Change Your Gardening Habits to Help Roots Thrive.* Occidental, CA: Metamorphic Press, 2007.

Logsdon, Gene. *Holy Shit: Managing Manure to Save Humankind.* White River Junction, VT: Chelsea Green, 2010.

McKibben, Bill. *Eaarth: Making Life on a Tough New Planet.* New York: Times Books, 2010.

Mollison, Bill. *Introduction to Permaculture.* Rev. ed. Berkeley: Ten Speed Press, 1997.

Murray, Christopher, Sara Ishikawa, and Murray Silverstein. *A Pattern Language: Towns, Buildings, Construction.* New York: Oxford University Press, 1977.

Pollan, Michael. *The Omnivore's Dilemma: A Natural History of Four Meals.* New York: Penguin, 2006.

————. *Second Nature: A Gardener's Education.* New York: Atlantic Monthly Press, 1991.

Stegner, Wallace. *Where the Bluebird Sings to the Lemonade Springs: Living and Writing in the West.* New York: Modern Library, 2002.

Sacrament

Cairns, Scott. *Recovered Body.* 2nd ed. Wichita: Eighth Day Press, 2006.

Capon, Robert Farrar. *The Supper of the Lamb.* New York: Modern Library, 2002.

Cassian, John. *Conferences.* New York: Paulist Press, 1985.

Chess, Richard. *Third Temple.* Tampa: University of Tampa Press, 2007.

Chittister, Joan. *The Liturgical Year: The Spiraling Adventure of the Spiritual Life.* Nashville: Thomas Nelson, 2010.

Chryssavgis, John. *The Heart of the Desert: The Spirituality of the Desert Fathers and Mothers.* Bloomington: World Wisdom, 2008.

Davis, Ellen. *Proverbs, Ecclesiastes, and the Song of Songs.* Louisville, KY: Westminster John Knox Press, 2000.

————. *Scripture, Culture, and Agriculture: An Agrarian Reading of the Bible.* Cambridge: Cambridge University Press, 2008.

Ekblad, Bob. *Reading the Bible with the Damned.* Louisville, KY: Westminster John Knox Press, 2005.

Heschel, Abraham Joshua. *The Sabbath.* New York: Farrar, Straus & Giroux, 2005.

Kamenetz, Rodger. *The Jew in the Lotus: A Poet's Rediscovery of Jewish Identity in Buddhist India.* Updated ed. New York: HarperOne, 2007.

Kierkegaard, Søren. *Provocations: Spiritual Writings of Kierkegaard.* Ed. Charles E. Moore. Maryknoll, NY: Orbis, 2003.

Kline, Francis. *Lovers of the Place: Monasticism Loose in the Church.* Collegeville, MN: Liturgical Press, 1997.

Merton, Thomas. *The Seven Storey Mountain.* New York: Harcourt Brace, 1948.

————. *Thoughts in Solitude.* New York: Farrar, Straus & Giroux, 1998.

Rilke, Rainer Maria. *Duino Elegies and The Sonnets to Orpheus.* Trans. A. Poulin, Jr. New York: Mariner, 2005.

————. *Rilke's Book of Hours: Love Poems to God.* Trans. Anita Barrows and Joanna Macy. New York: Riverhead, 1996.

Robinson, Marilynne. *Housekeeping.* London: Picador, 2004.

Romero, Oscar. *The Violence of Love.* Maryknoll, NY: Orbis, 2004.

Schmemann, Alexander. *For the Life of the World.* 2nd ed. Yonkers, NY: St. Vladimir's Seminary Press, 1973.

Tolstoy, Leo. *The Kingdom of God Is Within You.* Lincoln: University of Nebraska Press, 1984.

Waskow, Rabbi Arthur O. *Seasons of Our Joy: A Modern Guide to the Jewish Holidays.* Philadelphia: Jewish Publication Society, 2012.

Wirzba, Norman. *Food and Faith: A Theology of Eating.* Cambridge: Cambridge University Press, 2011.

Index

Abraham, 117, 219
Acteal, Mexico, 58, 59–60, 68
Acts of the Apostles, 67, 100, 122, 136,
    138, 143
Adam, 8, 124, 178, 196–97
Adam (crew boss), 220–21
adamah, see soil
Adamah Farm, 196–242
Adela, 192–93
Advent, 1, 12, 18, 25, 26–27
Africa (garden), 108–11, 113, 116
AIDS, 153
Aitan, 205–6
Alexander, Christopher, 109
All Souls Episcopal Church, 95
Alter, Robert, 120
Amish, 29
Amos, 229
Anathoth Community Garden, 1–14,
    21, 31, 84, 86, 96, 106, 129, 130, 161,
    174–95, 197, 244, 248, 251
  Cedar Grove's relationship with, *see*
    Cedar Grove United Methodist
    Church
  communal nature of, 31, 93–94
  community service kids at, 160,
    183
  potluck dinners at, 182–83
  racial equality at, 131
  visitors to, 5–6
"Angel from Montgomery," 95
Angelina, 73, 74
Anna Karenina (Tolstoy), 201, 221
Anne, Saint, 49
Anthony, Saint, 32–33, 47
Anthony-Maria, Brother, 31–35
Apogee Homes, 185–91
Apostles, 143–44
Apostolic Farming (Doherty), 243

Arabs, 143
Arcadia broccoli, 6
Armor, 111–12
Arturo, 62
arugula, 196
asher yatzar, 216
Asheville, N.C., 82–84
Asheville Citizen Times, 83
Ash Wednesday, 175
asparagus, 23
Augustine, Saint, 8, 120
'avad, 178, 179, 193–94
avodah, 200
Avodat Bayit, 200
Avodat Lev, 200
Avodat Sadeh, 200, 203
Azazel, 198

Babylon, 117, 128–29, 130
bacteria, 2, 4–5
Bahnson, Elizabeth, 21, 23, 25, 54, 84,
    96, 99, 126, 128, 239, 245
  as animal lover, 121–22
  in divinity school, 120–21
  family problems and, 4, 7, 8, 9
  farm sold by, 243
  Fred's courtship of, 117–19
  marriage of, 84, 120
  orchard planted by, 23
  singing by, 232
  as Yokefellow, 163–64
Bahnson, Fred:
  boys of, 4, 7, 8, 9, 21, 54, 239, 244
  childhood of, 48
  coffee roasted by, 149–56
  community garden idea of, 127–28
  courtship of, 117–19
  daily reading of, 67, 76, 109
  desire for family of, 77

Bahnson, Fred (*cont.*)
    fair trade coffee business considered
      by, 59, 61–62, 71–72, 77
    family difficulties of, 4, 7–8, 9
    farm sold by, 243
    ideal daily schedule of, 243–44
    marriage of, 84, 120
    as missionary child, 10
    New Testament taught by, 10
    as nonviolent Christian activist, 56–81
    as prayer leader, 97–98
    as worried about calling, 75–78
    as Yokefellow, 163–64
Baker, 121
Baker, Heidi, 144
Barry, 185–86
basil, 114
Bassie, 160–61
beans, 65, 129, 204
Beautiful Garden, 108, 112, 113
bees, 96
beets, 180
Beit Adamah, 202
Benedict, Saint, 22, 25, 27, 34
Benedictine monks, 16
Berger, Janna, 203, 221–22, 224–25, 227
Berkshires, 12
Bernard, Saint, 26–27
Berry, Wendell, 67, 107–8, 117, 137
Bertha, 186, 189
Bible, 178
    see also specific books
Big Egypt, 44–45
Bill, 87, 88
blackberries, 158, 170
Black-Eyed Susans, 89
Black Mountain, N.C., 92
Blake, William, 223
blueberries, 170, 182
blueberry bushes, 7
Bo, 90–91
Body of Christ, 116
Bones, 142–43, 161–71, 194, 229
    visions seen by, 148
Bonhoeffer, Dietrich, 101
Book of Hours (Rilke), 19
Book of Pilgrimage, The (Rilke), 132
borage, 89
borders, 252

Boyz Town, 203, 218
bread, 196
broccoli, 6, 156, 157, 185, 203
Bronze Arrow lettuce, 6
Brown's Feed & Supply, 175
Brussels sprouts, 8
Bryan, 185–86
Buber, Martin, 233
Bumblebee Democracy, 95
Burley, 183–85
Burlington, Wash., 133, 143
Bush, George W., 101
buy local, eat organic movement, 13

cabbage, 79, 157, 203, 225
cafetales, 60–61, 74, 75
Calvin, John, 120
campamentistas, 61, 77
Canal Street, 240–41
cancer, 153
Čapek, Karel, 181
capitalism, 61, 83–84
Capon, Robert Farrar, 74
Carrboro Farmer's Market, 187
carrots, 1, 6, 12, 25, 157
Cascades, 133
Cassian, John, 19, 20, 30
Catherine of Siena, Saint, 89
Catholicism, 60
cats, 122
Cedar, 71
Cedar Grove, N.C., 124–26, 176, 243
Cedar Grove United Methodist Church, 3,
    5, 127–30, 148, 174, 177, 192
Celebrate Recovery, 250
Center for Cultural Proliferation, 215,
    220, 221
Central America, 97
    dirty wars in, 136
Central Carolina Community College,
    114
Central for Cultural Proliferation, 203
Central Methodist Church, 82–84
C'est si Bon!, 183
Chandler, Sarah, 227, 229–30, 238
Chapel Door, 101
charity, 107–8
chastity, 54
Chavi, 209, 214–15, 240

Chekhov, Anton, 114
chenek, 73–74, 75, 77
Chess, Richard, 219
Chiapas, Mexico, 9, 55, 56–81, 106, 107,
    115, 148, 181, 243, 244
China, 180
Chittister, Joan, 26
Chorizo (pig), 121
Chosen, The (Potok), 171
Christian, Father, 28–29, 46
Christianity:
    subdivisions of, 95
    table fellowship and, 93–94
Christian Peacemaker Teams (CPT),
    56–57, 58, 61, 64, 65, 66–67, 71,
    76–77
Chuleta (pig), 121
Cîteaux, France, 22
civil rights movement, 40
Clarence, 191–92, 193
climate change, 8, 206
clover, 4, 6, 87
coffee, 11, 74, 80
    fair trade, 59, 61–62, 71–72, 77, 136
    protest burning of, 69, 70, 71
Cohen, Leonard, 238
Coleman, Eliot, 121
collards, 203
Collected Poems (Berry), 67
Colombia, 56, 75, 77
community, 24
Community Supported Agriculture pro-
    gram (CSA), 156, 201–2, 223, 248
Compline, 37, 51–52, 54
compost, 4–5, 38, 41, 88, 114, 122, 180
Compton, Dwight, 176
Conferences, The (John Cassian), 19, 20
Congregational Life Meetings, 123
Cooper River, 53
co-ops, 83
Copper, Mrs., 167
Corinthians, Letter to, 93
Coriolanus (Shakespeare), 171
corn, 64, 65, 70–71, 73, 80–81, 87, 90, 129,
    158–59, 175, 182, 243
cottage farming, 122
cover crop, 3–5, 87, 181–82
crack addicts, 129
Cretans, 143

Crognale, John, 92
Crossfire United Methodist Church,
    249–51
cucumbers, 159, 170
Czech Republic, 116

Danny the Rabbinical Rapper, 215–16
Dante Alighieri, 108, 109
David, 80
Davis, Ellen, 178, 226–27
Days of Awe, 198
DDT, 187–88, 189
"Dead Flowers," 95
Death Caps, 246
Desert Fathers, 22, 41
Destroying Angels, 49, 246
Deuteronomy, 168, 186, 188–89, 212
dinosaur kale, 6
Dismas, Brother, 17, 25–26, 43, 51
    monastery left by, 54
    mushroom work of, 31–33, 35
dogs, 122
Doherty, Catherine, 243
Dominic, Saint, 248
Donny, 177–82, 194
Doris, Sister, 31, 131, 191, 192–93
drip irrigation, 252
Dry Salvages, The (Eliot), 174

earthworms, 2
Eastertide, 84, 86
Ecclesiastes, 225–27
echinacea, 89
eco-kashrut, 237
Eden Village Farm, 209
edges, 115–16, 252
Ekblad, Bob, 133–43, 145–46, 148–49,
    150, 153, 169, 173
    Ph.D. acquired by, 133, 140
    prison work of, 136, 142
    speaking in tongues by, 147–48
Ekblad, Gracie, 133–34, 137, 138, 140, 150
Elijah, 48, 123
Eliot, T. S., 126, 174
Emma, 85–86, 103–5, 194
Erika, 209
eruv, 198, 213
Eucharist, 10, 27, 31, 77, 94–95, 191,
    194–95

Evangelical Free Church, 60
Exodus, 207, 211–12
Ezekiel, 171

fair trade coffee, 59, 61–62, 71–72, 77,
    136
Fairview Christian Fellowship, 91–95,
    100, 101, 104, 118
Fairview Town Crier, 92
Farmer's Credit Union, 175
farming, as art, 107
Fear and Trembling (Kierkegaard), 67
Feast of Booths, 210
Feast of Ingathering, 211–12
Feast of the Immaculate Conception, 51
Ferrell, London, 248–49
Fiebre del Norte, El, 140, 158–59, 161
Finlandia, 30
food and faith movement, 10–11, 245
Food for Fairview, 87, 102
Fox, Vicente, 61
Francis, Saint, 155
Fred, 164
fundamentalism, 139
fungi, 2, 19–20
Fusarium, 114

Gaia's Garden (Hemenway), 109
Galilee, 124
Gandhi, Mohandas, 76
gardens, as metaphor, 8–9
Gardens (Harrison), 9
garlic, 182
Garrett, Levi, 188
Generous Garden, 86, 90, 91
Genesis, 8, 136, 178, 196–97, 223
Genesis Farm, 248
Gethsemani Abbey, 18, 30, 38–39, 46,
    52
Gift of Good Land, The (Berry), 107
Giving Table, 249
global food crisis, 8
global warming, 8, 206
goats, 12, 121, 122, 196, 219
God, 8, 10, 13, 127, 141, 173, 211, 227
    Adam created by, 8, 124, 196–97
    Hebrew names for, 214
Godfather, The, 170
God's Garden Community, 249

Good Friday, 77
gospel, 247
Gospels, 67, 77, 124
grace, 97–99
Grace, Pastor, 125–26, 127, 128, 131
Grand Silence, 25
grape vines, 23
grass, 5
gratitude, 53
Great Depression, 82–84
Greeks, 2
Green Christianity, 248
Greene, Graham, 59
GreenPrints, 94
Greenville, N.C., 87–88
Gregory, Brother, 16–17, 18, 28, 45, 46,
    47, 51–52, 66
Guatemala, 137
Guerric, Father, 22–23

Hackney, Grace, 6
Hakurei turnips, 25
"Hallelujah," 238
Hamilton, Susie, 99–101
Hamilton, Will, 84, 99–101
Hammer, Jill, 211
Harmon, Harvey, 80, 81, 108, 109–14,
    117, 179
    soil treated with reverence by, 113
Harmon, Mrs., 111, 113–14
Harrison, Robert Pogue, 9
Havdalah, 237–38, 241–42
Hazon, 201–2
Hebrew, 200
Hebron, 56, 77
Hemenway, Toby, 109
hepatitis C, 153
Heschel, Abraham Joshua, 196, 197, 211,
    213, 222–23, 227, 232–33, 234–35
Hickory Nut Gap Farm, 99, 119
Hildegard of Bingen, Saint, 89
Hoke, Bob, 134
Hoke, Chris, 134, 141, 142–43, 144, 161,
    162–63, 164, 173, 249
    Bones's relationship with, 165–70
    coffee roasted by, 149–56
    visions seen by, 148
*Holy Shit: Managing Manure to Save
    Humankind* (Logsdon), 181

Holy Spirit, 50–51, 122, 123, 142, 143, 146, 148, 152, 153, 155
Holy Week, 58, 60, 77, 91–95
Honduras, 136–40, 141, 150, 152
Hope for Homies, 163, 166, 171
horarium (Divine Office), 16, 25
Horeb, Mount, 48, 123
horses, 122
House of Representatives, South Carolina, 40
human manure, 180–81
Hurricane Irene, 210, 217, 223–24, 227
Hurricane Lee, 224–25, 227
Hurricane Sandy, 227

imperialism, 139
individualism, 76, 202
industrial agriculture, 180, 181–82
Inferno (Dante), 108
Introduction to Permaculture (Mollison), 109, 115–16, 118–19
Iraq War, 101, 128
Irenaeus, Saint, xi
Irene, Hurricane, 197
Isabella Freedman Jewish Retreat Center, 196–242
Isaiah, Book of, 27, 56, 62–64, 67–68, 69–70, 77–79, 138, 191
Israel, 123, 136–37, 158
"Itzikel," 239

Jackson, Wes, 133
Jacob, 219–20
Jaime, 199, 224
jam, 209
Jeremiah, 117
Jeremiah, Book of, 7, 128–29, 130
Jericho lettuce, 254
Jerusalem, 117, 128–29, 198
Jerusalem Temple, 124
Jesuits, 62
Jesus, 7, 10, 28, 75, 93, 123–24, 155, 162, 168
    Advent of, 26–27
    appearance to Paul, 162
    ascension into heaven of, 143
    food shared by, 77, 79, 94, 168–69
    Last Supper of, 61, 77, 91
    Resurrection of, 41, 68, 86

"Jesus Rocks" motorcycle rally, 249
"Jew and the Carrot, The," 202
Jew in the Lotus, The (Kamenetz), 229, 241
Jewish Farm School, 204, 206, 207, 209
Jewish Food Movement, 201–2
Jews, 93
Jo, 186
Job, Book of, 67
Joe, Father, 27
Joel, 148
John Deere, 175
John the Revelator, 123
Jordan, 209
José, 58, 60–61, 62, 70, 72–76, 79, 80–81, 117, 229, 243, 244
Joseph, Brother, 18
Joseph, Saint, 48, 49
Joy, Zach, 134, 142, 194
    coffee roasted by, 149–56
    drug use of, 150–51
    visions seen by, 148
judaism, 196–242
"Judaism and the Garden" program, 205
junk food, 94, 166

Kabbalah, 233
kale, 1, 6, 25, 99, 100, 156, 157, 185, 188, 203
Kamenetz, Rodger, 229, 241
Kaplan Farm, 202–3
Kent State, 41
Kevin, Father, 27, 49, 54, 246
    Gregory taken to hospital by, 51
    moments of silence recommended by, 53
    on monasteries, 21
    on prayer, 17
Kfar, 198, 200, 230, 231, 240
kibbutzim, 136–37
kiddush, 228, 237
Kierkegaard, Søren, 67
kimchi, 25, 203, 204, 215, 220–21, 245
King, Bill, 124, 128, 131
King, Martin Luther, Jr., 213
Kingdom of God Is Within You, The (Tolstoy), 67
King James Bible, 164
Kings, First, 67

Kings, Second, 67
Kline, Francis, 19
Kohelet, 225–27
kokosh, 74
kosher, 203, 238
Kourik, Robert, 190
Kuri squash, 5

labor, 21, 30, 35
La Conner, Wash., 133
Lake Miriam, 198, 200, 205, 210, 213, 230
land, 251
landings, 43–44, 45, 47, 50
Laos, 111, 180
Larry, 102–3
Las Abejas, 56–81
    anti-violence stance of, 57–58
    coffee burned in protest by, 69, 70, 71
    paramilitary death threats against, 66
    soil treated with reverence by, 113
Last Supper, 61, 77, 91
Lauds, 24, 25
leaves, 5
lectio divina, 18, 53
leeks, 225
legumes, 181
Leonard, Father, 40–43, 53
lettuce, 156, 196
Leviticus, 198, 207, 211–12
life, authentic, 11
Life of Saint Anthony, The, 32–33
Light in the Darkness (coffee), 151–52
lime, 73
Lino, 64–67, 70, 71
Linville Gorge, 118
Little Egypt, 44, 45
Liturgical Year, The (Chittister), 26
Logsdon, Gene, 181
Loma Linda, 137
London Ferrell Community Garden, 248–49
Lord's Acre, 82–106, 161, 211, 248
    Holy Week at, 91–95
    idea for, 94
    synergy between Christians and non-Christians at, 91, 95
    tour of, 87–89
    watermelon thief at, 84–86
    Welcome Table at, 92–93, 95
    workdays, 95–99
Lord's Acre Plan, 83–84
Lord's Prayer, 30, 50
Louis, Father, *see* Merton, Thomas
Lovers of the Place (Kline), 19
"Love Song of a Celibate Man," 51
Luke, Book of, 10, 60
lust, 34

McClure, James G. K., 83, 84, 99–100, 119
machines, 253
Mack, 185, 186, 187–90, 194
maíz, 64, 65, 70–71, 73, 80–81, 158–59, 243
manure, 180–81
Maria, Virgin of Guadalupe, 33
Marie, Miss, 186, 187, 188, 189
marigolds, 129
Mary, Virgin, 33, 57–60, 62
masa, 73
Matisyahu, 230, 237, 238, 239
Matthew, Book of, 136
Maundy Thursday, 72–76, 91–95
Mayans, 55, 56, 61, 64, 76
    see also Las Abejas
Medes, 143
Mennonites, 64, 122–23, 177
Mepkin Abbey, 15–55, 82, 148, 211, 243, 246
    funerals at, 40–43, 53–54
    geography of, 46
    mass at, 16, 18, 25, 27, 47, 78, 200
    retreats at, 43–44
    trails at, 44–45
    tree stands in, 48, 50, 52
    Vespers at, 15, 25, 26, 50–51
Merton, Thomas (Father Louis), 18–19, 27, 30, 46, 52, 171
Methodism, 126, 128
Meti, 191
Mexico:
    low-level war against indigenous population waged by, 58, 60–61, 66, 72, 75
    mass in, 62–64, 68
Micah, 228–29

migrant workers, 129
mikvah, 214–15, 218
milpas, 65, 157
Milton, John, 8
Minas de Oro, Honduras, 138
Mohammed, 160, 161
Mollison, Bill, 109, 110, 115–16, 117, 118–19, 179
Monastic Guest Handbook, 16
monastics, 11
Monsanto, 204
Montpellier, France, 133, 140
Moon & Stars, 85
Moravian Church, 116
Moses, 117, 219, 240
Moses, Abba, 15
Mother Earth News, 88–89, 94
mountains, 2
Mugabe, Robert, 111
mulberry tree, 110
mushrooms, 11, 12, 17, 19, 32, 34, 38, 39–40, 49, 246
mycelium, 19–20, 32, 50, 247
Mycelium Running, 19
mycorrhizae, 19

NAFTA, 130
Napa cabbage, 185, 187–88, 221
Napoli carrots, 6, 25
Ndebele, 111
"Necessity of a Socialized Spiritual Life in the Countryside, The," 82–84
nematodes, 2
New Earth Farm, 134, 155–58, 160, 161
New Heaven, 191
New Testament, 10, 93
Neyland, General, 37
niacin, 73
Nick, 156, 159
Nigeria, 10, 108, 114, 199
night soil, 180–81
Nile delta, 133
Nina, 79–80
nitrogen, 4, 71
Noise Corps, 160–61
Norris, Steve, 90, 95, 104
Nuevo Yibeljoj, Mexico, 57, 67, 68, 70, 72–76, 77, 79, 114, 243, 245

procession of Virgin Mary in, 57–60, 62
Nut Gap Farm, 83

obesity epidemic, 94
Occupy Wall Street, 96–97, 106
Odell, Miss, 186, 188–89, 190
oikos, 23
Old Testament, 123, 140
olive oil, 196
Omnivore's Dilemma, The (Pollan), 98–99
ora et labora (prayer and manual labor), 21, 30, 35
Orange County, N.C., 120
Orange County Correctional Facility, 163–66
organic farming, organic food, 11, 90–91, 94, 133, 136, 175, 187
Overrein, Duncan, 250, 251
oxygen, 5
oyster mushrooms, 24, 31–32, 34–35, 39–40
oysters, 246

Pablo, 62, 79–80
Palestine, 75
Paradise Lost (Milton), 8
Parasols, 49
Parthians, 143
Passing of the Peace, 27
Passow, Nati, 206–9
Patmos, 123
Pattern Language, A (Alexander), 109
Paul, Saint, 93, 135, 162, 168, 190–91
peak oil, 8, 248
peas, 157, 182
pellagra, 73
Pentecost, 143–44, 148, 211, 222
Pentecostal churches, 139–40, 142–43, 145
people, 253–54
People of the Corn, 158–59
peppers, 182
Peretti, Frank E., 145
permaculture, 76, 81, 109, 110–11, 115–16, 118–19, 203
Pesach (Passover), 211
pests, 253
Peter, 93, 148

Pharaoh (Bible character), 178, 204
Pharaoh (prison inmate), 164, 229,
    245–46
Pharisees, 168
pickles, 204, 209, 223
pigs, 121
Pinchas, 241–42
plants, 19, 122, 253
Plotkin, Sam, 203–5, 207, 220–21
pole beans, 121
Pollan, Michael, 13, 98–99, 166
pollo con mole, 96
Porky, 160, 161
potatoes, 157, 182, 183, 204
Potok, Chaim, 171
poverty, the poor, 129, 137, 139, 184
Power and the Glory, The (Greene), 59
prayer, 17, 20–21, 30, 50, 98–99, 201, 247
Presbyterian Church in America, 101
Presence, 126
Prine, John, 95
protozoa, 2
*Proverbs, Ecclesiastes, and the Song of
    Songs* (Davis), 226–27
Provocations (Kierkegaard), 67
Psalm 34, 232
Psalm 51, 16, 200
Psalm 57, 16–17, 18
Psalm 65, 119–20
Psalms, 12, 31, 41, 42, 200, 207, 247
Puget Sound, 132
pumpkins, 225
Purpose Driven Life, The (Warren), 164

rabbits, 122, 187
raised vegetable beds, 87
Raphael, Danny, 210, 212–13, 233, 238
raspberries, 158, 170
Reading the Bible with the Damned
    (Ekblad), 136
Reagan, Ronald, 101
red cabbage, 185
Red Yurt, 200, 202, 212, 213
restlessness, 140–41
Resurrection, 41, 68, 86
Revelation, 191
rhizobium inoculant, 4
Ricky, 144–45, 146–47
Rilke, Rainer Maria, 19, 42, 107, 132

Rimmer, Mr., 175–76
Robert, Brother, 18, 27–28, 44–47, 48,
    49–50
    arthritis of, 44, 45–46, 47
    landings constructed by, 43–44, 45
    sleep patterns of, 46–47
Rolling Stones, 95
Romans:
    Jewish Shabbat disdained by, 235
    Second Temple destroyed by, 198
Romans, Letter to, 67, 168
Romantic poets, 22
Romero, Oscar, 67, 76
Roosevelt, Franklin D., 82
roots, 2
Roots Demystified (Kourik), 190
Rosetta's Kitchen, 96–97
Rosh Hashanah, 198, 208
Ruiz, Don Samuel, 58
Rule of Saint Benedict, 22, 27, 34
rye, 4, 6, 87–88, 181

Sabbath, The (Heschel), 196, 197, 211,
    213, 222–23, 232–33
Sadeh, Shamu Fenyvesi, 196–99, 202–3,
    217–19, 224
Sadeh (field), 217–18, 223–24, 225–26,
    232
Saint-Exupéry, Antoine de, 89
Salvio, 156, 157–58, 159
Sam, 191
Sánchez, Elías, 137, 138
San Cristóbal de las Casas, Mexico, 56,
    59, 64, 77
sauerkraut, 209, 245
Savage, Nigel, 201–2, 213, 216–17,
    235–37
Sayings of the Desert Fathers, 43
*Scripture, Culture, and Agriculture: An
    Agrarian Reading of the Bible*
    (Davis), 178
Seasons of Our Joy (Waskow), 211, 240
Sebastian, 62
Second Temple, 198
Seedleaf, 249
seeds, planting of, 187
Selma, Ala., civil rights march in, 213
Seven Storey Mountain, The (Merton),
    18, 30

Sext, 36
Shabbat, 199, 200, 209, 226, 232–35
Shakespeare, William, 171
shalom, 12, 75, 129–30, 247
shamar, 178, 193–94
shame, 146
Shavuot (Pentecost), 211, 222
shehecheyanu, 228
Shekhinah, 234
shiitake logs, 36, 116, 246–47
shmita (Sabbath year), 204, 206, 207–9
Shoah, 228
shot-callers, 159
Sibelius, 30
Sides, Susan, 84–97, 101–2, 247, 248
    Emma given soil by, 103–5
    and theft of watermelons, 84–86
    Welcome Table started by, 92–93, 95
Silberstein, Garth, 227, 229
silence, 21, 25, 27, 28, 39, 43, 53
Simone, 209
Sinai desert, 210
Sith, 111
Skagit County Jail, 136, 142, 155, 156,
    167–73
Skagit River, 132–33
Skagit Valley, Wash., 11
Skelton, Judge, 167
Smurf, 162
snap beans, 181
Social Gospel, 83
soil, 2, 4, 5, 8–9, 10, 12, 38, 49, 113, 138,
    181–82, 251
    ecosystem in, 2–3
    as sacrament, 13
soil erosion, 137
solitude, 24
Solomon, King, 211
Solomon (goat), 218
Song of Songs, 230, 238
Sonnets to Orpheus (Rilke), 107
speaking in tongues, 143–44, 147–48
Speckled Trout lettuce, 5
spinach, 7
Sports Parlor South, 37
squash, 87, 182, 225
Stamets, Paul, 19
Stan, Abbot, 18, 21, 42, 52
Stations of the Cross, 77

Steep Canyon Ranger, 117
Stegner, Wallace, 76
Steve, 151, 155
Stone, Becky, 100
Stone, Pat, 94, 95, 100
strawberries, 180, 192
Sugar Babies, 85
Sugarsnap peas, 5
Sukkahfest 5772, 238–39
sukkahs, 209–13, 228, 230, 237, 240–41
Sukkot, 198, 203, 205, 209–13, 222, 223,
    226, 227
Supper of the Lamb, The (Capon), 74
Sustainable Agriculture and Food
    Systems, 205
sustainable farming, 137, 138, 139–40,
    141
Sustenance Farms, 76, 79–81, 111–31
    edges at, 116
swale, 113
sweet gum, 116
sweet potatoes, 180, 196
symbiosis, 19, 20

tachliss, 205
Tales of the Hasidim (Buber), 233
tamales, 96
tamari, 196
Tasmania, 115
Tattoos on the Heart (Boyle), 167
Taylor, Scenobia, 125–26, 128, 130–31
Taylor, Valee, 125
técnica, la (sustainable farming), 138,
    139–40, 141
Tempest, The (Shakespeare), 171
Terce, 31
terra animata, 8
Thailand, 180
Theophilus, Brother (Alan), 17, 36–40
Third Temple (Chess), 219
This Boy's Life (Wolff), 171
This Present Darkness (Peretti), 145
thistle, 96
Thoughts in Solitude (Merton), 18, 27, 171
Tierra Nueva, 133–73, 211
    communal ethos of, 134, 138
    ex-convicts at, 141
    speaking in tongues at, 144
    see also Underground Coffee Project

tilling, 8
Tishri, 196, 199–206, 231–42
Tolstoy, Leo, 67, 76, 201, 221
tomatoes, 121, 129, 170, 182, 209
tools, 252–53
topsoil, 224–25, 226
Torah, 200, 201, 207, 211, 236
transcendence, 216
Transition Town movement, 248
Trappist monks, 11, 21, 35
    asceticism of, 21–22
    coffins eschewed by, 41
    habit of, 51
    as largely vegetarian, 24, 40
    silence of, 21, 25, 27, 28, 39, 43, 53
    see also Gethsemani Abbey; Mepkin
        Abbey
Trombatori, Barbara, 92
tulips, 158
turnips, 1, 25, 175
Tzotzil, 62, 64, 69, 71, 73, 74, 75

Underground Coffee Project, 134,
    149–56
Unsettling of America, The (Berry), 117
USAID, 139
Utopia, 108, 112, 113

Vaughn, 174–75, 194
veganism, 91
Vespers, 15, 25, 26, 50–51
vetch, 4, 6, 87
Vicente, 69–70
Victoria, 156, 157–58, 159
Vietnam War, 66, 169
Vigils, 15–16, 18, 25, 27, 47, 200
Vincent, Brother, 34–35, 41, 54

Violence of Love, The (Romero), 67
"Virgen de la Masacre, La," 59–60
Virgin Mary, 33, 57–60, 62
Voltaire, 9
Volunteers for Youth, 160, 183

waj, 71, 73–74, 75
Wallace, Henry, 82–84, 105–6
Warren Wilson College, 95–96
Waskow, Arthur, 211, 228, 240
water, 252
watermelons, 84–85, 87, 103–4
Weasel, 96–97
Weisberg, David, 230
wells, 252
Wesley's Storehouse, 251
whole foods, 13, 94
wild blackberries, 116
winter, 1, 7, 121–22
Winterbor kale, 25
winter squash, 79
Wirzba, Norman, 223
Wolff, Tobias, 171
World War II, 83
Wren, 189

X'oyep, Mexico, 58, 68

yellow pine, 116
Yibeljoj, Mexico, 74–75
Yoder, John Howard, 101
Yokefellows, 163–64
Yom Kippur, 198, 199
yovel (Year of Jubilee), 208

Zapatista peasant revolt, 57, 61
Zuccotti Park, 96–97, 106

About the Author

Fred Bahnson is a writer, permaculture gardener, and the director of the Food, Faith, and Religious Leadership Initiative at Wake Forest University School of Divinity. He is the coauthor of *Making Peace With the Land,* and his essays have appeared in *Oxford American, Image, The Sun, Orion, Christian Science Monitor,* and *Best American Spiritual Writing 2007.* Bahnson has received a number of awards, including a William Raney scholarship in nonfiction at Bread Loaf Writers Conference, a Kellogg Food & Community fellowship at the Institute for Agriculture and Trade Policy, and a 2012 North Carolina Artist fellowship in creative nonfiction from the North Carolina Arts Council. He lives with his wife and sons in western North Carolina.